The Existential Itch

THE EXISTENTIAL ITCH

Religion,
Socially Accepted Neurosis
and Existential Psychotherapy

Steven Eserin
Gestalt psychotherapist

Edited by
Ananthi Parekh

A Publication of the Gestalt Journal Press

CONTENTS

CONTENTS

ACKNOWLEDGMENTS

Thanks

I would like to thank everyone who read my first draft and gave me so much useful feedback. That draft was very raw and unfinished. In particular, I would like to thank Gill, I think you taught me more about grammar in that initial feedback than I learned in my entire formal education. On my second draft, Ananthi, my editor, who made such a massive difference with her exceptional skills, to me it was like a magic trick, watching you move a word in a paragraph and making it suddenly work. And to Molly Rawle, my publisher, who has been frank, honest and supportive consistently, without whom this volume would not have become what it is today. Heather, for putting up with me whilst I wrote. Its hard enough living with a psychotherapist, living with a writer too? not many people would sign up for that. Lastly I wish to thank all the clients who agreed to let me share their stories within these pages, it has been my absolute pleasure to know you all. You have made my life rich indeed.

INTRODUCTION

"People tend to find books when they are ready for them."
Neil Gaiman (*Why Our Future Depends on Libraries and Reading*, 2013)

One should only read books which bite and sting one. If the book we are reading does not wake us up with a blow to the head, what's the point of reading? A book must be the axe which smashes the frozen sea within us. (Franz Kafka, 1904. *Letter to a Friend*)

I decided to write this book because of my growing concern at the number of clients I am seeing who have been adversely affected by religion or religious behaviour. I frequently see clients who can trace the root of their maladjustments and neurosis to religion, a religious upbringing or some abusive event justified by religious edicts or religious people. I have heard tales of controlling behaviour and abuse, often systematic abuse dressed as a religious necessity.

Frequently, these effects have been brought about by people for whom religious behaviour has become a mask for abuse. Yet what is most clear from all these conversations is the way contact with self is subverted, not just for the client, but for all concerned. For a long time, I have been seeing how religious behaviours interfere with contact, reducing man's ability to be, the removal of agency and sublimating of will. Much of the rules for suppressing our desires, needs and feelings come from our society and frequently, religious sources. Challenging them is not simple for the therapist or client, therefore, I intend to explore options and unpack some of my ideas in this book in the hope that others will find my professional insights useful. Given the subject matter, I suspect for many people this book will be Kafka's axe.

In the title I refer to the vague awareness of existential concerns hiding under layers of neurotic roles and religious behaviours as 'the existential itch.' It is a feeling that won't quite go away, a little irritation which we occasionally find ourselves scratching only to find that it's now bleeding, like the proverbial gnat bite, so we stop itching, distracting ourselves instead of dealing with the gnat or the bite. However, we cannot avoid the itch forever, everyone must at some point come face to face with existential problems, at the very least we must all acknowledge that this life we have will end, that death is inevitable. The intention behind this book is to draw attention to the 'existential itch' rather than ignore it.

I will be discussing areas of conflict between religion, existential thought and the ontological self, within the framework of psychotherapy and Gestalt therapy in particular. There are many apparently beneficial aspects to religion or spiritual exercises, and I do not wish to detract from those or the beneficial aspects of some behaviours with a religious overtone or origin. These aspects of religion are discussed at great length in many other publications, whereas, delusional behaviour, religious belief as a mental construct, restrictive religious ideology as the source of developing neurosis, and its inevitable conflict with psychotherapy has rarely been raised directly as a pathological concern. Therefore, my primary focus is to explore how neurotic behaviours are created and supported by religion and ideologies, with the principle aim of understanding the role of delusion in religion and the impact upon the human psyche within the framework of existential psychotherapy and Gestalt therapy.

It may appear to some that I am espousing a form of extreme egotism when discussing contact and free expression of self; I can assure you nothing is further from my mind. In discussing the concept of contact with self and self-expression I am envisioning a person for whom the appreciation of his co-created being and the awareness of impact upon others will make it hard to do harm or be entirely self-centred. We are taught that expressing self and the needs of self are in some way selfish and wrong, unless wrapped up in individualism encouraged by western culture. What I am suggesting is, if you are in good clear contact with yourself and others you will act for the betterment of all. John Bowlby said, "We're only as needy as our unmet needs."

I have established early on the premise that personal responsibility is key to living well and to good mental health. Selfishness is, I think, rooted in a lack of love for the self. Certainly, modern greed as expressed through selfishness stems from the insecurity that self is not enough. It is an expression of self-loathing, in a life devoted to goals he has not even considered, let alone accepted, his greed is an expression of that fixed system. Compassion for or love for the self-eradicates the need for greed. Once satisfied with self, material gain for the sake of gain, beyond necessity, becomes pointless. I have shown that religion jumps on this bandwagon, often increasing or utilising self-loathing in order to maintain control.

Although I have incorporated numerous other techniques and theoretical knowledge, my approach to psychotherapy and counselling is primarily Gestalt.

As such the contact cycle, the paradoxical theory of change and the five layers of neurosis are central to my understanding of inter-relational behaviour, human interaction, neurosis, ego function and contact boundaries. In the appendice I briefly provide a basic overview of the main psychological theories I refer to throughout the rest of the book. Particularly how they relate to awareness or contact, and in the case of the 5 layers, the dissolving of neurosis. I am providing only the very basic aspects; this book is not the place for a full discussion of these ideas and many other excellent volumes have already been written about these theoretical views by other authors.

The book pays considerable attention to the interpretation of subjective experience and how it is tainted by ideals and expectations; within this framework, I also explore the role of religion in building and supporting unhealthy ideals or expectations, primarily through the introduction of fixed valence systems of virtue and behavioural introjects.

The terms "role" and "neurosis" will often be used in discussing the impact of religion on self and self-expression. Sigmund Freud described neurosis as the 'inability to tolerate ambiguity', he was well known for his views on religion as a mass neurosis; despite being written 80 years ago, this quote from Sigmund Freud's *Moses and Monotheism* (1967) shows how little we've come in terms of the grip religion has on society:

> Religion is an attempt to get control over the sensory world, in which we are placed, by means of the wish-world, which we have developed inside us as a result of biological and psycho-logical necessities. But it cannot achieve its end. Its doctrines carry with them the stamp of the times in which they origi-nated, the ignorant childhood days of the human race. Its consolations deserve no trust. Experience teaches us that the

world is not a nursery. The ethical commands, to which religion seeks to lend its weight, require some other foundations instead, for human society cannot do without them, and it is dangerous to link up obedience to them with religious belief. If one attempts to assign to religion its place in man's evolution, it seems not so much to be a lasting acquisition, as a parallel to the neurosis which the civilized individual must pass through on his way from childhood to maturity. (Freud, 1967)

I handle religion throughout this text with evident disdain, although I try to remain objective and respectful, I am not always. I am constantly confronted with the harm caused by religious attitudes. You may take offence if you choose, the nature and foundation of offence is also being a subject I cover too. However, my own feelings toward religious behaviour and thought are not hugely important, aside from how they inform my personal reactions. What really interests me is the way contact is hindered between human beings by these neurotic behaviours. Within the context of therapy, it is contact that will promote healthy choices and contentment. It is awareness of contact which eliminates the need for expectations and their impediment to the expression of self. My irritation is mine, developed through years of hearing horrific stories of people's interactions with religion. But it is tempered with my genuine concern for those I see as delusional and the knowledge I was once amongst that group.

You will find I make a clear distinction between spiritual experience and religious behaviours, we are spiritual beings, capable of being moved by contact with other beings and our environment, including esoteric abstractions. I will explore how religion can impede spirituality and reduce contact with the spiritual aspects of self.

I begin with a little foray into freewill, something that cannot be avoided, as it is too intricately tied to self-expression and introjects. I could easily have continued the issue of free will for months without achieving much but circular arguments therefore, I decided to keep it in as the backdrop to religious thought and part of the tapestry of an impediment to contact.

Choice naturally falls across many facets of this book, along with motive and will. I'm of the opinion that we must know and explore all of these in our personal therapy in order to be relevant as therapists and if we are to experience clear contact with self and other, I explore these and how they interact with religious thought in some detail.

I want to be very clear, this is not a how-to book, or self-help book. I am not telling therapists how to be or act within the therapeutic space. There is no list of tools, no bullet points to follow, no behavioural procedure. Each therapist will have their own style and subjective viewpoints to encompass. I do not believe there is a single way to work with neurosis supported by religion, there is no singular path to freedom from neurosis.

In Fritz Perls' book *Gestalt Therapy Verbatim* (1992, 1969), he specifies 5 'layers' that offer a blueprint which is relevant to all, but the details, the content we work with, are always different. To suggest there is one solution to fit all such would be to belittle the client's individuality and undermine their knowledge of themselves and everything they can teach us about them. I suggest that healthy contact is our best hope for good therapy and a fulfilling life. It remains key to exploring aspects of life undermined by religion and fundamentalist thinking.

While reading this book I invite you to attempt exploration without prejudice of your own reaction to the statements I make. Perhaps take them to your therapist or supervision group. Your reaction will teach you about your own introjects and any single-dimensional viewpoints you may maintain unawares.

I take a glancing look at some neurological patterns and human evolutionary traits exploited by religious and superstitious thought, specifically the threat detection system and pattern recognition. It is important to highlight these as we now understand much of where superstitions are generated or upheld within the neurological net. What's more, we can see that discussing fundamentally held ideologies will trigger the threat response system. Avoiding overt conflict within the therapeutic exchange is usually desirable, so I undertake to explain a little of why reactions to a challenge of belief can be so emotive.

I will also highlight the importance of myth for society in general, particularly for individuals, while exploring the hidden dichotomy inherent in myth and the impact of mythic tales on the human psyche. From here I explore the use of myth as a motivator within religious structures. The importance of mystery within myth in order to allow creative exploration of archetypes vs holding myth as truth we commonly see portrayed by some religious groups will be discussed.

A discussion of religion would not be complete without aspects of psychological transference being highlighted. I cover in some detail the effects of terminology in religion which inspire transferential feelings. I think it important at that point to consider our own feelings toward parents and how we may bring them into our relationships with our own beliefs. Within this section, I will give a sample of attachment theory, specifically because transference is easier to understand once you understand a person's attachment style and people's expectations of adults in their lives. Attachment styles also seem to make a difference as to the kind of role people will take up within a given religious structure. Shame also plays its role, related as it often is to a deficit of early contactful attunement. I tackle shame as separate from transference, yet they are frequently indivisible.

Throughout the book I cover elements of existentialism within psychotherapy. All too briefly — as it's such an enormous topic. Currently, I am specifically concerned that many restrictive aspects of religion appear to actively dissuade exploration of those existential questions we all must face if we are to live a joyful, contactful life. The obstacles to existentialism engendered through religious thought are explored quite thoroughly. As such I cover topics such as will and meaning, death, isolation and separation, freedom and responsibility. I attempted to cover these from a phenomenological perspective, attempting to avoid over intellectualising and trying to promote a connection between the reader and personal exploration of the ideas.

Most of all and perhaps most essentially, I hope you will allow your thoughts to run, mentally chew up this missive and take from it what truth you can allow for you. Spit out the rest, if it's not your truth, give it back, I do not need you to believe as I do if you can believe the opposite, feel free.

In the appendice, I will go through some of the basic psychological theories I use throughout this book. Not in extensive detail as there are many books on the subject. My reason for including them is for those new to counselling and psychotherapy, in training or just an interested layperson; the appendice will introduce and explain concepts common to Gestalt theory. If you are unaware of Gestalt therapy or theories surrounding neurosis please read the appendice first. However, if you are already a practitioner you may wish to refresh yourself or skip the appendice and get straight into Chapter 1.

Chapter 1

Free Will, Motive and Choice

The animal twists the whip out of its master's grip and whips itself to become its own master —not knowing this is only a fantasy produced by a new knot in the master's whiplash. (Kafka, *Zurau Aphorisms of Franz Kafka*, 2006).

The issue of free will

At what point does a choice become our own, and can it ever be said to be our choice? Do we as individuals ever exercise choice?

It's a difficult set of questions for therapists, we spend much of the therapeutic hour enlivening awareness of internal and external stimuli and experience in order to facilitate clearer choice. I describe many aspects of my role as enabling awareness so that we may have clearer choices, that I want my clients to be free from automatic behaviour enabled by unhealthy introjected data. Yet I am struck by the lack of choice still inherent in what remains, for both myself and for my clients. This in turn requires that I ask myself "do I really have free choice? Or is it illusory?."

I will start with an easily accessible everyday example. Did we choose to wear makeup today? And moving beyond that, how did I "choose" this example. As a functional expression of ego, are we wearing makeup to beautify, to shock, or to mask? Are we aware of our motive at all or is it so automatic and inbuilt that we have no awareness of why? Or you might be saying "Of course not, I'm a man." Which suggests you are still not freely choosing; you are just following society's views about gender roles which may dictate that you as a man shouldn't wear makeup. If you don't wear makeup because society has told you it is wrong for a man to do so, you are not choosing but following the flock. Let's examine this simple everyday choice made by millions of people across the world every day.

Can you say you choose to wear makeup? Certainly, you can, you think I shall put my make up on now, you find your comfy niche, sit down and apply it, often with great attention to detail and skill. That sounds like a choice, right? That sounds like free will and you move under your own volition, your hands take up brushes and pens, you prepare your skin, it's all deliberately applied with practised artistry. But is it a choice? Or is it a role we are playing to appear as something other than what we are?

Why then do we apply makeup? Do I wear makeup because some significant other told me that I would look better with a bit of makeup on, or maybe as a teenager, someone told me I'm spotty and pointed to foundation and concealers? Perhaps you bought into the advertising which told you you're not so worth it so you had better cover up your natural appearance and put on this fake version of you instead. In order that the rest of the world will admire you or even accept you; even if that acceptance contains the tacit understanding that it is only the covered version of you that is acceptable. Can you leave your make up and go out without it? Or are you reliantly dependent in order to feel confident enough? Have you ever considered these reasons before and if not, are you choosing to wear makeup or are you choosing to assuage your anxiety about being seen as you are, without the mask, exposed to others thoughts and judgements? And what of my judgments are implicit in this line of questioning? It's not like I have the right to question you or mention your makeup at all, but still, the question of choice is interesting and clearly not obviously delineated. I'll revisit this in the discussion of expectations and their impact on free will, choice and motivation in Chapter 7.

Could it be that you are projecting your insecurities onto those around you and imagining their judgements; then wearing makeup to help you disown your thoughts about yourself? Why would you give so much credence to others' judgments anyway? However, we choose to explore this, I can think of few examples when the choice to wear makeup is a free choice, uninfluenced by the environment or historical precedents. Even reading this brief foray into choice will now figure in your awareness when faced with situations involving makeup; and will change your perception of it as a process.

In the west when we celebrate Halloween, when many of us dress up and don makeup to join in the fun, are we aware of how we choose to join the group? Your motives for the sugar skull death mask or zombie head makeup? Are we trying to impress, or fit in? Does it have to be better makeup than the neighbours? Is there an element of competition? Or perhaps we can enjoy hiding behind a mask and exploring being something more exotic for a night, and we are free to do so because everyone else is. Then are we so repressed at other times that we refrain from the same behaviour because the majority are also refraining? Or because without the mask it is no longer safe to do so?

We see then that we might feel we make our own choices; yet it is likely these are not necessarily of our own making. Realistically our choices are governed by motives created within our social context or imagined within our minds with the influence of our environment dictating our reactions. Be that via advertising, peer pressure or social constructs about beauty and acceptability. Where is the freedom then, where is the free will we all aspire to? Or is that just another lie we tell ourselves in order to feel in control? Another great delusion. Can you imagine a single instance in which you make a choice? A clean choice, any choice that is not influenced by other matters?

Take my choice to use makeup as an example. This choice is another good example. I'm sitting here debating its inclusion, simply because I don't want to be seen as interfering, or trying to tell people what to do, that they can/can't, should or shouldn't wear makeup. So even here, just writing this chapter I am influenced by judgements of mine and others, rather than going with my first instinct, that this is a good example of choice clouded by introject.

We are born and you might say free, except that, of course, our immaturity at birth leaves us totally dependent on our primary caregiver. However, we are at this stage relatively free of influence from others in the emotive, rational sense. We live and grow with our caregiver, gradually absorbing experience. Our developmental environment for good or ill, will impact upon our thoughts and feelings throughout our entire lives. We all had one, some were healthy enough and others less so. Some were damaging, and some nurturing. It was in this initial environment that we developed our attachment style and had our first experience of attunement which shaped our own attachment style which we carry into our adult lives.

My Choice

I chose to write these words, certainly, I decided to sit and write today. The subject was chosen by my interest in and interactions with others, in a way I guess, co-created, either within my social circles, family or through work, and in part by my struggles with religion in my past and in general within therapy. In part, I am writing to attempt to further my understanding, coalesce my thoughts into a more meaningful whole. But also I am writing to impress you, my reader, with my ideas, for the kudos associated with being an author. It's a role, of course, something to perhaps mask my real feelings about my intellectual abilities. Part of me also wishes to help people stop and think for a moment about their existence and mine, about the roles we play and why we play them. It is a grandiose thought and a complicated process, there is no one clean motive, and there may be other motives which have not yet become apparent.

Suppose I am writing that I might affect others through you, that this thought process might start something bigger than both of us. Am I choosing that then? It is certainly a plausible possibility, but I wasn't aware of it before I started to write this paragraph. It occurs to me now but was furthest from my mind when I began with my earliest struggle with the idea of will, choice or religion in the therapeutic context.

What I want to express here is that even now the judgments of others are sitting behind all our motives and actions. I will however take responsibility for sitting here and writing. I choose to continue, and that is as close as I can come to free will and choice because I am aware of the events leading to this moment.

Perhaps the separation of choice and motivation is in order here. The difficulty being, if the motivation is held out of awareness can we ever say we choose an action? This path seems the most trampled with the feet of the masses. We choose endlessly, often badly when faced with a crossroads, we evaluate with limited or no information. Robot style we blithely wander on, not noticing the fork in the road or our reasons for our blinkered vision. Blame sits then at the crossroads of choice, no matter the motivation that engineered the crossroads or paths, blame sits with the one who chose this path over that. That seems bleak to me, at least give me all the information, name the roads, give me a map, bring my unaware impulse to figure and let me see clearly why I have to choose and what my options truly are, with antecedents all. That, I think, is my aim in therapy, to bring a modicum of awareness to difficult choices which would usually be made in a state of unawareness. That feels a good goal to seek, to unmask the roles we play, to see them for what they are. Choice and motive is a theme that winds its way throughout this book. It is inseparable from religious belief and Psychotherapy.

Introjection and change

Coupled with this local bubble, our close relations and family, we were born into wider society, a society which imprinted upon us its values and concerns. We learned its laws, its social niceties, its religion and myths, this we call our culture, or from a psychological position, our wider environment. It is part of our field of experience. We ingested much of this as an introject, without thinking, without mentally chewing it up. As Fritz Perls said in *Ego Hunger and Aggression* "introjection in itself can be a normal process, they" – speaking of previous psychological thinkers and pioneers such as Freud – "overlooked the fact that introjection means preserving the structure of things taken in, whilst the organism requires their destruction." (1947, 1991, p. 129)

Gradually we were moulded into people fit to live in this society or be condemned by it. Condemned because if you don't fit the bill, you will be considered an outsider. One of the keyways a group expresses its identity is by saying not just "this is what we are"; but also, and usually more frequently, "we are not like that." In saying we are not this or that, we are building an imaginary line between us and the other and limiting ourselves to this group with this experience. I could say I am English for example, and we are not like the French because they drive on the other side of the road and eat snails, or because they speak a different language. It's a limited vision of the self, defined by the definition of others and judgements of difference; Usually sweeping statements of generalisation, not concrete positive statements. It says little about me and more about the other, yet as a societal group, this is often our mode of differentiation and exclusion. If I step outside of this, I might find I like eating escargot and that driving on the other side of the road might work too.

This is also one of the key ways religious groups define themselves. We are not like those people over there, they believe in a different god, or they have different rules. Even within religions, you have many sects all of which define themselves against other groups within the same religion. We split from the main body because we no longer adhere to their doctrine, we think your belief is false, so we are going to set up our own club of like-minded people who also believe that belief is false. After a while of course the belief is replaced with another. Other's behaviour can then be defined as heretical, wrong or evil. By saying I am not like you I set myself apart, whilst creating for myself a safe clique of people who share enough of my ideology for us to fit together without too much friction.

It is through this shared difference with the 'other' that we can overlook the aspects of ourselves which clash with members of this group. The emphasis is on otherness. As with any fundamentally held belief or ideology, from socialism through to communism, capitalism or fascism; where the difference is used to delineate boundaries, hatred will be projected onto others. We see time and again arguments between churches of this group or that group where one holds the other in contempt and attacks them. We saw it all too clearly with the holocaust of the Jewish people during the Nazi uprising. We are not like them, they are not even fully human, we must eliminate them. Taken to its extreme in this case, it caused immeasurable harm, as entire racial groups or ideological groups are scapegoated. The expectation to be this way or that is so strong that entire groups of people can be persuaded to act contrary to usual moral boundaries in order to remain a part of the group. I'll look at this a little more when I come to masochism in Chapter 12.

Eventually, all these systems fall into chaos because when the difference between you and I is used to define, as soon as the object of difference disappears, or as soon as it can no longer be blamed for how I think and feel, a new enemy has to be found in order to protect myself from introspection, a new schism forms and the group divides again.

All the introjects we learned in early life will combine to create the motivation behind role enactment; each also becoming an impediment to contactful engagement. All this role playing is the result of choices we think we have made from a place of free will. Introjects are another's rules we could not assimilate; they have nothing to do with free will.

I might "choose" to wear a suit for example. But as we have seen in other examples it is rarely because it is what I want to do, or even because I have willed it so, though it's a valid choice to make if I can make it from a place of free thought. It is usually because my society says I must, that I am unacceptable unless I do, perhaps because my suit represents a business persona, or because a friend once told me I looked attractive in a suit, and I like the feelings associated with being admired. I want to be seen as attractive and if my society says I need to wear a suit or tie to be a businessman then I am likely to go ahead and do what is required of me, despite any discomfort incurred. Can we say then that the choice to act is ours, but the motivation is not? We need to look closer at awareness of motivation and the role it plays in our choices, the use of psychotherapy to increase awareness and thus promote healthier choices, whatever they may be.

We can eventually release ourselves from introjects, but we must wrestle still with the idea that choices are never free, even if subjectively we experience them as such. We are products of our environment, though responsibility for action, the carrying through the choices still lies with us.

Arthur Schopenhauer suggests in "Two Fundamental Problems of Ethics" (1841), his essay on the freedom of the will, that we are born with a character and that character is unchangeable. Employing the adage, once a thief always a thief. Counter wise, once found to be trustworthy, always trustworthy. In many ways, that argument would seem to hold water. If I want someone reliable to look after my kids, I choose someone I have experienced as reliable. That much at least seems self-evident, but this is just a process of threat elimination, I can't guarantee this person's behaviour, or assume it will be as before. How can I be certain that there isn't something sinister lurking behind the mask which I have yet to encounter? All I am doing is picking the best alternative I can find to doing the job myself. That is not part of my character so much as an innate caregiver instinctual response evolved over millions of years, inexorably linked to the pattern recognition mechanism described later.

Introjects form a large part of our character structure, but they are alien, later I will explore how we might challenge them along with our other beliefs. We are still left with the issue of change. I will admit that we are continually growing and changing as people; therefore, we must allow that within the p, including but not exclusively limited to value systems; change is possible, abandonment of unhealthy beliefs is possible. I have seen people you would characterise as totally untrustworthy; change so vastly through the therapeutic interaction that I would personality trust them entirely. We are after all neuroplastic, malleable, we can change throughout our lives if we wish to make the effort to face the requisite fears or if we have an external stimulus as a catalyst.

I include the external stimuli here because it is often explosive life events which provide much of the incentive for change. A promotion or loss of a job, moving home, getting married, having a child or losing one, the death of a parent or friend, or the diagnosis of a life-changing illness or indeed entry into therapy. Events which have not before been assimilated into our usual threat pat   tern analysis. Whatever the catalyst, people come to therapy in order to make changes as much as to feel better about this or that aspect of themselves or their lives as they perceive them. The essential character of the person is intact, but aspects of it can and do change. On this point then I differ with Schopenhauer, though I recognise the enormous influence his thoughts have had upon mine. He was operating before the birth of psychotherapy and as such had fewer data and a different environmental field to work from.

Our total experience is created and sifted through interrelated tendrils of perception, sparked by internal and external stimuli and filtered through the myriad aware/unaware memories, introjects and concepts we bring, like a time traveller, from the past to the present moment. It is a dynamic system which contains fixed gestalt, these fixed gestalts hinder or colour choices. Nevertheless, we are constantly evolving, we are neuroplastic. Our perception of ontological experiences is added to our pool of awareness. All this is focused by the loci of our dominant need; the figure which has sprung from the field of our perception. In this way no one is separate, we are all co-creating our now, inseparable from the field of our existence, our environment.

Integration of new experience, when contacted fully, is not only possible, but also essential. Requiring its disintegration for assimilation to take place. Health and recovery are not only possible but created directly by the integration of new experience. The moment when contact with others becomes a reality, a creative figure arises from the interaction. It is at this moment where integration takes place, and the fixed Gestalt is undone.

We can say that we must choose to change, we must act toward. However, it is not going to take place of its own accord. Scrooge, as depicted in *A Christmas Carol* by Charles Dickens (1843), is a good example. A moral reprobate, repugnant and devoid of warmth for his fellow man, faced with an existential crisis, being visited by the ghost of Christmas past, present and future. It was upon seeing his future, seeing his death, standing at his own graveside, experiencing his fragility and the finite nature of his life, the lack of mourners, the lack of friends at his side when he dies that he realises for the first time that his wealth means nothing. He cannot take it with him, and he is wasting his life. In a dramatic change, he becomes outgoing, benevolent and warm toward his kin. He must accept his new awareness and act upon it. He chooses to make different choices as a result of his existential realisation. Although it is a work of fiction, like all great myths, we see a kernel of truth hidden between the lines.

In therapy, we do see a change of this magnitude happen. The confrontation with existential elements such as death, meaning, isolation, will and responsibility for self is often the catalyst. When these aspects are brought into focus the resulting awareness is likely to have a tremendous impact on us and drive us toward change as we become aware of and re-evaluate the introjects, we have swallowed. It cannot be ignored, that in order to change we must choose. We must choose to make ourselves vulnerable, to experiment, in order that we might change what is and accept responsibility for personal development.

When the Choice Is Not Our Choice

Change we must and change we can. We can learn for example ways to be angry without being abusive or violent. If I grew up in a household of bullies and violent people, I could learn to be something else. I can learn to take a breath first, to pay attention to my entire being, not just the angry part. I can choose to express myself with assertions, without abusive adages or violent effects. I can choose to explore my vulnerability in the face of my significant others' rage and accept my own impact upon the world. It would have to be my choice though, right? I mean I couldn't change unless I wanted to. I must put in the effort, build the awareness and move toward a different way of being. No one can make me change, I must desire it, though sometimes external events are so overwhelming I may seem to have little or no choice.

What if my wife says, "I have had enough, I want you to see a therapist and do something about your behaviour or I'm off, this is your last chance." So, I go to therapy and make the changes required to stay with my partner, or I don't. The choice then is to acquiesce or to leave and have another type of life elsewhere. But are either of these choices really mine? If faced with this situation I must make the choice and I do choose, either by action or inaction. Yet I might not have even considered those options if left without the prompt. I may never consider therapy without the entreaty to change. Can I say then, I choose therapy, or I choose to leave because I do not wish to change? Either way, the choice is foisted upon me.

In the above instance it may appear I am being blamed for being me as I was created by my environment and I will in turn, more than likely, blame him/her for not accepting me as I am. Yet even the simplest folk amongst us will agree that change in this instance seems healthier than sticking with behaviours which are outmoded, inappropriate, abusive or limiting intimacy. Or is that just the influence of our societal norms talking through us as well? We must, for example, allow people to choose to make an unwise decision or we risk the loss of independence and dignity. It's a complicated equation, which has no definite solution.

The other important question is does it matter if it was foisted upon me or I found it via my own perception. Now I am face to face with this mirror, I can no longer avoid the awareness of my impact on other people or my environment. My awareness that my behaviour has been so abhorrent that they have had enough of me. This alone will have a lasting effect on me, on my perception of myself. Even if I make no choice and bumble on until choice is taken from me, and no choices remain. The awareness has now become a figure, of the opportunity wasted, will still have a lasting effect as my perception of myself is irrevocably changed as a result.

I think from my theoretically subjective position as a therapist, but also considering my phenomenological experience as a human being within my society, that choice is always complicated by expectations of others. Complicated because we are frequently faced with choices we do not want to make and the expectation we should be other than we are. Hobson's choice, as it was called when I was growing up, good old Thomas. not to be confused with the doubting kind. I know part of the therapeutic process is to promote a healthy choice. Yet it's not always an easy choice to make or a choice we want to make, because a healthy choice might mean leaving someone we are attached to or doing something which, in the short term might be painful.

What we are really promoting during the therapeutic hour, is a strengthening of the client's figure until it is bright, until their awareness of the situation is such that they must choose to act or choose to stay with what is in all reality, damaging. We bring to awareness the repressive mechanisms by which our clients suppress feelings and contingent behaviours. Exploring them in the present moment, through creative experiment or contactful expression; in the hope that the resulting awareness will lead them to find other, hopefully healthy ways of being. We are then helping to make choices intentionally rather than automatic. Reiterating my first example, there is nothing wrong with wearing makeup; and I would argue it is good to have clear awareness as to why we do so. Though that awareness might drive us to seek other options, it's still not ruling out makeup, it's just making the choice and the motivating factors underpinning it, more explicit.

In therapy we see choice and freewill intermingled in client's ideals. Clients often come respectfully expecting change but are unaware of the motoric resistances they employ to prevent the clarity and expression of choice. The awareness we offer does not always make the choice easier, though it might make the path more visible.

If I see someone sitting across from me stifling tears, I might see the clinching, reddening cheeks, the tightening around the eyes, the holding of breath and the swallowing back of what wants to come out. I don't say "do you want to cry" or "you should be crying." But I might say "be aware of your throat," or "what is going on here?" while pointing to the area on myself. I'm not being prescriptive, telling them not to inhibit or disinhibit themselves, I just draw their attention to the mechanism by which they do that. Then they, in turn, have greater awareness and can choose, do I continue to suppress my tears, or do I allow them?

Following the awareness of how I stop my self-expression, questions will arise, why am I afraid to allow my tears? I am sad, why do I not allow my sadness? The choice is now clearer; the motoric resistances are now in awareness. You have options to explore them and experiment with differences each time that awareness becomes apparent. Next time you feel like crying you can choose between allowing and suppressing. Perhaps initially allowing a little shift with observation, in order to experiment or to clarify catastrophic expectations.

The choice is now aware, not automatic. We are organic beings that experience a continuum of emotion, we are also sadly beset with other people's ideas about what is good for us to express or repress, and this has turned us into automatons. It requires enormous courage to do something we have perceived as or been told is dangerous, wrong, evil, sinful or threatening to others. To allow our vulnerability and remain in contact with other people and our own emotional experience requires great courage. As a therapist I am privileged to be there during these moments, to offer containment for chaos, and a mirror to the introjects that they might be divested of power, chewed over and spat out.

Choice and Motive

Returning to the choice of clothing analogy. If I choose to wear a suit, a skirt, a headdress, a type of shoe etc. because society says I must; though this thought pattern is held out of my awareness, it is still the motivating factor. Who then is to blame for my choice to wear it? Once my awareness is raised of each antecedent factor, then, of course, I then have a clear choice. My choice is and will always be subject to introjected beliefs. Awareness is required in order to challenge introjects; would I become aware had not some significant other, friend, partner or therapist not drawn my attention to my angst at being me without this thing I am told to wear, or would I choose to wear it anyway as an expression of my ego which is not to mask, but rather to play at being something else?

Case Study One
Angela

I'm going to introduce a short case study here. In all the case studies I use in this book I have changed the person's name, often age, some personal circumstances and often gender. I do this in order to make the person unidentifiable. This first case study has little to do with religion I admit but is a good example of how we can behave according to others wishes or design without awareness. The role played is believed by the actor to be their true self, we run through the script that was given to us and play the role faultlessly. Though the role is born of an introject and we lack the awareness that the role even exists. It is a creative adaptation which made part of our earlier life more bearable. Continuing this behaviour into our adult life is perhaps unhealthy in most cases, but often never even noticed. In accepting the role as self, the existential guilt over the negation of the true self is not felt directly but will be evident in other ways.

Angela's Motives

Angela appears to be successful by society's standards, a successful businesswoman, self-made in the entrepreneurial sense. She has started several businesses, but at some point, became bored with each. As Angela has become disinterested in all of them, she either resolved to sell them or wind them up, in each case this was preceded by a withdrawal from the business and a sense that this was not what she really wanted to do after all.

Angela comes to therapy because she feels she has a lack of interest in life and a lack of meaning. Complaining that everything she does comes to nothing, she is unfulfilled and wants me to show her how to find fulfilment. The first part I disabuse her of is the idea I might have a magic wand or some secret formula which if she follows, she might then find fulfilment. I suggest we meet for 6 sessions and that we could concentrate on how she contacts the world and herself, to see if that throws up any possible solutions. She is curious about this contact thing but does not really grasp the meaning.

Manic Input

During the second session, Angela seems distant, as though she is not quite with me. I ask her where she is because she does not seem to be here. Her response was an irritated snapping at me. I ask her to consider how she is feeling now and to bring awareness to her apparent irritation, but she replies she is not irritated with me, just frustrated at how expensive this is and how she is making no progress. I was slightly taken aback, as this is the second session, Angela's expectations of me or herself must be intolerably high. I ask what is important about making progress quickly? To which she sits in silence, perhaps for the first time. Then begins to explain to me how she always likes to get things done, and quickly "that's just how I am" she went on to explain that it's part of her success. When she has a new idea for a business, she does like to get things done, to move on quickly. She talks about losing interest and that she rushes ahead to get started before interest is lost. Angela still sounded frustrated, her voice snappy. I said, "I feel like I'm being told off, your voice, your mannerisms toward me, are you telling me off?" Angela waved my concern away with a smile. to which I replied, "now I feel as though you have brushed my question aside, with a smile and a wave of your hand." Angela then looked right at me but ignored my responses. If looks could kill.

Angela went on to describe periods of frenetic activity, as soon as she had a new idea for a business, she would enter a sort of manic phase. For the duration of those time periods all other concerns were secondary, her kids, for example, were left to fend for themselves for all but the most basic needs. She was out on business most of the time, her contact with herself seemed to be limited to considerations of business needs. She was excited but not grounded and the interest in the business would take on an obsessive quality. The mania would eventually wear off and Angela would settle into running the business.

As a businesswoman she was competent, and her determination often strayed into ruthlessness. A trait which is often common amongst those for whom commerce is a primary focus.

I wondered aloud if she was approaching therapy as though it was another business idea, something to get stuck into and accomplish before she lost interest? Angela denied any such connection.

On week three Angela described how she becomes bored with projects. And that she often realises it was not her idea, after all, usually it was sparked by a comment someone else made, or a friend's wishes, or her husband's desire for something. Once the business is set up and running, she starts to withdraw, unable to remain in contact with an idea which is not her own. I asked her what she was doing with her own ideas? A question ignored. We focused on how she latched onto others' suggestions and jumped at them without considering if she was really interested. How she overrode her lack of interest with manic behaviour, which kept her out of contact with what she was really feeling until she was already embedded in the process of setting up the venture. I remember this session as being a little sparky. Angela seemed to resent every question or remark, and I challenged her to tell me about how she felt now, at this moment when we discussed various aspects of her business history. Angela also spoke a little about her dad and how proud he was of her achievements as a businesswoman, how he was easier now than when she was young. Back then he seemed austere and aloof. She had no physical contact with him, she could remember no hugs.

At the end of the session, Angela said she didn't think the session had been useful and wasn't sure she would come next week. I said I would leave the session open and for her to confirm a few days before if she wanted to come after thinking it over, I reflected that she had a tendency, from what she described of her behaviour, to expect results very quickly and to back off once the manic phase had diminished, was she perhaps doing that again in our relationship.

Angela did return the following week. She seemed quiet and low in mood when contrasted with the previous high energy, out of contact businesswoman she presented in the previous sessions. She said she had a disturbing dream, a dream she couldn't forget or let go of. When I suggested we explore it she looked quite shocked and claimed she had not realised I did that sort of thing. But maybe I could tell her what it means. I replied that she did that in the first session, asked me to provide the answers, and again she became quite belligerent, "I am paying you for your time, and I expect results." She was not in contact with me, and she didn't want to take any responsibility for her dream either. I explained gently that the awareness must come from her. "If I interpret your dream for you, it is my truth, it is what it means to me, not what it means for you. Let's just work the dream and see if you can find the insight for yourself."

Angela was reticent. But we worked on the dream for 20 minutes. The dream was of a faceless man, he wore a dark pinstripe suit, and moved as though he was very strong. He had a powerful voice which she couldn't quite recognise. "It's like when you have a name on the tip of your tongue but just can't grab it." Angela went on to describe how in the dream this male figure came into her front room, picked up one of her favourite dresses and ripped it into pieces. Angela screamed at him to stop but he pushed her away and said, "it's a waste of time." Having torn the dress, he disappeared. Angela was transported to her first place of work, where she was in telesales. She sat at the desk holding the phone in hand, wondering why she was there, aware this was in the past, she didn't work there anymore. Angela woke to feel disturbed, out of place and alone.

The dream had been vivid, we explored various parts of the dream, I asked her to do different things within the dreamscape to gain different perspectives on the content. All of which seemed to be fruitless as Angela seemed incapable of staying with anyone aspect, kept leaving the process by opening her eyes and kept placing judgements on what she was doing, as though her every step was wrong.

I reflected on the process and suggested we continue to look at the dream next week but use the remainder of the session to explore her reactions to the way we were working. Angela was imagining I was judging her. When working the dream Angela said she felt foolish being the dress because it's not even a person. I asked her how she experienced her foolishness, physically. She spent a moment getting in touch with her flush and sense of embarrassment but then became angry with me. When I enquired about the anger, she said I was judging her. I asked her to look at me and tell me what she saw. When she made contact with me she allowed herself to see I was not her judge. Angela was exasperated, frustrated and angry. Eventually after much back-and-forth Angela said "So, if you're not judging me, I am judging myself, is that what you're saying?" We explored that for a time until I asked her what she might get out of judging herself. At that moment when I asked her to be the dress in the dream, what was the payoff? After a few moments of silence, Angela responded: "I guess I don't have to get in touch with being the dress, but that makes no sense?!" In essence the dress was also a projection of her unconscious, or part of her unconscious and part of the natural process of dreaming. The projecting of judgement onto people outside of oneself is common, but neurotic in nature.

The judgement was a projection. I can say this because I wasn't judging her, aside from appraising her response. Angela's internal critic was being projected out onto me, an older male. The dream figure had been a male who was also critical, but Angela had not made that connection yet.

I asked her if this was a familiar sense, being judged by others. She described several instances in which she walked into a party, a room with people in or even the doctor's waiting room and felt as though everyone was judging her. In exploring the feelings that arose she decided it was a feeling of embarrassment. So, I asked the same question, what's the payoff? Then after a little silence, "If you were not feeling embarrassed what would you be feeling? First thought?" her response was, "I would feel as though they were looking at me, enjoying what they see." She looked shocked; Angela's hand quickly moved to cover her open mouth.

"So, if I wasn't being embarrassed, I would be enjoying it, being looked at... (angry tone) I'm not sure I like that; it seems a bit creepy." We spent the remainder of the session exploring her dislike of the thought she might enjoy being seen, the judgements she had introjected about being a show-off or being admired for being her. Then explored how she may be projecting that out onto others, imagining they dislike her instead of enjoying her attractiveness and the thought people might be attracted to her.

Eventually, I asked her about her anger with me, and if that was linked. She decided it was and that I might find her attractive, which would be somehow wrong. We had come to the end of the session, but we picked the theme up several sessions later. At which point Angela had enough trust to say that she had been attracted to me and she felt a bit weird about that because I was her therapist. It appeared she had projected her distrust of her own feelings onto me, assuming I was attracted to her and not allowing her own attraction or attractiveness.

The Second Dream

Session 5 came after a 2-week break: Angela had been ill, a flu type virus. The night before the session Angela had experienced another dream. It is noteworthy that Angela's dream occurs the night before therapy is available. This is often the case. Clients may well unconsciously prepare for therapy and allow things to come to the fore in the days leading up to a session. Dreams of significance frequently occur the night before a session.

This time the man without a face had become her father, he was the exact same image, but the face had been added to the mannequin. He was standing at a desk in a dark green room, tearing up all her clothes; but these were not clothes she had bought or clothes she had worn, these were clothes she had made. Each one was torn to shreds. He looked stern while doing this and shouted, "I told you this was a waste of time." Angela was bemused and informed me that he had never said that! So, I asked, "Since when do dreams follow the rules of reality?" which provoked perhaps the first warm smile I had experienced from her. Angela then talked about her dad, in the dream and in real life. She kept it very surface level, she didn't stay in the dream space, which would be my usual way to work a dream but just spoke quietly. It was surprisingly bland and subdued considering the lack of warmth she experienced from him as a child and young woman.

Then toward the end of the session, she talked about how when she was leaving school, she had wanted to study textile design, and her dad had been furious, telling her what a waste of time that was and she should do something where she was going to make some money. It was the end of the session, so I pointed out how Angela had talked in the blandest, most banal way since describing the dream, but now when there is no time left, she brings up something interesting and emotive. I suggested we meet again and begin where we left off.

Angela returned and was engaging from the outset; more contactful than the previous session, less obtuse, less snappy. She returned immediately to the conversation with her dad without prompting. Having had a week to think about it, Angela had realised what she really wanted to do was to design textiles, to have her designs turned into clothing, bags and even chair covers and curtains and felt excited when she imagined it. The discussion was lively and bright, Angela was angry with her dad and herself. Angela was bemused as to how to proceed from here as, "I can't make a living from designing textiles." I wondered aloud why she had to make a living from it? I used 'two chair' work for Angela where she explored the two aspects of herself currently presented, the self which was interested only in money and income, and the creative self which wanted to design textiles. It appeared to be fruitful and certainly not dull, as Angela switched chairs and personas while each aspect of her described the other and told each other what they were thinking and feeling. Toward the end of the session, we went back to her anger with her father, I asked Angela to reflect on the lack of hostility or reproach from her toward me in this session and the difference in her willingness to explore. Angela brushed this off with a throw away comment and conciliatory smile, "Yes, well I wanted to explore this" and smiled at me. I also smiled and suggested she had just deflected my comment again. Which earned me a joking mouthful of scorn for seeing too much. It was a turning point, in the therapeutic relationship and in her approach to therapy.

Over the next 3 months, Angela explored how she had given up her desire to design, had done what she thought her father wanted and went into business, indeed, her business acumen was the only thing in which he showed any pride in her. She explored the lack of warmth she experienced from him and began to grieve the parent she would never have. Angela explored the need to follow his lead in order to feel accepted. Angela also acknowledged how she had at times abandoned her own family in order to pursue business, and how she wasn't sure how to have a relationship with her own kids.

Angela as a Role, Not Authentic Self

Angela had chosen to play a role in order to garner acceptance from her father. A man who had never really accepted her, particularly her creative side but someone whom she longed to get affection from. The role of businesswoman, she played the role so well she had become wealthy, materially speaking. But at the expense of her creative self, at the expense of relationships. She had driven her creative side underground in order to get limited contact with her father. The role she assumed had become her persona for most of her adult life, but as it was at the expense of her authentic self, her creative self. As a result, Angela never felt fulfilled. Angela had introduced manic activity in order to force limited contact with things she found quite dull. She had given up herself, her interest in textiles and design, that part of herself was lost to her, put away. Now aware of her process, the ways in which she shut off contact with herself and others in order to please a man she had no relationship with, but with whom she desperately longs to have one. She explored her sense of isolation and her lack of meaning. From here she now has a clear choice whenever the businesswoman persona begins to appear.

At various points in this book, I will look at how people give up aspects of themselves in order to follow a path laid down by parents, by society, by religion, and how in doing so, abandon aspects of self which cannot be expressed along those paths. I will look at how difficult it is to go back and explore those lost potentialities, the guilt and grieving which often accompanies such exploration and how hard it is to leave the supportive fictions created by others; as that means taking personal responsibility and perhaps taking the risk and being creative, making ourselves vulnerable. All of which requires courage.

Control and Will

Most, or all of us imagine we have control, we imagine a cut-off point and say from here, from this point I am in control, of my actions certainly and of the environment. We say to ourselves I will do this; I am doing this, I am responsible. If we detect no external push or pressure to make a choice of one sort or another, we assume we are making a free choice. Yet free will, it seems to me, is anything but free. More a conglomeration of judgements, memories and introjects, a response to external concerns expressed through our personal population of selves in order to be perceived in this light or another. Often, we are just playing a role, like Angela, in order to be accepted by a person, by society, by a group, to alleviate our isolation. Sometimes what appears on the face of things to be free will is a prison for the self. I cannot think of a single instance in which my choices are not governed by antecedent stimuli or conditioning or manipulation of self in constraint to others. If we can allow awareness of these shackles to grow, perhaps we can shed some of them for good.

Individualism is in many ways an illusion we have used to convince ourselves we have personal power and make choices with clean clear awareness. We are not free from external constraints if we are to be in contact with other members of our society. We are co-created and totally interdependent. We can be individual only within these limiting confines. We might think we want our children to be independent and desire them to develop the ability to think critically, we want them to be individuals. Yet we educate them within a schooling system which is more concerned with the outcomes for society than for the individuals. We train them to suppress feelings which do not fit our ideals and expect them to conform, wearing uniforms and fitting into timetables. None of this is intended to promote individuality, all of it is there to promote conformity. We are limiting their choices by limiting their available reactions and emotional responses, we force them into curriculums which fit only a few, in order that our capitalist society has enough skilled workers to fill its ranks. But we ignore the frustration, the resentment, and the imposition of roles which prevent the expression of the authentic self.

It is hardly surprising that the current generation of young people is having trouble feeling, we have systematically stopped them expressing what they feel, it is a short trip from there to not feeling. Then when they become depressed, we pathologize their responses and put them in boxes and give them medication, when really, we need to give them permission to be.

A word from Fritz Perls (*Gestalt Therapy: Excitement and Growth in the Human Personality*, 1951, 1994) "Social often means being willing to introject norms, codes and institutions which are foreign to man's healthy interests and needs, and in the process to lose genuine community and the ability to experience joy."

Chapter 2

Spirituality vs Religion:

The Exploration of Difference, Morals, Ethics, Single-dimensional Viewpoints and Blame

"When one person suffers from a delusion, it is called insanity. When many people suffer from a delusion it is called a Religion." Robert M. Pirsig, *Zen and the Art of Motorcycle Maintenance: An Inquiry Into Values* (1974)

Spirituality vs Religion

I suspect that there are as many definitions of spiritual experience as there are people. Given a choice between spiritual or religious, I am positive most of us would opt for spirituality. People sometimes begin therapy because they have had a "spiritual" experience. Often this experience is not immediately tenable, they may have difficulty staying with it or its implications. Often people cannot find words to describe it, many spiritual experiences are hard to put into words. Imagine trying to describe to someone a colour you had seen for the first time. These experiences are often elusive and unsettling as well as exciting; they represent a disturbance to what we think we know.

There is often a disconnection, people have no sense of where this experience has come from or what it may mean, this may create a little anxiety about the unknown. Almost all are curious about it, in my entire practice only one woman wanted it to go away and never come back. That's a rare stance though, driven by fear of the unknown rather than curiosity toward the experience. This same person thought we should never be angry, or anxious and that tears were for children. This was what she described as being mentally strong. When people are bound by introjects to the point of virtual non-expression anything novel can be perceived as a threat to equilibrium. Under these conditions, life is not contacted fully, and a stultified existence ensues. I think many people I have discussed spiritual experiences with want to explore further and look to therapy to unlock or coalesce some thoughts about the experience and its personal significance; putting a boundary around its wider impact or exploring how to encourage its development.

Therapy then can be used as a space in which we explore spiritual matters as they pertain to our phenomenological experience and our judgments of related awareness. In this way, we could say that therapy itself can be a spiritual experience and often does have a spiritual aspect which we dismiss at our peril.

I am also fully aware that my main training was in Gestalt Therapy. Fritz and Laura Perls, Paul Goodman and Ralph Hefferline were all influenced by, and wrote to some extent about eastern traditions. Mindfulness, for example, is a key component of Gestalt therapy. Gestalt is a here and now therapy, we are encouraging awareness of experience in this moment. Particularly, the observational stance of awareness or mentalising, from which we can retain a sense of self and allow self to be, while simultaneously not becoming embedded in emotional distress. We allow it, we let it be, we don't get in the way or try to stop it, and we achieve this with tools or practices often explained or at least touched on, within the meditation practices of Buddhism, yoga and other ancient traditions. There is a healthy correlation between spiritual practices and psychotherapy. I spend time every day in meditation, you could say this is a spiritual endeavour. In my reality, however, I find it helps me become more observant and act from a place of grounding and balance within which I am more aware of my somatic response to and evaluation of my environment. It is good for my mental health and my clarity of thought. It is a means to develop my observational stance, which is a skill that can be practised and honed just like any other.

Humans, indeed, humanity itself, is in a constant state of emergence and transformation. Existentialism and existential psychotherapy aim to explore and bring awareness to the phenomenological and ontological aspect of our experience. Whether we seek to express this through art, music, dance, poetry, philosophy, therapy or some other interactive, exploratory or expressive medium; in attempting to express we bring awareness to our existence and moment to moment experience. The science of being can only be experienced in the here and now. If I am reading Kierkegaard today, I might be influenced by, excited, stimulated by his writing from centuries past, but the impact is being experienced now, both physiological and psychological, in the here and now by me. This is separate from the man who wrote his thoughts so many years ago.

While being in the moment; if I pay attention to the impact, the thoughts stimulated, the connections I make now with my own musings and other experiences I have had while paying attention to connections of experience and others expressions of their own, I am experiencing an observational change in myself and my own thinking. This change is a constant, ongoing process of immersion in being and the emergence of new, at least to me, ideas, thoughts and potentialities.

The internal observation of my change and being is not constant. I could read the same book tomorrow and be closed to myself and the impact, or I might be distracted and not fully comprehend the meaning or allow my reaction to develop. I might interrupt myself by worrying about some future event which will never take place as I fantasise it will. That lack of awareness of self and its interaction with being, in this moment, inhibits growth in the human personality. The existentialists and existential psychotherapy, hold that awareness of the present moment is existence, and this is where growth in the human personality is observed. The word existential comes from a root which means to emerge, to grow into existence. This is what we observe and encourage through psychotherapy.

What Is Real?

My reality is not your reality. We are objectively different beings, and subjectively we will always hold a different perspective of reality. When I am in contact with myself in the present moment object and subject merge. I am the object I am aware of and the subject of my observations, at that moment the dichotomy of observer and object is dissolved. From every moment of awareness, I emerge anew. Transformed to some small degree by my experience. Sometimes momentously, in seemingly life-altering flashes of insight and growth; more often gradually through minuscule perceptual awakenings over illusory aspects of my felt reality, or again through the gradual building of integrated awareness. I consider this awareness, of the path of change in this moment, a spiritual experience.

Therapy can be seen as an attempt to explore, analyse or determine the process unfolding in this moment. I can make an educated guess at what is taking place within you, but only you have the direct link to your experience, you are the expert on you; your choice to share it will be doctored by previous experience and layers of neurosis and repression. Vulnerability in this present moment is risky because it allows the other person in the interaction some tenuous blurry vision of what it is like to be us. We are laid bare and have no control over their reaction when they see us as we are, or even that they will see us clearly at all. The best I can hope for is that someone will be willing to be with me in any tender state and allow me to be, without trying to rescue me or get in my way by supplying explanations and labels to my experience. In that place, I may find the courage to look upon my naked ego and not despair but at last, let go of the fetters that have bound me to others perceived realities.

I liken this self-observational aware state of being to awe. It's the best descriptor I can find, though finding words to describe what is so often ineffable seems a clunky task. By way of example, there have been moments when I have been outdoors for long periods, and when I feel closer to the earth, to myself, when the noise of the world has abated, I may experience a quickening within. It's like I become aware of the universe, its immensity. More than that I feel connected to it, part of this immense unknowable thing. In that moment I know myself differently, as though I become aware of knowledge that was distantly held, just out of my perception. There is a moment of awe, induced I think, in part at least by my smallness within this vast expanse. In that moment I have a sense of knowledge I could not grasp previously, a knowledge which is part of me but also seems to encompass all. I describe it as a deeply spiritual experience. I cannot manufacture this experience, I cannot contain it or control it, I cannot choose to continue it ad infinitum. It is. I experience it and then it is over. I do not, however, consider it a passive activity, in as much as I could at any moment stop it should I choose to. Instead, I allow it to continue and observe myself within the experience.

Some people might try to add some religious construct and try to explain it away. I prefer to just allow the experience and let it be, let myself be and experience myself as I am in that moment. This is the self-same experience I have at that moment when part of an introject has dissolved and I emerge from beneath. My somatic response feels almost identical, I am aware of my changing emerging self and feel awe at the possibilities. I experience a momentary reconfiguration of the whole and feel an invisible restraint undone. It is a moment of clear contact with my authentic self.

There is also a similar experience of sensation when I have a moment of good, clear contact with a client. When we really meet, with no expectation, when contact is no longer clouded. I feel moved, it's as though we have shared something momentous and for that brief moment met without the need to be anything other than what we are here and now, it is often moving, and I frequently experience joy and contentment as a result. I think this is the experience Bauber described as the 'I-thou' experience. He thought it was the presence of God joining him and the other in the room, enabling access to information otherwise unavailable and quickening the experience of contact.

The description of God as a person is indispensable for everyone who, like myself means by 'God,' not a principle (although mystics like Eckhart sometimes identify him with 'being') and like myself means by 'God,' not an idea (although philosophers like Plato at times could hold that he was this: but who rather means by 'God' as I do, him who – whatever else he may be "enters into a direct relation with us men in creative, revealing and redeeming acts, and thus makes it possible for us the enter into direct relation with him. (Martin Buber, *I and Thou,* 1937 p.169)

I don't add God to the equation, I don't see the need to explain away or give some causality to a supernatural fictional entity, for what is in effect a relational phenomenon, which does not need another presence to explain it beyond the ones already present in the room.

Religion and Reason

Being, in relation to religion is a difficult tangle to unfurl. The imposition of rules creates binds and hurdles we are often unable to overcome enough to be authentic. The separation of the felt self, the organic, authentic you is accomplished through the hindrance of contact by the imposition of imagined constructs, and the encouragement of stultified intellectual reason.

Being and the need to feel and own felt experience is regularly denied by the moralistic rules imposed. Deterministic regulation leaves us with the inability to know ourselves and thus separates us from our psychological being.

Leaving us limited avenues of expression and diminished awareness of consequence beyond the overwhelming desire to belong.

It seems to me pointless to set up alternatives to religious thought within the framework of psychotherapy. We are at odds with much of what is achieved by religious thought and the process of lived religious attitude. Rather than the bounds of religion we seek to enable freedom through choice and expression, where religion all too often restricts and devalues the autonomy of man, we seek to enable re-engagement with a felt reality. As therapists, we are in a rarefied position, in that we can observe and promote exploration of the behaviour lost underneath religious ideologies or other restrictive idioms. In bringing light to those dark recesses, we begin to enable support of the nonreligious framework expressed through human psychology and relationship, laying the foundation for greater understanding of self, awareness and self-expression within the co-created whole.

Freud considered religion to be a collective neurosis, a repetition of the childhood experience, where the Godhead takes the form of transferential father. Under these conditions man is unable to come into adulthood, to take responsibility for self and become fully human. Doomed to always be the child, under the sway and dominion of parental influence and choice for behaviour; maturity seems forever just out of reach.

Seen in this light religion of all types, despite some possible beneficial outcomes, seeks always to limit the extent of growth, placing bounds with laws, rules, edicts, morals and ethical concerns which in turn become swallowed as introject by extended communities. This extended community contains the collective neurosis and lends it credence, calling it normality. A challenge to this cultural norm is a challenge to the collective neurosis likely to invoke the threat response for the culture as a whole.

In any true sense of the word religion is a fiction, created by men through fantastical imagination, to control the populace, to offer a source of cohesion so larger groups can coexist and co-operate. It serves to give salve to existential angst and a container for the perceived chaos of existing without answers to those questions. It is not an object that exists, it is rather a collection of ideas gathered over time by a variety of people. By encouraging people to believe in an illusion. Religion also impoverishes intelligence by the prohibition of critical thinking. Extant texts become a source of knowledge despite the dubious origin, and exploration beyond these bounds is at a minimum frowned upon and frequently prohibited entirely. Unfortunately, this reduces adherents' power of reason across all spheres. All observable reality becomes filtered through the limited framework provided by the religion, excitement and growth as such stultify, reason is lost. The religious framework provides a balanced plateau of possible thoughts, these become more and more commonly employed.

For example, what are the chances that spontaneously, quite by chance you, while reading this suddenly think of a horse? Very slim, unless you are an equestrian about to go to the stables. But now the possibility has been increased because I have mentioned the word horse; horse has now become a more likely thought for you, in fact, I'm guessing you have just pictured one. Similarly with religious doctrine and ideals, once taught that this law or premise applies to a situation when that situation happens you are more likely to find that belief pop into your mind. The balanced plateau of thought probability has taken over, removing your need for creative thought or discerning reason. A wise man once told me "A belief will only find itself."

The truth of something is a subjective judgement of intellect. Religion says this or that is true, thus in following blindly without recourse to critical thought and the process of reason, truth is no longer explored and discussed as a fluid entity; rather it becomes a fixed standard with which to bind humanity and thought.

I can say it is wrong to kill someone, and we would probably agree on the truth of that statement. Many religions hold this as a basic tenet. Thou shalt not kill, being an obvious example. New king James version of the bible saying, "you shall not murder" Exodus ch20 verse 13. other versions alternating between kill and murder. However, what if the person I am about to kill, would if left alive kill hundreds more in a terrorist attack? I might then feel justified in killing this individual if I can prove with certainty this would be the outcome. If a robber enters my house and threatens my family, I will relax my belief that I should not do violence to people. The truth of these situations is fluid. The maxim, "Thou shalt not kill," seems good and plausible, but if we are held rigidly by this belief, we risk harm of another type. I suspect we never really consider good and bad, right and wrong, in the polemic sense. On average most people make judgements based on familiarity, familiar/unfamiliar. If your tribe are cannibals, you may have no qualms about eating your enemy; you won't feel guilty about eating another human because the familiarity of the act makes it ok. The familiar/unfamiliar polarity is more useful to moral thought than good or bad, it leaves out judgement and introduces fluidity.

Ideology does not have to be called religion in order to have fundamentalist followers. Marxism, Socialism, Communism, Materialism, Fascism, Conservatism, Existentialism, pretty much any ism you care to add, are religion in all but name. They have charismatic leaders and their fair share of fanatic fundamentalist followers. There is a code of belief, usually called a manifesto or statement of core values. People will blindly vote Conservative or Labour or Democrat or Republican or whatever else they vote for. Not out of reason and considered judgement, but rather familiarity. All too often from a position of religious adherence to an ideology. Frequently people vote as their family has always voted, doing as their father has done. We learn our values from our parents, so it's no great leap to see why we would automatically collude in such issues as religious adherence and political alignment. Its why you can safely say a country is a Muslim country, or Hindu or Christian because the children of those who went before are indoctrinated by familiarity.

In *Psychoanalysis and Religion* (1950), Eric Fromm described religion as "any system of thought and action shared by a group which gives the individual a frame of orientation and an object of devotion." (21), using this description it is easy to see how all belief systems, religious and political can be framed as doctrine-based religion. Each of these systems can be seen as a hindrance to intrapersonal and interpersonal contact. Each has rules or norms which will inhibit contact with self in one form or another.

Contentment and satisfaction can be gained from a unified sense of equilibrium, encompassing our intellectual and felt processes, married with a sense of self-direction, or realised action through the process of living. Removal or interruption of any one of these aspects creates a deficit which disturbs the ontological equilibrium sought. Religion and religious thought of all types is frequently counter to these stated aims. Individuals restricted by religion and dogma will inevitably then struggle to find equilibrium/satisfaction and continue to devote themselves to neurotic behaviours in the misguided premise this behaviour will bring relief or satisfaction eventually.

Looking to God is an expression of this need for equilibrium and satisfaction. E.g. "I do not understand how this came into being, therefore God..." The desire to relinquish personal responsibility and pass it on to God/Gods is a key element. The mistaken belief that a fictional supernatural entity with parental overtones, will somehow look after us and give us the sustenance we need, does nothing to detract from the intention. The ignoring of this self-evident fiction is testament to the clouded vision we receive from our supportive environment. Sadly, the desire remains unsatisfied and drives people toward neurotic solutions which leave them with less ability to respond authentically. The neurotic solution also allows for overlooking and justification of very simple contradictions and flaws. Reason being lost, it is no longer employed, and justifications enshrined in dogma back what would otherwise be considered nonsensical.

Dichotomy of Existence

We all need a frame of reference; we all need to make sense of our existence. At times all of us struggle with existential considerations and the dichotomy of living in the knowledge that we must one day no longer exist. This need will play out within the framework provided by our local environment. Whether you worship celebrity, money, God, animals, the wind or the personification of evil, all these are idols to which we render our reason and wit.

Aside from religion creating or fostering neurosis, neurosis can also be seen as a private form of religion, in the same way, religion can be seen as a mass neurosis. Within the framework of neurosis, we play our roles in order to placate and manipulate the environment; to make ourselves safe we distort ourselves into something we are not. These distortions become so second nature that we hardly notice them, so adept are we at playing the role that our authentic selves are hidden and even the role is played without awareness. Break through that role, even for a moment and you will find fear: fear of being found out, fear that our true self will be exposed, fear that our defence has been breached, fear that our authentic self will not be accepted. The fear may at first be nebulous and we may tend to project it onto anything we can grasp at; beyond this initial clamour, we will find a vulnerable aspect of self which has never been supported. We use neurotic behaviours to disguise fears and religion can be employed in much the same way.

There is an important difference between a personal neurosis and a mass neurosis like religion. Chiefly isolation, another of the existential mainstays. We avoid isolation and the realisation that we are alone by being part of the larger group. The group existing only because of a fictional premise is secondary and overlooked as the primary aim is to stave off awareness of isolation. Even an ideology we might consider evil may give comfort if it is accepted by enough people. It accomplishes this by virtue of providing a group to reduce isolation. In joining the group, isolation is banished from our minds. The actions of the group can be justified, like any other religious tenet, once reason is diminished by religious adherence to man-made ideals. In recent history we have seen with incredulity how far man will act contrary to perceived concepts of right and wrong, in order to be part of a group or to at least remove the threat of being separate to the group, even if joining is not the desired option.

When man projects his own power and ability onto God, man no longer owns them as his own, he relinquishes more of his reason and ability to function with contactful awareness. Waiting for God's command, for supernatural entities to take responsibility from him is justified with edicts. Now he no longer must deal with his concern over making decisions and taking personal responsibility. Eric Fromm on responsibility:

> ... most irrational tendencies to be found in man, namely, by
> an unconscious desire to be weak and powerless; they tend to
> shift the centre of their life to powers over which they feel they
> have no control, thus escaping from freedom and from
> personal responsibility. We find furthermore that this mas-
> ochistic tendency is usually accompanied by its very opposite,
> the tendency to rule and dominate others. (Fromm, *Psycho-
> analysis and Religion*, 1950, p.54).

This need for both freedom of expression, to be self-directing, and the desire to be bound, to give away responsibility to others is a dichotomy present in all human beings. We derive contentment from being self-directing, yet seek comfort in giving control to others. In many ways, we still long for our parents to take care of us and provide direction when we are faced with difficult emotions and challenging situations. The intellectual ambiguity created in relinquishing reason stifles the growth required in human personalities. The full development of reason is dependent upon the ability to accept responsibility and attain freedom from ideals that are not our own, the ability to respond. Within this concept of ideals, I include the term "introject," Perl's description of the introject, as being foreign, alien in nature, unassimilated but present as a hindrance to full contact. Freedom to be our authentic selves allows and promotes reason, beyond judgement and belief. Likewise, the relinquishing of introjects promotes freedom of expression and offers greater awareness of our extant environmental field.

A seemingly well-adjusted person (taking 'well' as tongue in cheek), may play the role of the good citizen, the churchgoer, the placid man, the hard-working employee. However, in doing so his adjustment to his environment has left little room for the expression of his authentic self. He can no longer be self-directing in the true sense. Guided only by rules to which he must adhere. He is mired in endless guilt and regret, entangled by limitations he has taken on from his forefathers. His authentic self may well be a good man, we may look at him and see a good person by our own standards and judgements. Though that will only be our judgements, not his reality. In being so bound in neurotic automatic behaviours he limits his options for contact with the environment. Excitement is stifled; passions are diminished, expression stilted. The fulfilment of contact with life is no longer open to him, the opportunity for joy becomes limited.

In order to undo this position, we must accept that we are separate, isolated and alone. In this separate place knowing also that we are inextricably linked to the rest of humanity. We are one, and we are co-created and co-creating our existence moment by moment, yet always separate and distinct.

"Then you will know the truth, and the truth will set you free." John 8:32 is a well-known biblical quotation I used to use to 'bible bash' people into thinking my way when I was a devout Christian. I still agree entirely with that quote. While adding the addendum that if someone else has told you what the truth is, it's probably not your truth. I can tell you the sky is blue, but if you are colour blind your experience of blue will be totally different from mine. Truth is so very subjective. My truth is not yours. I must be intellectually and emotionally free to find my own truth in order that it be mine. Considering this, if I have not challenged my thoughts and beliefs, they are never truly mine.

Following another's truth inevitably leads to worshiping not the God you profess to love but the cult that has sprung around it, the sect you align yourself with. Your attachment to them as a group, your worship of them as a body has become more than the devotion to the deity they represent; that 'godly' devotion has taken a secondary role now that it has brought you into the incestuous heart of the faith. The likely awareness of this fact and of isolation is diminished behind the need to belong.

Single Dimensional Viewpoint

Fundamentally fixed/rigidly held beliefs, of any school, no matter the motive or intention will disable contact with felt experience and the ability to see the world from another's perspective. They are by nature singular, excluding other possibilities. The use of single-dimensional viewpoints allows a very limited capacity to maintain other possible views of a given situation. It is a vital aspect of healthy relationships and contactful behaviour, that more than one world view can be entertained, explored and allowed without interference. This skill is a key aspect of mentalizing. Mentalizing is the ability to reflect on the here and now experience and to make interpretations after the moment of the nature of interactions. In essence, mentalizing is the observation of contact. I use the term as described by Fonagy in *Attachment Theory and Psychoanalysis* (2001). We could also use the term reflective stance, though in the moment I tend to use the descriptor, awareness.

People unable to maintain more than one viewpoint leave no mental space for interpretation of external stimuli. A close relationship with other people demands we allow them to be other than us and accept without the expectation that they will not be or must become like us. The observant position of mentalizing encourages growth through contactful behaviour by allowing conflation of disparate experiences. Without the observant awareness of the mentalizing stance, embeddedness tends to overwhelm the observer. In an embedded state people experience being controlled and overcome with emotion. The emotional state seems to have them in an overpowering and frequently frightening way; rather than them having an emotional reaction which they can experience and observe through allowing themselves to be with it. It is a challenging skill to learn as it requires a degree of metacognition. Having a singular world view hinders metacognition by funnelling all conclusions through a tightly limited path. Without the ability to explore beyond those limited boundaries fear of what is beyond will restrict interactions to a narrow channel of experience.

The observant stance requires active self-scrutiny. For us to accept parts of self which may exist contrary to our ideals, to accept that we may be biased. Fundamentally held views prevent this from occurring; when backed with religious edicts which induce shame and invoke the triggering of the threat response system, it becomes challenging for those beset with the guilt, shame or righteous anger to see past their embedded state and grasp the intangible aspects hitherto eluding them. Adding more descriptors does little to disrupt the circular arguments likely to ensue, contact is lost and often irretrievable.

This ability to mentalize and use metacognition seems linked to the security of an ego state. If you are feeling insecure you will be more likely to resort to controlling methodologies in order to feel contained. The fundamentally held beliefs of religious constructs fulfil this role by creating the framework, the scaffolding, which supports the fragile self while the facade is built. The exploration and trust in a solid self would require a secure autonomous attachment style, or the growth into something approximating this, through mirroring and experience of a relational style akin to secure attachment.

As therapists, we hope to provide a relational space in which this can be developed or experienced, maybe for the first time. Though it can take a long time for clients to accept that there are other ways of being, or that they can, in turn, be different without expectation or judgement. We must also expect there will be backward steps as the client experiments with new behaviours outside the therapy room. In this they may be rejected or attacked, as they were in past relationships, by people who feel threatened by emotional intimacy or emotionally contactful relationships. We cannot assume people will behave toward our clients with the same empathy and compassion we ourselves express. Learning that these moments of rejection say more about the rejector than the client, requires a reflective stance and the ability to observe possible alternative subjective realities. The realisation that the embeddedness of single dimension viewpoints must become an awareness, from this, the limited view is dissolved by allowing other possibilities to exist simultaneously.

Our likely response to and development of a secure attachment style then will enable tolerance of self-observation against a background of security in the knowledge I will not disintegrate if my personal beliefs are challenged, or the other people in my environment do not accept those parts of me. In this state, I can hold my beliefs much as we might a cupped hand of sand. If needed, I can allow the fingers to open and release the sand, leaving space for new knowledge and understanding. In short people with a secure attachment style are better equipped to approach new knowledge with flexibility, to see life in shades of grey rather than as black and white. In contrast, religion and fundamentalist single-dimensional viewpoints of any nature tend to encourage polarised thought patterns, allowing few flexible alternatives or exploration of substitute behaviours or ideas. We only must look at the Christian Church and its continued adherence to out of date judgemental concepts of sexuality, its inherent inflexibility in accepting women into positions of power or embracing change. Its dogmatic insistence that it is right; even within this more tolerant society belies its inflexible nature and shows us the single-dimensional viewpoint limits contact with, and acceptance of otherness.

Clients with Single-dimensional Viewpoints

In clients who hold rigorously to single dimensional viewpoints, we should be looking to offer effectively attuned responses, modelling through feedback and behaviour the kind of contingent flexible approach to exploring the here and now which is alien to the client. Through the intrapersonal dynamic of the therapeutic dyad, recognition of and possibly exploration of alternative views could become a possibility. The message recovered from observing self in relation to the therapist is that allowing otherness does not mean it will obliterate us. We can tolerate otherness; the difficult feelings associated with these moments can be expressed and explored. In allowing the exploration the client and therapist co-create a microcosm where newness is encouraged without fear of annihilation, isolation or merger.

Once triggered the threat response system will respond with anger, frustration, sometimes rage. We can allow this to wash over and past us. We are not the source. We can model acceptance of otherness by allowing the threat response in the client to play out and in acknowledgement, enable processing of the interaction. Awareness of the response is useful in defining the boundary of the belief and its impact on communication. All our clients will resist letting go of neurotic behaviours, the alternative is to face the fears and move to authentic behaviours. Responsibility for the self cannot be palmed off on another once we are operating from the authentic self.

In my practice, it has been my experience that religious people will most likely be those clients who offer the hardest resistance to a softening of their attitude towards difference. Clear explored contact will do more in this regard than any intervention you can provide. Eventually, the accepted self will explore vulnerability and open single viewpoints to the vast horizon beyond.

Religion

Giving up on the idea of God as a real entity was something of a Copernican revolution for me. Nothing changed aside from my perception; and as a result, my understanding of everything changed. When I talk about giving up religion, or the illusions contained, I am imagining the disintegration of some religious aspects of the self. This has little to do with spirituality, as religion, in my experience, is not essential to experience our spiritual self. I suspect the reverse to be true, frequently religions hinder spiritual experience.

Letting go of my religion was like the dissolving of many restrictive, underpinning or impeding elements of my mental map which hindered my interaction and contact with the world. I envisage these compartmentalised aspects of self as brittle pillars which when tested, crumble to dust because under duress they have no substance to sustain them. Letting go of these is to invite freedom, but also the realisation of responsibility.

Metaphors aside, as a therapist I cannot in all conscience push a client into this experience, if not ready to undertake this journey of their own volition, the consequences for them and our therapeutic relationship would likely be catastrophic. Responsibility for undertaking such a trek must rest with the client. I will always be glad to walk alongside and explore alternative roads to tread, the choice of road can never be mine. If, however, the client starts to dissolve introjects of a religious nature of his own accord, I can assist in directing awareness to the present moment and the effects of the disintegration. I might bring awareness to the experience of the change or support the fear and the emergence of excitement by encouraging breathing and observation. I will offer enough containment for the client to experiment and interact with novelty.

Our experience of the present moment, of the now, is where the change happens within the client's personality as well as my own. Even the experience of being a therapist in those moments of tragic clarity is profoundly moving, creating a ripple through my own psyche I can never ignore. The full awareness of the moment as a rarefied event is, in my experience, a moment of utter beauty. Where the self emerges from behind the fears and takes its place as I, while connected to thou.

Modernity has created an environment in which it is so simple to distract ourselves from the present moment it has become almost inevitable that we will. Our western societal ethos seems intent on constant stimulation, through our mobile phones, through our unending devotion to noise and distraction. The intentionality of constant doing in order to eliminate the need to be. Yet in being, in experiencing the moment, we find the opportunity for growth and development. Being has been obliterated in favour of doing, as such we are losing our capacity to experience change and awareness of self.

Most of the population would disagree, they would conclude they know themselves intimately and they assume they know what they see. Very few however have challenged the perception they have of themselves and attempted to step beyond, to robustly examine rules handed down from parents or society. Even fewer have experienced that moment when object and subject distinctions disappear, and awe is experienced throughout the observation of the emergent self.

Where single dimensional viewpoints exist, blame and blame shifting is usually evident. The narrow viewpoint prevents full contact as I have described, but to maintain that viewpoint often there must be blame apportioned.

In order to make you fit my viewpoint I would have to attack yours as though it was, well let's use the term "a sin." In so many religions this concept encompasses so many elements that it is easy to pronounce judgement on people who behave in ways counter to my viewpoint. If I considered all skirts shorter than full length to be provocative. If I create a rule for my sect that says you must always have your legs covered. If you do not adhere to that rule, I can then use this as a vehicle to blame you for my inflamed feelings and sensual desires. Projective behaviour is sanctioned at the expense of another's personal freedom, and in doing so I also get to feel self-righteous. Blame can be apportioned to support any unfounded edict, the shame induced is then a powerful deterrent to challenge of unfounded beliefs.

The Blame Game

I suspect this is where the existential lion named 'responsibility' lies panting in the shade. How do I take responsibility for my actions, if my choices are driven by motives not my own but given to me by others? And if none is taken then blame will surely be apportioned. As a species, we love to blame. From the myth of the Garden of Eden and the passing of the buck by God to mankind with a juicy ripe apple, right through history we see "it wasn't me it was him or her." If only… if only she would do this or stop doing that if only, he would work harder, if only she would hoover up, if I had more time, if I had more money, if if if. We are going to see the all-pervasive thread of expectation raise its spectral presence here too. How good it feels to bask in the light of our expectation, that others will be exactly as we want them to be, and how gratifying to attack them when they are not. Expectations, as we will see later, are a block to contact with self and others. Blame is at the heart of expectation of behaviour types, blame enables us to attack others when there is little or no justification to do so.

Blame is useful of course, as we established our fictional entities to govern us, we also created laws and punishments in order that society might work for the majority, if not for the minority. Without blame we could not punish the criminal: those that attack society's values to get what they need instead of manipulating it like everyone else must be brought to account for their actions. I do of course allow that a few, a very small few do not manipulate the world to get what they need, but ask directly, but so few and far between are those they hardly seem worth mentioning. I'm not in that camp for sure, I might ask for what I want sometimes, and I might even get it sometimes. Most of the time I subtly manipulate the environment without even being aware of it, with smiles, stories, laughter, music, a handshake, a wink, a word, a well-timed intervention, even this missive. All my actions bar the very few are designed to elicit a response and impact upon my environment, thus they are frequently a manipulation of the environment to get what I need, be it love, praise or money. I'm just honest about it when I catch myself doing it.

Blame then can be justified as a useful tool for society as it helps society stay cohesive and offers us a chance to feel superior and righteous. In many ways, the blame of one person, forces the remaining individuals closer together. Here we all are separate from them because we don't behave like that, this at least we have in common, even if I don't really like you or the way you bring up your kids or the way you drive. At least you don't do drugs... well not those drugs. It is a feature of defining ourselves by defining other phenomena touched upon earlier.

Frequently blame is also used to draw forth compensations for the aggrieved party, be they words of apology, deeds of restitution or financial reparation. Without blame, who would you ask for compensation? Which then begs the question, who drew the line in the sand? The one that says I am right, and you are wrong.

Morals, Ethics and Other Imaginary Lines in the Sand

When political power for the individual is diminished, the loss of agency must be compensated, or rebellious thoughts will arise. Creating the concept of the individual soul, a thing for which I, the powerless individual, have ultimate responsibility is one step on the path to restoring a sense of agency. This is a part of "self" which cannot be corrupted or contaminated by another human being. I am, through diligence and virtue, able to build my self-esteem and some semblance of power by taking care of this soul; despite the subject, the soul, being illusory. If I, through faith, hold it to exist, I can convince myself of my power over it, in turn, I no longer feel powerless, and my imagined agency takes the place of my displaced lack of actual political power. By shifting my focus to a fictional concept, I no longer worry about my lack of power apparent in reality.

Religion then can be said to promote social powerlessness, asking people to accept the situation they find themselves in. By introducing the illusion of soul and imbuing virtue as a sacred duty, people are convinced to accept their previous powerless state. The virtues themselves not only become the focus, instead of my relative political weakness, my impotence, they also become a source of pride for the powerless individual. Often the religious virtue converts a positive influence into a negative one by the change of emphasis. For example, it might be a virtue to suffer in silence, which negates the possibility of standing up and doing something to alleviate the suffering. Where virtue is made of a negative expression or the suppression of the self, we find the driving forces of masochism and sadism at play.

Political impotence then is redressed or masked with the soul and its sustenance. An ethereal object given us by some universal deity. A fictional thing to nurture and care for. Not being of this world is of far greater importance than my political impotence or even my physical self and therefore, psychologically it can take centre stage. Conveniently reducing the angst about the current condition of the devotee whilst suppressing the urges to do something positive about the real situation to enable change in this world rather than the imagined next. The desire for a more fulfilled existence is transferred to the imagined world of the future and hope is called upon to fill the remaining void.

Morals are born of the herd's ideals enshrined in virtue. Common virtues like hope, love and charity. Oppression of or deviation from the path of virtue is transformed into sin, crime and failure; the punishment of which is inevitable. The punishment itself creates for the punitive figure another layer of pride and virtue. Ironically the punishment may itself be an abhorrent expression of sanctioned sadism. Righteousness is what religion and society approves of unrighteousness is its antithesis, but just because it is approved does not make it healthy.

The concept of sin is in truth a prison, by any religious standards we have all sinned, so there is no escape from it. If you accept that perspective as a personal standard to live by, you accept that you have sinned and will forever carry the guilt for that sin. Even if you accept redemption in one form or another, the memory that you have committed the sin will still be there as a heavy reminder of your sin tainted nature. I will explore this concept more in the discussion of shame in chapter 6, though it underpins much of the concepts explored throughout this book.

The forcing of virtue upon the ontological self, often by cruel removal of contactful expression and the introduction of veiled masochism, or in the case of self-harm, such as flagellation, starvation or purging, is less obvious and more acceptable as pious behaviours. Disguised as virtue these perpetuate the battle between self and other, self and doctrine, self and introjected norms. That is not to say that there is anything wrong with love, charity etc. It is the use of these manipulative tools in order to engender observance of social constructs which creates imbalance and disharmony. The imbalance appears in the psyche while removing it from society. One is sacrificed for the other. Individuality sacrificed for homogenised conformity.

A criminal may attack society in order to preserve himself, steal for food, to pay for shelter or to satiate a desire built from learned behaviours which are unhealthy; or perhaps just because he has never learned or indeed been taught another way to be in the world, and with his surfeit of skills, attacks society in order to exist. A drug addict may use his drug to numb the pain of past terrors, an all-pervading sense of loneliness and isolation or to excite an otherwise dull, meaningless existence. I feel nothing, but I wish to feel something, or I feel too much, take it away. This is deemed intolerable and unjust by society and must be punished and suppressed, though rarely understood or offered supportive intervention beyond criminal justice. Presumably, because it highlights our own powerlessness and impotence in the face of existential realities.

For example, in 2020 while I write this; currently locally and in general in the U.K., you cannot get addiction counselling or therapeutic support for addiction until after you have come off your drugs or alcohol unless you are willing to pay for it privately. There are some charitable bodies providing this much-needed service. However, local and central governments have, in the main and with few exceptions, taken the position of no support for those still using. It's a little like saying, we won't teach you to drive until you have proven to us you can drive. As a society, when we catch the thief, mugger, addict or political agitator etc. in order to preserve ourselves and our society; we will and can justifiably cause injury, mental and often physical, by incarceration or fine or in some societies worse still. Yet this is ok because this injury is perpetrated by people on the ethical side of the law.

In short, if someone locks me up against my will, which is clearly a violation of my desire to be free. Society can, with no sense of remorse, guilt or irony, do the same to him/her. This reveals that ethics are frequently the justification of injury by necessity, and when we look a little deeper often mask sadism. We look back on history to see in hindsight how brave men and women were persecuted when they attempted to change a political system, and justly so for they were acting against the law. A law we now see as unjust. In our topsy-turvy hindsight, we see a courageous struggle. Yet had we lived at the time would we have seen it as such or would we have seen the agitator as up to no good, set on destroying what we have worked so hard to maintain? The line in the sand has moved, and now this agitator is a hero of folklore.

Religion as the Drug of Choice

Religious dogma can be seen in a similar way to the drug of choice, though applauded rather than attacked. Because piety and religiousness are allowed, expected and even lauded by society. Man creates a rule and uses it to elevate himself in the eyes of his peers. Let's take sexual desire as an example. I choose this because I have heard many religious people wax lyrical against the expression of sexual desire outside of marriage, or in same-sex couples. It is a subject which many religions have described as a terrible sin, depending on various parameters, like marriage age and gender.

Often this sinful urging "lust" must be fought according to religious dogma. In this following example, our protagonist seeks to subjugate his natural urges, his sensual desire, because he has been told it is wrong to lust after women he is not married to. Thus, a conflict is created within his ontological self, that part of him which genuinely finds women attractive and alluring. This schism takes up much of his time, in some ways you could say it becomes something of an obsession: fighting the good fight and suppressing himself and his natural state. It is all vanity in the end though. If he succeeds, even for an hour he can say I am doing God's will, I am a good this or that or whatever we are calling ourselves these days. He can say to himself, "I am fighting the good fight, what a good man I am to struggle so and be so holy." etc. etc. Thus, he builds himself up in his own eyes and in the eyes of others with similar beliefs when he accidentally lets it be known how he has been struggling and how he has won through. All of course by the grace of his deity, though secretly feeling very pleased with himself.

The struggle itself is a source of great pride that he is so very strong in the face of such terrible temptation. It is also the justification for attacking anyone who does not live the way I live, someone who is attracted to members of the same sex for example. They may be excluded, vilified, seen as weak, as giving in to a lifestyle choice, when our sexual desire is no more a choice than our skin colour. Still, it has been my experience that religious people tend to ignore the immutable in favour of unsubstantiated ideas, especially where sexual preference and gender are concerned.

Of course, this charade requires that the desire remain, in order that he may fight it again and again. He can never be rid of it, if it was to disappear, what would define him as a good man of God? Likewise, the desire is frequently projected outward, seen as something other, not of the self, induced by perhaps an evil spirit, a demon or the devil incarnate. Let's call it the spirit of lust and in doing so make it something other than self, an attack that must be repelled. Perhaps, "It was her and those short skirts, she made me do it." The projection of personal responsibility is clear and often remains unchallenged and even promoted. A client of mine told me how her mother had responded to her rape with, "What do you expect going out dressed like that." No concept of the perpetrator's guilt and a new layer of shame added to what was already a horrific experience.

The motivation then ultimately is vanity, pride, hubris, but that is masked behind layers of guilt and shame, the guilt that secretly, possibly even hidden from ourselves, we enjoy these sensual feelings and occasionally let them spill out so that we can revel in them, and our shame that we fail. In that last regard, Christianity is unremittingly harsh. Not only do Christians give themselves the supremely hard task of living the spotless life but, they compare themselves to Christ, that they might be like him. In doing so they set the goal so high that it is unattainable. There can be nothing but failure and therefore shame and self-punishment for being so lowly and sinful. This, in turn, creates a constant sense that the self is not enough, will never be enough, that we will never be able to measure up. All this built on a myth, that I might fill my life with meaning and avoid thoughts of death with the promise of heaven, if I measure up.

The attack of people who hold a different belief is inevitable. Ugly though it is to us looking on, to a fundamentalist thinker, the very idea that someone could hold the opposite idea to their own to be true, is experienced as an attack against their very foundation. That foundation being a fiction held to be irrefutably true. It is experienced as a personal attack because that belief is a pillar of a fragile ego.

Let's stick for now with the idea that sensual pleasure is somehow wrong. If that is my belief and I spend a great deal of my time attacking my inner desires and urges in order to feel good about myself; if another comes along who is free and clear of remorse about such impulses, what does that say about me? It says I could be free too, that I could allow my sensuality full reign and it would not be the end of me. I would have to face my fears, my avoidance of contact with sensual behaviours, the excitement. I would be faced with how I have prevented myself from living life fully, the fear of rejection and vulnerability and the reality of all the opportunity lost in the years of self-debasement. To choose to attack the other as being sinful or even evil is convenient. Not least because it reinforces my beliefs that have no empirical basis; but also, because it allows me to feel like a good man again, for fighting the good fight, win-win. Unless you are the one being attacked, in what is usually a tyrannical display of bigotry which is inevitably harmful.

When a religious person says this or that sexual behaviour is a sin or forbidden, when they choose to ignore the immutability of sexual desires origin, what they are really doing is trying to avoid their own desires, whatever basis they take. It is also the mechanism by which I can engender pride for myself as I recall what a good person I am for not giving in to such detestable urges. Of course, the downside is the shame of failure, because ultimately, the urges and desires remain, no matter how vociferously denied or stoically contained, they will spill out, often indirectly and all too frequently with horrific consequences.

I will never have clear contact with another if they are able to express something I repress. If I contest the desires and behaviours of others, if I say you must be like this in order to fit in, I am in contact not with the human being I am talking to, but rather my expectations of otherness and that they must be like me to be acceptable. While in contact with these expectations I will never be in contact with myself or the other. We will never have a meaningful meeting because the expectation will always interfere with contact.

Chapter 3

A brief look at the brain functions used in the creation of religion and superstition.

Yet mystery and manifestations arise from the same source.
This source is called darkness. *Tao Te Ching,* by Lao Tzu,
translated by Stephen Mitchell (1988).

The problem of patterns.

Religious ideas, ritual and superstition arise within the human community through the implementation of mental abilities we all require for everyday survival. This includes our social networking, pattern recognition, threat detection, intuitive reasoning, attachment and bonding etc. There are many areas of brain function we use in order to create, and exist within, groups of humans that can work together.

Religion appears to use aspects of all of these in its construction. Unfortunately, where religion is concerned the logical reasoning aspect becomes sidetracked and lost. This group of neurological systems are responsible for multifaceted patterns of behaviour which we employ every moment of every day. I have found the technical information about how these systems work and intersect to be invaluable as background information to have as a therapist. It will give us a larger framework within which we can understand and respond to the needs of our clients struggling with changing, or exploring, different behaviours within their own relationships.

Our hunter-gathering long-dead cousins required pattern recognition to survive. The mechanism appears on the face of it quite simple: when two events are perceived they are compared with previous memories and experience. If these events are similar, they become linked mentally as similar. If there is a correlation, a perceived cause and effect is looked for. Initially, this may be so we can avoid threats: If I see an angry face and it has been followed by physical violence my brain will link the two, and on seeing an angry face in the future, this recognised pattern will pop up and warn me I might need to avoid conflict. Also, I will remember this specific face and even if it is not angry, I will be on alert just in case. My mind unconsciously remembers the correlation. I have, in this example, also used facial recognition as well as threat recognition and pattern recognition. I will have developed some form of creative adaptation to deal with this situation based on previous experience and my own physicality. The effect is remembered and regularly accessed and updated with new data. As part of our threat response and evaluation mechanism, it is constantly active. It is also one of the methods by which we can judge another person's emotional state just by a glance at body posture, breathing and facial expression.

Hyperactive Agency Detection

If I see a wasp, and it stings me I will remember that little black and yellow bug will hurt if it lands on me. However, we are looking for a threat all the time, so when a black and yellow harmless hoverfly or a stingless wasp comes into the room I will react as though it was a wasp, until that is, I am reassured that this is a harmless bug. On the other hand, I will never look at a wasp and think this is a harmless bug. This process is called hyperactive agency detection, it never really turns off. Even when you're sleeping if you hear a noise, you will wake and stay awake until you are sure all is safe.

Religious thought hijacks this mental response mechanism, in part to insinuate its way into a person's belief system and in part to support itself. It is via this mental mechanism that superstition is developed; in turn, this response also makes it hard to give up a belief system. When the faith is threatened by an extraneous thought or someone else's divergent ideas, the alert system kicks in to protect the threat being realised. I'll come back to this in a moment but first, let's look at intuitive reasoning and how this marries up with the threat detection system.

Intuitive Reasoning

Intuitive reasoning is a fascinating aspect of the human mind. In attempting to comprehend our situation we try to see the whole. If we have partial information, we literally fill in the blanks until something appears to make sense. You will see many examples in therapy books explaining intuitive reasoning, like the black and white pictures that can be seen as either vase or faces. The ability to fill in the blanks is important to our survival and incorporated as an integral aspect of our threat and response system. In essence this helps us predict possible outcomes to new situations based on previous patterns.

Having developed a threat response system based on ritual and pattern it is very hard to overturn it. We are hardwired to respond to and monitor for threat; ignoring our threat response is not an evolutionarily advantageous trait. If every time I saw a lion walking towards me, I learned to climb the nearest tree, I stand a good chance of surviving. But if I override that threat response and stay on the ground, I might well be eaten. In the past, there may have been people who chose to stay on the ground, they may have been more likely to challenge the automatic response of the intuitive threat systems. If they did exist, they and their genes would more than likely have died off before regularly passing on those genes responsible for the behaviour.

Similarly relinquishing the threat response developed through superstition will of itself be viewed by the mind as risky behaviour. I must first experience support to know I am safe before I can consider letting go or even beginning to challenge my previous modus operandi. Through therapy, we might call this process of support, containment. Containing a person while they explore alternative behaviours which might have been perceived as threatening is a slow process, which requires trust and courage in equal measure.

Superstition and Intuitive Reasoning

Superstition is really the belief in a supernatural agency to affect me and my world to beneficial ends or to curse my enemies' world to my beneficial ends. The building of that belief requires that we develop imagined causal links between events that are no more linked than a banana and a ball bearing. We try to make sense of the world as we perceive it on the fly. In doing so we search for patterns of cause and effect, which fill in those blanks and become part of our threat detection system for us to stay safe.

As part of a process of danger avoidance, if a situation presents danger, we must find out what chain of events has created this threat and how best to return the environmental threat to a state of equilibrium, so that we can rest. There may be no determined threat, or it might have been an event with no preventable cause, or possibly there is a cause we cannot discern. The human brain, in looking for links between threat and event, will in these cases fill in the blanks between events: it will tell us, maybe this or that happened, and after a while, we will perceive our thought as reality because we can find nothing more suitable to fill the gap in our understanding. It is a creative leap of mental gymnastics which renders floating anxiety less likely as a physiological outcome. I use the term floating anxiety loosely, there is really no such thing, by this, we might mean anxiety for which I have yet to determine a cause.

We are thoroughly unreliable as eyewitnesses simply because everybody fills in the blanks and has a different take on the situation at hand. If I sit in a room with a couple I am working with and ask them how they feel the session went, I might be thinking it was a terrible waste of time, one of them might have thought it was useful and the other may have discovered something I had not even seen. Even though we have all experienced the exact same event, our subjective experience is built from our relationship to our historically familiar experience and our different perception of the same 50 minutes. Our evaluation centres, threat perception and intuitive reasoning give us all a different input and we all then have a differing view of what happened. Add to this the filters of transference and introject and we have a canvas for some very creative adjustments. Even with something as seemingly obvious and straightforward as a crowd watching a car crash, every witness will give you a different picture of what happened. That may include differing focus, different colours to objects, a different chronological order to events etc. Importance will be lent to alternative aspects by different personalities, as such no two stories of one event will be the same, though similarities will arise and with more witnesses, an average can be attained, which we like to label as truth. It is always relative to the observer; truth is in truth always subjective.

Superstitions we form are used by the mind to fill in the blanks and ascribe agency when we imagine agency should exist, but when there is none. We build religions from groups of superstitions around which we add ritualistic behaviours. The result is a complex set of rules or guides to living which relieve a little of our ontological anxiety. We also do this partly to construct larger groupings of people that can work together. The faith or commonality of shared belief becoming a binding agent or prevalent goal. In turn, the goal is presented as a reason to cooperate, the tenets derived creating a unity of purpose. Culture is then attached as trappings around these, and culture further serves to allow people to feel connected. Be that through art, music or any other expression. As such it is the creation of such superstitions from nothing but the subjectively perceived patterns in life, combined with intuitive reasoning, that underpin much of the rituals propping up religious belief. All of this is guarded by the threat detection system, as though we are hardwired to follow our cultural norms.

Superstition and Intuitive Reasoning in Action

By way of example, I wish to run through the process of how a belief or religious ritual might develop or become ascribed to actions it has nothing to do with. This is an oversimplified version of what is far more complex than this, however, I hope this example gives a little insight into how this process might work.

— Brain Functions Used in the Creation of Religion —

Let's assume I live in a dry place where there is little water, and which is reliant on rains which are infrequent. If my tribe needs water, let's say it's the dry season, it's been a few months and the wise man who talks to his invisible friends tells us that tonight it is a full moon, if we dance under the moon the gods of rain may favour us with water. We are desperate so we let him teach us the dance. We dance, the dance brings us together for the evening at least, we are even happy, it was a good night. Dance complete, the next day the heavens open and rain, blessed rain falls on our jubilant faces.

Point one, we see a link between our dance and the rain; We were told it would work that way after all so why not believe it? We are ecstatic, something we have done seems to have affected the universe in order that we might get what we need. We are imbued with a sense of agency, in the belief that this dance, let's call it a rain dance, so pleased the gods as to bring the rain. Now we have a way to make it rain but also a way to talk to what... the Gods. God? Better ask the wise man he clearly knows about this stuff.

Point two, the wise man was right, he must be really wise, we should really stop mocking him because his friends are invisible and do as he says when there is trouble. Also, maybe promote him to village shaman or holy man. I mean just imagine if he were to use that kind of power against us! Maybe give him an income to keep him happy. Also, if we give him food and shelter, he doesn't need to hunt so he will have more time to do his shamanic things which are clearly important.

Point three, It's the dry season again the shaman tells us to dance, but this time it does not work, so we are confused, full of doubt. We go to the Shamen and tell him he's full of it. He replies in mocking tones "but you're dancing all wrong, last time you got it right, the fault is yours, try harder to please the god of thunder and rain."

So, the blame is shifted onto the devotee, not the god, and subtly the god is no longer just the god of rain but also of thunder, well that's a bit scary, he could throw thunderbolts at me. I had better dance well tonight. We dance again, and it rains again in the morning, just soon enough for us to feel full of agency once again and for the shaman to bask in his brilliance and extract his apology.

As modern humans you and I look at this and might smirk, we know better, we have a broader knowledge of physics and natural science with which to recognise this for what it is. Yet once upon a time, it was believed to be true, and not so very long ago either.

As we have seen, we are hardwired to see patterns, it's a survival mechanism. We see that when Bert ate this mushroom, he got sick, and when he ate that mushroom, he was well. We learn that eating this mushroom is good and that one bad. It is a pattern we use to survive and a pattern we can pass on through communication, through tales and stories and even myths, to other members of the tribe, or to our children and their children. We find patterns in everything, in facial recognition, in language, in all that we do. It is an integral, important part of how we survive. Unfortunately, we frequently take these patterns and build them into more than they are.

The ascribing of agency where there was none becomes inevitable in order to fill in gaps in understanding of events which we cannot fill with fact. If I pray and something happens, quite separately to my prayer. There is no cause and effect here, my prayer not having the least power. I may see a pattern anyway, I see that I prayed, and this happened, my mind fills in the blanks because it needs to make sense of the world. Ergo, God must be real, he hears my prayers and prayer must really work. That is if I pray in the right way and God in his mercy deigns to listen and act upon my wishes.

— Brain Functions Used in the Creation of Religion —

Over the centuries events like these are accumulated, often written down, and become a tome of belief, supporting religious ritual which must be adhered to, despite being frequently at odds with our ontological experience. At some point someone, often a man, who wants power takes over. In doing so he becomes the head of the church or the state religion or the tribal hunting grounds. He uses this position to instil more social control through the medium of religious ritual, dogma and moralistic teachings. Thus, organised religions are created to make social control more palatable and enable the cooperation of thousands where once only a handful could cooperate.

That part is useful, as a glue to adhere the disparate elements of a social order spread over miles, into one cohesive paradigm. But at a cost to the self and self-expression which is often unhealthy.

I don't want to be seen as bashing the shamanic circles either. I have read plenty of descriptions of tribal communities, who through shamanic understanding, use what appears to be a kind of group therapy to heal troubled souls. Taking the entire community and saying this person is ill therefore we are all ill and must work together to find the remedy. This is a shorthand version but there is clearly some truth in cohesive compassionate groups being healing for individuals when they are well-intentioned and well-led by competent individuals. Particularly when the leader of that group has been ascribed power by the attendees. There is a natural therapy within that context of being with and being part of the whole, which is intrinsically healing. We are social beings after all. I suspect they would scoff at our individual therapy as unrealistic and unlikely to get results. I suspect that may also be key to why group therapy is so very valuable. There is always something to be learned. It doesn't really matter if the superstition is a belief in a rain dance, tarot cards, lucky totems or astronomy. If we have created for ourselves a belief system based on superstition, we are looking for agency where there is none; more importantly, we give away personal responsibility in order to ascribe agency to a fictional system.

Our prehistory ancestral cousins did not have the scientific insight in order to understand or make sense of this process of superstition creation, so we can forgive them for jumping to conclusions and forming superstitions. Today though we do have these insights and yet we are still following religion as though it is more than superstitious fiction. What's more, those religions are jealously guarded and protected, often by the state.

Chapter 4

Delusion and ideas, the basis for religious behaviour and its conflict with personal responsibility.

A man cannot live without a steady faith in something indestructible within him, though both the faith and the indestructible thing may remain permanently concealed from him. One of the forms of concealment is a belief in a personal god. Kafka, *Zurau Aphorisms* of Franz Kafka (2006)

Religion as Delusion

Fair warning. If you have a faith or religion, you may find this chapter particularly challenging. I can only hope you will try to keep an open mind. I hope it will stimulate discussion. Try to notice if you are feeling combative or angry and ask yourself how this has come about, and how you experience it. These are my thoughts I am writing here; you do not have to agree with any of it, just try to allow a healthy debate between those aspects of you that are angry and those parts that can explore the ideas I present.

I want to express my concern that we imagine we have control just as we imagine we have free will. Both of which are often intimately related to religious belief and introjected behavioural norms. I struggle with religion as a therapist, however it's also a personal thing as well as professional. I would once have defined myself as a "born again" Christian; actually, I suspect I was an opinionated, judgmental, unaware mess of a human being hiding behind the façade of religion and moral inflexibility. Looking back at those years, my choices, my statements to others, the beliefs I swallowed, I consider myself to have been delusional throughout that period.

The Diagnostic and Statistical Manual V clearly states, "An individual's cultural and religious background must be taken into account in evaluating the possible presence of delusional disorder.." By definition, it considers religious belief not to fall into the delusional bracket, perhaps because it does not want to suggest religious belief is a mental health problem. I suspect I am not alone in this assumption that delusion is at the heart of religious belief, I wonder then at the inclusion of religious belief as an excuse in the DSM V. The taking into account statement seems to allow for acceptable levels of delusion. The delusion that is cultural or religious in origin, which is accepted by the society a person originates from.

If you look for a general definition of Delusion you will find something along these lines:

A false personal belief that is not subject to reason or contradictory evidence and is not explained by a person's usual cultural and religious concepts (so that, for example, it is not an article of faith). A delusion may be firmly maintained in the face of incontrovertible evidence that it is false.

The part of this definition that I have always struggled with is; "and is not explained by a person's usual cultural and religious concepts (so that, for example, it is not an article of faith)." Essentially, we are saying that you can have a delusion if it's part of your religion and we won't challenge it, even if it's plainly nonsense. I struggle with this because as a therapist it is my job to work with and support the movement away from delusional behaviour. The dissolving of delusions creates an intrinsic freedom of choice, within the limits already discussed; it also re-engages a person's personal agency stemming from their authentic self as personal responsibility is re-established. However, when faced with religion, I am suddenly defanged and told to just accept it. Today it might be considered discriminatory to suggest to someone their religion is based on a delusion, but I suspect there are other reasons why challenging it is taboo.

I am not suggesting cultural institutions such as a society's religion or any social construct, would not be taken into account when accessing character types or their formation, we are all co-created within our extant environs. But I do think the ignoring of nominally accepted delusions is harmful and incongruent to a profession seeking to promote mental health.

I feel as though that last part of the actual description has been added to appease the fundamentalists in our society. I can't see that it was added by virtue of reason as it seems self-contradictory, making the boundaries fuzzy and unclear. Perhaps It was added for fear that if we say, as Nietzsche did, that God is dead, we risk a confrontation with half of humanity. It is worth asking the question, is this why the description of delusion, as is commonly held by the mental health community, is fudged? Is it because awareness of our expectations and motivations always brings clarity and motivation toward change, which means a very different society would exist? Would people be in a better position to choose for themselves?

For the purpose of this book, I define delusion as "A personal belief that is not subject to reason or contradictory evidence. A delusion may be firmly maintained in the face of incontrovertible evidence that it is false." If we remove the cultural excuses, it is far clearer.

Religion as Idea

Religion, when viewed from my perspective, is just a group of man-made ideas formed into a set, linked, often tenuously, by an overarching ideal, such as the existence of heaven and hell, reincarnation or a messiah, a specific God/gods or some other pivotal belief. Ideas are not immutable and should not be treated as such. Ideas are free to be challenged and discussed, in much the same way I would challenge any idea which I felt conflicted with my perception of reality or which I did not fully comprehend. The challenge and exploration of beliefs are enacted in order to gain a deeper understanding and to give expression to curiosity.

I do not need to challenge everyone from every religion, I'm not an evangelist for atheism, I don't "need" you to give up your beliefs or your gods. Professionally, I am only really interested in those damaged by religion or seeking to hide an authentic self behind religion, and that last, only if the client wants to explore it. I know many devotees of religions who might otherwise get a diagnosis of schizophrenia, and because their voice is saying nice things, they never get seen by the likes of me. It's not an issue if you have an angel who follows you around and tells you really nice things about yourself, why seek treatment. I don't need to undo that, and I don't want to find problems where there are none, there is enough to deal with already.

Likewise, I don't want to get rid of religion overnight either. If we suddenly removed religion from circulation, there will be millions upon millions of people without a safe group space, who regularly hear the voice of God/Gods/angels/the Devil but would have no one to share it with, they seem happy enough sharing it amongst their group and in many respects, it seems to act as a therapeutic tool. We can leave well alone where no harm is done. Sadly, we do see much harm being done by religion and religious people of any persuasion, as a result, I am no longer comfortable with ignoring the delusion I see.

Dangerous Ground

As a therapist, as part of the therapeutic community, we have been told not to touch religion. I feel uneasy about this, it looks like an avoidance, which ironically is exactly what we as therapists are supposed to spot and challenge. That is, I guess what I am doing here. I should stress that we don't need to challenge it in the sense of trying to make people listen to reason. We don't have to attack them or their beliefs. That is what religious people do to us when they turn on science, particularly biological science. We don't need to take that approach, it's not helpful to fight, and would stimulate an automatic response. Given that the hyperactive agency detection mechanism inherent in humans is fired when threat is perceived and that this same system is used by the brain to ward off attacks against faith; attacks against said faith will generate a fighting response, during these episodes, reason is lost as the imperative need to defend kicks in.

I do not challenge my client's religious beliefs head on, not because I have been told not to, though originally that was a motivating factor behind my choice. Rather, I choose not to challenge a client's religious belief because it's counter-productive and creates a conflict where there need not be one. I am aiming for a compassionate relationship, not a combative one that tears people down. I do have to hold in awareness my dislike of the apparently delusional aspects of religious behaviour in order to remain congruent and in contact with the client.

Often, I really want to challenge a delusional reality couched in religion. I have to hold myself back from pointing out inconsistencies and the lack of evidence. I would not be fulfilling my role if I ignore delusion where I find it though. Later I will give some case studies and explain how the delusion was not challenged directly but rather through other awareness development it became a problematic figure or inconsistency for the client. When the client brings it, it's a different matter. They are setting an agenda, not me. For me, though it is a struggle at times; a struggle which I have no doubt is noticed by my clients as they comprehend my unawares expression and their intuitive perception of me during sessions.

I think much of my desire to point out the obvious stems from my previous delusional state and escape from it. I do genuinely want people to be free from the religious dogma that inhibits and denigrates. But they are not me and I am not them. What is good for me is not always good for them. Instead, I look upon working with this, in the same manner I would be working with someone who has an imaginary friend. I don't have to tell them the friend does not exist or convince them to get rid of them. What I can do through therapy is to enable re-integration of those aspects of self that have been split off to form that invisible friend, for them to start a dialogue about what they get from that friend. Often that can be obtained elsewhere, though it requires courage. If they can get that need met elsewhere or if that correlates to any aspect of themselves which does not get a voice, the exploration of the missing contact kickstarts the healing process of reintegration.

Regularly these fantasy constructs are wishes and desires projected onto an outside agent and religion has oftentimes been the source of the conflict in the self. This is particularly the case in those that feel threatened and powerless. It is not a coincidence that religious beliefs are frequently held by those that feel powerless without the religion that supports them. The projection of power onto an omniscient, omnipotent, omnipresent being is a common theme throughout many religions, particularly monotheistic religions. Coupled with the ability to speak and be heard with the mind alone or through ritual or liturgies, this illusory power is evoked and imbued with a strong sense of significance. The actual absence of power seems to be ignored mostly using blame, guilt and shame as deflection. Fritz Perls said in the discussion of neurosis in *Ego Hunger and Aggression*:

"That permanent projections like the creation of gods are an addition is obvious to anybody who does not turn this fact upside down (who believes that these gods created man.) but even with the believer, religion remains an "as if" fiction, a fact which can be realized by comparing a pious person with a psychotic suffering from religious delusions, who experiences God as a personal reality. Religion tends to prevent the growing up of mankind, tends to keep believers in an infantile state. "We are all children of one father - God!" Religion as foundation (1942, 1992)

As I said previously, it does little good to challenge the delusion directly. I do not believe we need to. We can assume this person lives with this belief for good reason, it underpins much of their actions and the way they live their lives. In moments when I feel combative or entertain the possibility of challenge, I try to take a step back and evaluate my motives. I must ask myself if this is productive. I have no right to challenge another's foundation. If used as a foundation for one's fragile ego, religion does a good job of sticking together parts that might otherwise disintegrate. Unfortunately, it also tends to prevent healing and growth of these parts of self through exactly the same mechanisms. If you cover up something which needs to be seen, you will never see it.

It could also be said therapy is my religion. It is certainly an ideology, much like any other it is constructed from ideas and gives us a moral code, a code of ethics, it has devout followers and is often evangelical. There are great and charismatic leaders to follow. Yet I do not believe it is based on a delusion, the science is rigorous and well tested. What is more, all psychological theories are open to challenge and extensive peer review. Tweaks and changes are made to existing theory, new ideas added, tested, verified or thrown out. It is a living thing, flexible and open to change. Yet in my role as a therapist, I often feel as though I am one of the new set of priests, people come to me, recount their failings and difficulties; we say the appropriate liturgies and send them away feeling unburdened and relieved. During the exchange, hopefully, awareness is gained to increase the likelihood of healthier choices being made next time. They pay of course, like previous priesthoods we gather our tithe, though I'm perhaps a little more upfront about the fees and the full extent of my powers.

But I do not work miracles, though it might appear that way at times. It is just the client working hard and having the courage to make momentous changes to the way they are, confronting the most challenging issues of life. It's not me, though accepting praise is seductive. I have no power to heal in the sense you might imagine a faith healer claiming. I say let's walk down this road together, and if they come, we have many moments of joy and pain, and we have them together, not in isolation, which is itself a considerable source of existential angst. In some way, that process of contact, immersion and acceptance generates change that does look incredible. If you were agoraphobic and now can leave the house, if you suffered from panic attacks and PTSD and now after a few sessions you are free from the burden of your mental health problem, then sure it looks amazing, bordering on the miraculous at times. More importantly to the client, it can feel like a life has been returned to its owner. But it is not me, I have no power to heal. I am well-read and experienced, I know some of the maps that might fit your purpose, I can lead you on the path, and hopefully, help you find the right one. I cannot make you walk or come with me. I cannot make you well, though well you may become. It will only ever be because you find the courage and take the responsibility to do what needs to be done. Responsibility because this is your life, no one else can fix it for you, and courage, because to face the pain, to allow your vulnerability and risk change, that takes courage.

Personal Responsibility

Belief in a personal god though, that part, that really hits my button. When a client is faced with a difficult choice, and they decide they will go away and pray and see what God says. That moment right there is a difficult one for me. Interestingly I'm not against prayer, it won't work in the sense that no deity will answer your call, but it does help you focus, it gives an outlet and may allow your brain to rest and collate, work through a problem and find a creative solution. Most importantly, it is you, not a god that provides the solution, and if it is you, then it is your responsibility, not Gods.

There is no God, Nietzsche proclaimed him dead in his 1882 book *Parable of a Mad Man,* and I'm inclined to agree with him on this; as I see no evidence to the contrary, or that he ever existed in the first place, beyond our own created image. It's your choice, you must take responsibility for yourself and your actions if you are ever to contact the environment in a healthy way. Giving the choice away to God will not help your situation. What I do see here is some delusional behaviour, a giving away of personal power and responsibility to the incumbent fictional entity. Projection in spades and transference that's off the scale.

Personal responsibility is a cornerstone of existential thinking. It is also the cornerstone of personal development. I don't see people recover from mental health issues until they take responsibility for themselves. People may scout around the edges, dip in toes, run away, hide, fight their anxiety, run from fears, blame others etc. None of this works. Change begins when people begin to take responsibility for who they are now, in this moment. Lasting change is likely to come about when we are supportive enough as therapists to allow the client to explore and experiment with different ways of being, but only after they have accepted what they are at this moment. Without feeling we can cope with them in all their distress, they will not allow change while with us. During the process of exploration, clients will find they have more resources than they thought they had, they will find themselves again and let loose the neurotic behaviours that have enshrouded them. Ultimately though, the responsibility for their change rests with them.

If it was a belief in fairies and leprechauns, which was considered a valid religion not so very long ago, would you call it a delusion? A widespread view held by seemingly rational beings. I know some still hold to this specific supernatural worldview and still leave bread and milk out at night for the fairies and leprechauns. I personally look upon that and see delusion. If a client said, "I'm going home to talk to the fairies in my garden, to see what they think." This looks clear, right? I'm not alone, it's a delusional reality that needs specific, compassionate treatment. So why then when someone says, "I'm going to pray and ask God." Do we ignore it? Is it any different to saying, "I'll be having a chat with my imaginary friend over here, he will know what to do"?

Heaven vs Living Now

Most of the world's religious influence is, of course, wrapped up in the cosy existential angst soother called the promise of life after death. No more the worry about dying and nonexistence because I will be magically transported to the heavenly gates, or wherever my religion tells me I will be going. Either way, some version of being transported by angels from my body to rest with a supernatural host; never to feel pain or sorrow again. What a beautiful thing, though how we know joy when we have no sorrow, is a point I have never really grasped. Yet to have the thought of death assuaged by the promise of heaven. That is it of course, that is the reason why we give up so much. It's a comforting idea that requires relinquishing self-expression and accepting conformity, but what a payoff for giving up a few "sinful" behaviours and following a book of rules. Alternatively, I might be taken to purgatory, or reincarnated, or many other options which still avoid the stark alternative reality of non-existence. If only it was real. By which I mean if only you could show me evidence that God or heaven existed. I too would be glad to know I will not cease to exist but can go on being into eternity. Alas, there is no evidence I can see.

Then there's the death of others to consider. If we lose a loved one we will feel a strength of emotion, the rich depth of sadness which is brought about by grief, separation from loved ones, isolation and heartache. It sounds awful I know, and yet, it is informing us we have loved and do love. It is an expression of our love, which I would argue requires us to feel. It is something which must be felt, experienced and expressed; all this in order that we may emerge from our grief with a true sense of us in relation to others, and the knowledge that we can still love and be loved.

We might conceivably seek to lessen the impact or emotive strength of our grief if we hold to a belief in an afterlife. By saying this is not the end I will see them again, in the next life if not in this, I give myself hope, but diminish my felt reality in the process. At the cost of inserting a fictional reality, which in overlaying my actual experience, becomes the blanket with which I soothe myself. I never get to feel the true extent of my grief, it is never fully expressed and instead I calm myself with fiction and tell myself this fiction is real. The authentic self is lost yet again, hidden behind a fictional trope. The experience of grief is not fully experienced, my sadness, anger, love, passion etc. never fully engaged with or expressed.

To Challenge or Not to Challenge

As with all delusions, this is someone's crutch, their subjective reality construct and their support. Even if the delusion is one of a horrific nature, it is still frequently serving the role of expression for darker aspects of a personality schism. Removal of the delusional aspect leaves clients nothing to prop themselves up with. Aside from the prospect of removing someone's meaning, remembering that meaning is also one of the pivotal existential concerns; we also have the issue of will.

The people holding religious beliefs are usually following their society, following parents. Frequently these are people who have been indoctrinated for generations, who's choice has been limited by obedience to external input, or at best they may have chosen religion to free themselves from such angst about death, isolation, meaning or personal responsibility that they would not function well without the religious structure. Abeyance from institutionally indoctrinated people is both unlikely and would be intrinsically challenging to their Self as they perceive it.

I am not in the business of arguing the points of delusion in religious belief or the profundity of personal thoughts on the existence of God or his/her/its/their many attributes. At least not in the counselling room. As such I have held back from challenging when clients speak of the soul as Apriori. There is no evidence I have seen or heard to convince me that a soul exists beyond the wish and imaginations of frightened people. Would that it were the case. I would love to say I have this immutable soul and know it will exist beyond the extent of my brief tenure on earth.

I never challenge religious belief directly, not in awareness at least (obviously this book is an exception). For example, I never ask Christians if they have ever read any of the other stories of Christ that have appeared in other religions before Christianity, or the myths of Mithras or point them to the numerous place's aspects of the story of Christ which have been lifted or adapted from previous iterations in religions that went before. If I make this statement, if I ask this question, if I kick this nest of hornets, is it kind? In short, in asking this or making this point does the benefit outweigh the probable cost to the client. If they have not seen this delusion for what it is; Is, it kind to demolish it? Or even useful? Probably not.

Again, to argue against miracles seems a pointless gesture. A person I know well told me his car was broken down but after prayer was miraculously healed. I incredulously heard what seems to me total delusion, yet this person formed from their imagination this amazing tale. When faced with not knowing what happened to cause this transformation and no one at hand to take responsibility, this person filled in the blanks using the belief system already formed. This served to reinforce a tenuous belief and no doubt made them feel quite special.

The very idea that God, despite having a universe to look over, millions of disabled, homeless, ill, impoverished, traumatised and pained people all seeking help in desperate pleas to the ether. Despite this clamour for assistance, God chooses to fix someone's car. That must feel wonderful of course. I can see the attraction, to think that God thinks so much of me, that I am so supremely special I deserve divine intervention when my car breaks down, when there is so much strife to deal with. How special I am then. Also, much cheaper than the RAC or the AA. From my outside perspective, I just can't imagine how anyone can really believe that God would be taking on the role of chief mechanic when there are so many important things to deal with. Maybe he's really interested in internal combustion engines?

Chapter 5

Understanding the Reduction and Removal of Belief its Effects and Pitfalls.

Yesterday I was clever, so I wanted to change the world. Today I am wise, so I am changing myself. Rumi (Essential Rumi, Jalāl ad-Dīn Muhammad Balkhī, 1995)

Solvent

I like the idea of Glue and solvent in therapy. Every day I offer glue to sustain and hold people through distress, yet also solvent to dissolve neurotic behaviours. Religion is like glue, we used too much and ended up affecting everything to do with life, now it's a messy ball of glue and human and we are all tied up with it. We don't really need to dip the entire ball of glue into solvent, if we did that it would just all dissolve and we would be left with a mess that isn't used to supporting itself without all that glue, it would literally disintegrate. The human psyche is resilient and adaptive, but there are some things we should avoid doing to it.

The second option, which is the one I favour as an approach in therapy, is to create a holding space. Then when the client feels ready, I give them the solvent and suggest we try it just on this little bit. Then we increase the holding space, we support them to tolerate chaos and discomfort as they dissolve small facets of those parts of them that are bound to delusion or neurotic behaviours. Eventually, the delusion is gone, mostly. A shadow or stain might remain which may take years to dissolve or may never quite leave us. Our job then as therapists is to gradually relinquish the support role, to gradually get the client to create their own support for their shape, within their own lives as their authentic self is revealed from under the layers of role and introject. A client that starts to take responsibility for themselves will organically begin to create appropriate support for what they are and want to be. We just need to hold some of the chaos until they can get to that point.

I would describe much of what I do at this stage as containing chaos. I provide some of the solvent, perhaps as directed awareness, but I also provide the space for containment and experimentation with all the bits that come loose. We don't want to drop them or get rid of them. The client can, if he so wishes, after chewing them up, decide to keep them or parts of them which still work or fit.

As beliefs only find themselves, it is unlikely that once someone has a belief in a specific deity that they will let that belief go without a considerable struggle. Yet it does happen. At some point someone may see a different reality beyond the one they have been inhabiting, they may perceive a chink in the arguments that support their delusional state and if not immediately dismissed the thoughts may continue to gather momentum. They will be suffused with a tremendous amount of angst. To remove my belief is to rock my foundation, the bedrock of my perception of all things. This is how I make sense of the world, if I remove it, I am left adrift.

Occasionally you will find people who have changed religion, by religion I mean from one entire system to another, not Christian sect to Christian sect, which is relatively common. Christian to Muslim, Muslim to

Christian or polytheistic to monotheistic. This is in a sense the person realising that their supernatural fantasy isn't working. Instead of moving to a more rational position and allowing the authentic self to take centre stage, another delusional reality is built in the place of the first. If you talk to people who have made this personal transition it has usually happened after a period of trauma or great stress. Change which was unexpected and which they were unable to deal with using the current religious model. A new model is found in the hope it will work better than the old one next time around.

Essentially this represents transferring hope from one broken system to another. The point at which this change takes place we might call the impasse in the Perlsian model (1941) of neurosis. Beyond the anxiety commonly experienced at the impasse, if we breathe, if we have support enough, we may experience excitement. To be blind and suddenly see, would be both exciting and possibly overwhelming. Our job as therapists at this point is to give support to enable the client to make his own choices, to experience seeing for the first time, those parts of self which have been hidden. To offer containment enough that the client feels safe in experimenting with letting go of the old system; rather than replace it with more supernatural fantasy, just allow it to dissolve and experience the angst it has been covering.

Remember the role of expectation in reducing contact. If the client has reached an impasse of the kind described above, is on the cusp of relinquishing neurotic behaviour, if I enter the therapy room with the expectation that my client will change in this way or that, I have already block- ed contact; blocked it with my expectations and will more than likely see no growth or change unless it is despite me not assisted by me. Equally, when the client reaches the impasse, their expectation that the transition will be this or that will lead to blocked contact with what is, being in contact only with what is expected and unable to feel or experience the now. If the experience is not exactly as expected the tension of the impasse may be lost until awareness can be gained again. Reduction of contact at this point is a common defence against moving through the impasse and experiencing the next phase. It's not an implosion as might be required for change. Often clients will need to be brought to the brink of the impasse many times before they are able to push through it and allow the implosion and necessary gathering of energy to take place.

Isolation Fallout

To remove my belief may be to ostracise myself from my family, my friends, my church, my ashram, my mosque. If I say I am awake after all these years of sleeping, to people who have also spent those years sleeping alongside me, it is indeed a great challenge to them and their belief system. I will likely and necessarily be cast out or any cancer I introduce may spread. Change of this sort is far-reaching and often painful. Though necessary if we are ever going to rid ourselves of the spectre of religious delusion.

I remember vividly when I gave up my religion, when I gave up the belief in God; of the hundred or so people I had spent several years meeting every week, people I considered my friends, not one came to see me, not one came even to ask, "how are you?" I was cast as the goat in the herd of sheep.

For me it was a long slow journey, starting with small chinks in the armour of righteousness I wore. I remember the first chink quite clearly. My minister, a kind man whom I loved, whom I considered a mentor and who presided over my marriage, gave a sermon on anger. I remember it now, so momentous was the day that 24 years later it is still fresh in my mind. I remember the chair, the position in the church, the wallpaper, the brightness and the clarity of the memory. The subject of this sermon was specifically that Christ came to destroy anger. I thought to myself, "Really?" It made no sense, it didn't fit well for me, I sat there in the sure knowledge that had been drilled into me for years, that the sermons were God speaking to us through the minister. Then I heard him speak. It wasn't God speaking, I knew this man. Through his words, I saw a picture of this minister, my friend, and his father. I realised this wasn't God's message, this was his message about his father.

This was transference in action. I knew his father had been violent at times, and vented fits of explosive anger. This was the pivotal moment at which I started to question everything when I saw his humanity coming through in projections onto his concept of God. Though at the time I had a limited framework within which to sit my thoughts. I knew I was observing his lack of contact with himself and could see him beaming with pride as he projected it onto God.

That may be a good thing looking back. My lack of technical knowledge meant I had to find a way to explain what I was experiencing. On the way out of church that morning, he was getting a lot of handshakes and praise for a great sermon. When I came up to say goodbye he was smiling and asked what I had thought, as he usually did. I politely explained that it made little sense to me, mostly because the bible explicitly describes Christ in a towering rage turning over money lenders tables and using a whip to drive them from the temple. I said it didn't fit with his sermon. Later that week we spoke again in private. He was irritated with me but trying to hide it. I pointed out how many times God had hurt people because he was angry, the largest calamity being the biblical flood. I told him I thought he was confusing his image of his own father with the image of God as presented in the bible. That he wanted to be rid of anger and assumed God did too. I also suggested that rage and violence is not all anger is, that there is more to it. That anger can be the driver behind passion; that it can push people to make a change for good, that it has been the source of amazing art and creativity. He couldn't accept it and we parted in disagreement. Sadly, he never took me into his confidence again, we never met together unless others were there. Our relationship did not survive the challenge of conflicting thoughts.

Fast forward a year, the next big moment in my transition was the birth of my first son in 1999. What a moment! That was the first time I experienced love at first sight, and in that moment my faith in Christianity made the final flight and dissolved. Interestingly it was the same for my wife, she too, in this moment of clarity let go her hold on the fundamentals of Christian thought.

I had been pondering the existence of evil, and God's part in the creation and maintenance of such, not to mention the lack of explanation of his part in it. After all, I had been taught that all things came from God, but no one could tell me, if that was the case why he had created evil, it was all starting to unravel.

Here was my newborn son, and I had a moment of perfect clarity of feeling and thought. One of those I-thou moments. One of those moments of awe. I looked at him and he looked back, despite being just 10 minutes after his birth, he held my gaze and I knew no matter what he did, ever, no matter how bad, I could never condemn him to an eternity of torture in hell. If I cannot do this then either my love is bigger than Gods, or God does not exist, or hell does not exist, or perhaps God was a despot? So many questions. Everything dissolved, all my beliefs seemed so fragile and founded on nothing. I realised, how many other lies I had swallowed? In that instant, my reality changed. I experienced the beauty of unhindered contact, of unconditional love.

My internal map of the world was torn up, I let go of the myth I had been taught about the biblical texts being the word of God. I let go of the concept of hell and with-it heaven. I allowed myself to see that this was all just people's words, not the words of God. Just fanciful Ideals I had clung to for many years and in letting lose my grip on these beliefs, I allowed myself to realise that the evidence I had been presented with for the existence of God was not evidence at all. That God could not exist, or if he did, he was responsible for all of it, everything, good and bad. This unravelling cascaded down through my thoughts and though it took a few months to complete, this moment was the point at which I look back and say I no longer believed the delusions I had held that God existed, that there was no personification of good or evil. I was alone and yet not alone. I was very aware of bright contact with the world.

It's amazing how many times my clients have sighted the birth of their first child as the awakening to the miracle of life and a new subscription to God as creator, yet my experience was the polar opposite. I still don't challenge them when they say that, and it's a common theme.

If I was to try and persuade you of my belief that God is a comforting myth, a fairy tale and religion a delusional reality to flee, am I not just giving in to my evangelistic desire to have others think as I do? It is easier to be part of a group after all. I can say I think these thoughts, that this is my reality; I have certainty, certainty beyond reasonable doubt. Is this mental construct of mine better than yours? Do I have the right to attempt to impose mine upon you? Difficult questions indeed given the implications of rocking foundational systems. Yet is it kind also to leave someone in a state of delusion? Two polarities to explore there and I mostly sit myself in the middle. Not on the fence, just aware of both poles without necessarily needing to travel to either.

Transference and Attachment in the Guise of Religious Dogma

Another aspect of the psyche we see used by religion is transference and in tandem, attachment. Ask any monotheist for his view of what God is like and he will more than likely give you a description of his own father's traits with a few supernatural abilities thrown in. Alternatively, an idealised image the opposite of his father if he needs his god to be something his father was not. The descriptions might be of a loving father or a puritanical tyrant. God the father is imbued via transference through our own experience of father figures. It might very well be a fantastical view of the father I always wanted, but however you look at it the opinions vary based on personal experience and desire. Similarly, attachment styles discovered and described by Bowlby and Ainsworth (Attachment Separation and Loss, 1973) are clearly visible in people's perception of gods and ministers of faith. Some religions use this to their advantage: openly calling members of the various orders, mother, father, sister and brother. Invoking familial attachment and attunement, guilt or shame through familial archetypes.

People are surprisingly subservient to authority, perhaps more than we would like to admit. In making the 'Mother' or 'Father' the head of the order, religion adds another layer of authority. It is far harder to challenge someone called 'Father Bob', even if he isn't your father and your father isn't called Bob. We have been conditioned to honour our fathers and mothers through religious edicts and social constructs. These constructs have built upon our innate survival instinct. It was our mother and father after all who brought us into the world, we owe them our very existence. In most cases, they then supported us until we could support ourselves. We owe them our lives, and in my experience, religions often play on that to manipulate people with guilt in order to exert control and obedience.

Loss, Promoting Vulnerability to Religious Thought

A group vulnerable to the uptake of religious/superstitious thought are those who have recently suffered loss or trauma. From the simple expedient that we are trying to make sense of, look for reason and meaning within the seaming chaos. Searching for those links in causality and for relief from the stress soon after trauma or loss. Add to this the need to feel community when we are naturally isolated, and we have a potent mix which makes us far more susceptible to religion and religious ideas which offer a community of sorts.

An all prevailing need to make sense of, in order to move on; makes us far more open to suggestion and looking for answers in places we might not usually look. It's seductive to hear someone with surety and authority state "this is the way, be like this and all will be well, in the next life if not in this." Add to this heady mix the transferential familial links of authority and the seduction is clear. In my experience as a therapist, many of the people I have worked with have become involved in monotheistic religion or new age style irrational ritual after powerful overwhelming or life-threatening events. The concept of mother or father looking after me when I am in distress is a potent image. Like I said earlier, we all want to be looked after, to return to a state of reliance in which our needs are taken care of. I am not suggesting that religions prey on the vulnerable intentionally. Many of the people I have encountered genuinely believe that what they offer to others is a valid solution, even when faced with incontrovertible evidence to the contrary. The delusion they hold effectively blinds them to other versions of reality. (See the section on single-dimensional viewpoints in chapter 2.) This blindness becomes evangelical when the desire to have others believe the same takes hold. It is far easier to maintain a belief in something ostensibly non-existent if more than one person holds the same belief. The group identity adds credence to an otherwise untenable position; Being part of the group also removes the sense of existential isolation the trauma may have awoken.

We can't avoid transference; it is one of the flags we might use in therapy to highlight a flight from the present state. However, I like to think we use it to bring awareness and greater choice, whereas religion appears to have hijacked it in order to manipulate people into greater obedience.

Transference in the Therapeutic Relationship and Religion

Transference between client and therapist is one of the tools we use to highlight problematic behaviours in one personality or another. Grasping the inescapable, all-pervasive nature of reciprocal influence in the therapy room is a challenging but fruitful task. The collaborative response and interplay are the co-created driver of therapeutic change. Once brought to awareness it is full of meaning and substance. Each layer of the interaction reveals ways in which client and therapist bring past experience to present here and now behaviour; whether as a filter or motivating factor; Either as transference or countertransference. Each area explored reveals more of the motivations behind individual behaviours, interactions and responses.

The therapeutic exchange suggested above is a mirror to the unconscious use of transference enacted by religion. We bring to awareness our transference and explore it to see how we are blurring our contact with clients or vice versa. Armed with this knowledge we can experiment with other behaviours which might be healthier. Religion in its presumably unaware state uses transference to exert control and force specific behaviours. In many cases this behaviour is unplanned, but I think many intelligent religious leaders have used this behavioural trait to increase control intentionally.

Attachment styles play a vital role in the transferential relationship between people or indeed between a person and their religion. The goal of psychotherapy and the goal of attachment are the same, namely the psychological integration of all brain function, sensory, limbic, motor, emotion centres etc. Secure attachment behaviour in relationships creates links between these different aspects of neurological functioning. Psychotherapy does the same, by offering a secure relationship within which attachment styles can be challenged, even modified through mirroring, modelling and experimenting with novelty.

The impact of attachment relationships registers in the interrelated, indeed overlapping domains of the body, the emotions, and the representational world, shaping the stance of the self toward experience in each. David Wallin, *Attachment in Psychotherapy* (2007, 61).

To function well we must initially have an internalised secure base. This base is built in response to our primary caregivers. Bowlby (1973) would describe us in terms of needing a good internal map. The map shows us roughly what to expect in given situations. We respond based on the map. If the map is poor, if we had a poor experience of attunement, our attachment models we developed as children would be lacking. The relational models we developed as children will, like the map, guide us through future relationships. This attachment is our internalised secure or insecure base. Through transferential triggers, such as the use of familial terms, holy father, the mother superior, sister, brother, these maps are invoked as though we are experiencing our family by proxy. If you had a good enough upbringing, you may be none the wiser, you might feel a sense of benevolent care and regard for Father Bob. If your father was a tyrannical despot, you may have a constant sense of needing to please and placate Father Bob or a nagging irrational fear when you are with him. At the very least in both cases, you will want to do as you are told because that is what children do with their fathers specifically, and authority figures in general. He is still the same priest; the only difference is your reactions to him based on your internal map and the imposition of the father archetype.

Religions and ideologies use this to their advantage, hijacking your inbuilt relational map and manipulating response through familial terminology and implementing authoritarian structures with similarity to familial ones.

The goal of therapy is integration, pulling together disparate elements of self and promoting coalescence of disparate parts to form an integrated self. When I talk about the organic, authentic self, it is this unhindered self I describe, the self that is integrated and secure in attachment. Religious movements tend to avoid many of the useful aspects of attachment theory, and in turn, frequently employ a dominating critical parental approach which hinders healthy attachment styles while extending the influence of ideals created from fiction. Polster and Polster (1995) describe the personality as *A Population of Selves* in their book of the same name; "Selves are formed by a configurational reflex which takes the disparate details of personal experience and forms them into a unified pattern. Such organisational reflexes result in shorthand identifications of clusters of experience." (7).

Each self is expressed at the contact boundary as a vehicle of communication and understanding. In this way I have many selves, they are all parts of me, I allow each and use each in order to function well in groups of human beings. I might have a trainer self, that I show to groups of people I am working with to train in therapy. I have my husband self, which is quite different, it has very different boundaries to my trainer self. My husband self, for example, has different boundaries around sexualised behaviour. I might also be said to have a father self, which has many aspects of the intimacy experienced through the husband self but more limits on physical contact. You could argue that I have an angry self, a sad self-etc. each of these modalities is different but not separate from me. Each is integral, and I have a sense of agency about disclosure and interaction. In the main, I decide which self appears and which self is expressed with which fellow human being. Ideally, I express as I need to without fear of judgement, without the need to sensor my interactions and expressions of self.

Not everyone has the awareness of these distinctions, or they may have distinctions, common ones being the work self and the home self. but each may be a role played in order to mask authentic contact. Let's take the intellectual as an example. Clearly, there is nothing wrong with being intellectual and exercising one's thought processes. It might feel to such, that an intellectual exchange is just that, but it might also be that intellectualisation is employed to limit contact, to play the role of expert, or to keep people at arm's length. Intellectualisation can be used to desensitise, if I am thinking about and talking about my thoughts around something, I am not feeling or directly experiencing. It might be a way to limit my internal connection with my felt sense of my experience. We might say I was in my head, not my body. That does not mean it is wrong to have a self which spends time in intellectualising, but it does mean that if it is a hindrance to contact the authentic interaction may be lost.

Religion on the other hand tends to judge many authentic behaviours and has ostracised people for having their authentic needs and desires. I remember being in church while a minister praised a parishioner for being brave, holding it together and not crying when her twin sister died. The message was clear, "Don't show your sadness it's wrong, bottle it up." I came away feeling trampled on, I felt as though I had just been told yet again that sadness was not a valid reaction to a death. I know now that the minister was operating from his sense of impotence. He could not cope with tears and sadness because he was a fixer. He can't fix sadness so he praises people that hide it, so he does not need to deal with his impotence in the face of something he can do nothing about.

The trouble with a position like this is that if sadness is not expressed it becomes something darker. If it is bottled up it will come out sideways as another manifestation of emotional expression. Usually, it will become anger or anxiety, it might be vented as sarcasm, it might become depression. As therapists we have all seen how the non-expression of sadness at the behest of another becomes resentment toward the person wanting restraint; this resentment all too often is retroflected as guilt. Instead of being resentful that you want to shut me up and be rid of my sadness, I might turn it inward and feel guilty that I have 'made' you feel like that.

Yet we all know sadness is a rich and powerful emotion, full of affect and energy. All the shaking, the sobs, the wracking heaving chest, the tears, the snot. Once allowed and expressed we release all our pent-up tension and the release transforms us, the sadness expressed we can once again return to our self and our love. For that is all sadness is, a recognition that something or someone we love is now missing. We are separated by distance, by death, by hurt, and once expressed we will gradually recover and return to our place of love. The place within us from which we can express our love, from where we allow ourselves to love and be loved, is an essential aspect of human relation-ships which becomes, in part at least, unavailable to us if we cannot express our sadness.

Sitting on sadness then is just one aspect of the control of emotional response that I have witnessed from religious leaders and indeed many other people in society. We can all recount stories of how religion has hindered expression with tenets which mean little or nothing outside of the religious dogma they support. The full expression of self is an integral aspect of attaining fulfilling relationships and having a fulfilled contactful life. When we are subjected to the rules of others we see atrophy of awareness, expression and response of emotionality played out on somatic and psychic levels. In short, the population of selves is replaced with a religious self, built on the rules of others. Contact, clear contact between humans in this condition is almost impossible. If I am always viewed through the veil of judgement and edicts of your religion, I will never clearly be seen or given space to be fully expressive of myself and its ontological needs. Your religious expectations will always act as a buffer between us.

Ironically it is through that contact, through clear healthy contact with others, that I am most likely to have that spiritual experience, the I-thou, the sense of connected oneness from which I can learn, experience and know beyond my usual limited capacity.

> As crucial as the role of contact is in the formation of selves, it cannot stand alone. It is interwoven with empathy and merger, which together compose a contact triad, circumscribing the experience of full contact. What empathy contributes to the contact triad is a sense of common experience and understanding among contacting people, one person reaching out to know another's experience. Polster and Polster, *A Population of Selves* (1995, 155).

Empathy is a key component in healthy contact. Though religions are good at promoting merger through confluence, this is not a healthy form of merger most of the time. Also, they are frequently poor at allowing empathy, despite protestations to the opposite, that they stand for God's love and promote love for one's neighbour. For all the professions of brotherly love, empathy is sadly lacking. When a homosexual person is told to change, that their sexuality is a sin, there is no empathy. They are being asked to ignore an immutable aspect of self and instead to merge via confluence and accept the "right" way to be, the way you "should" be, on the path of righteousness. When women are told to obey their husbands in all things, or prevented from speaking in church, or becoming a bishop, this denigration, this demotion to second class citizen shows no empathy, only controlling expectation. Empathy is so far from these exchanges as to make contact impossible. If dogma and expectation are included in any interaction, healthy contact is impossible. The expectation that someone else must be something other than what they are, will always block contact. Likewise, I cannot engage contactfully with my client if I expect them to be anything other than what they are.

Morality

We have a moral self, it's innate. We all develop one as a child and would do regardless of environmental stimuli. We have mirror neurons, when I see you hurt, I experience hurt, when I see you in pain I am pained. They are called mirror neurons because when we see someone suffer, let's say I see my son get stung by that pesky wasp. I see him flinch, in his mind neurons are firing to tell him he has been stung on the arm. In my brain, those self-same neurons (locations in my neural map) are also firing. I haven't been stung, but I experience a small measure of the expected pain. It is part of our empathy centres, it's also why we can catch a yawn, and probably why we laugh more when with other people than when we are alone.

We use this information to build our own moral codes. It essentially says this would not be good for me, therefore I will not do it to others. I know there are exceptions, and some pathologies don't allow for this experience in the same way you or I might experience empathy; it's not simplistic, but the pathologies which restrict empathy are few. Most of us have enough empathy to create a moral system that works well enough and likely to be acceptable to our local communities.

So, firstly we learn from this that we develop our own moral code, we do not need to be taught one. This idea we hear from religion that says, "Where would we all be if we didn't have this set of rules to govern us." Its topsy turvy religion has imposed extra rules to help societies coalesce and cooperate through conformity and control. That is not the same as a true morality. The difference might be said as follows: Morality is doing what feels right, religion is doing what we are told is right even if it feels wrong.

Mirror neurons are used, not consciously but instinctually. It is unfortunate that they are frequently Co-opted by religions to elicit a specific guilt response. For example, in many churches in the west Christ is still hung on the cross; hanging there to remind you, to fire those mirror circuits and see what was done "for you" so you had better toe the line, otherwise you dishonour his name and all he did for you. you get the picture. Guilt is created instead of empathy, via the firing of mirror neurons coupled with harmful dogma.

As religion uses ordinary cognitive mechanisms used for survival and social interaction to become and spread, we as therapists can use those same mechanisms to offer alternative solutions. We can support the client by modelling and refusing to take on the priestly mantle, the father figure, the mother; At the very least exploring those aspects when the client sees us in those roles. By being an adult and promoting a healthy adult to adult dialogue, no expectations, no need to be higher, better, greater, to control or diminish the other. No need to infantilize them in order to be powerful. We can offer an alternative experience. In that place of adult acceptance of otherness, as is, we start to suggest a different, healthy way to be.

Chapter 6

Exploring the Downside to Hope.
Personal Agency, Choice and Courage.

You can withdraw from the sufferings of the world-that possibility is open to you-but perhaps that withdrawal is the only suffering you might be able to avoid. Kafka (*Zurau Aphorisms of Franz Kafka*, Michael Hofmann, 2006)

The Problem with Hope

"The problem with hope" perhaps sounds a little pessimistic. Though I am smiling, I don't want to remove hope in the traditional sense. I do want people to explore what it means within the context of avoiding what is now. This being in the interest of better contact with self. Hope, looking forward to something tomorrow, planning well in advance, is often a mechanism used to deaden the feeling and experience of now. Hope that we will have this good time in the future is an opiate for now. Booking a holiday and daydreaming about it, for example, is a possible way to relieve intolerable feelings of now. You might be thinking that's a good thing, though, right? I would disagree. Not with the holiday, we all need one from time to time, but the hoping, the pinning our hope upon something tomorrow.

That intolerable feeling, we wish to flee from, is telling us we need to do something else; and that something else is not to flee. We need to wake up and change our world so we don't feel the need to flee from it, not spend our days daydreaming through time in the hope that tomorrow will be better. I'm not suggesting for one second, we should not have a break and a holiday from time to time, that's not it at all. But I do suggest that in daydreaming about the future, in entertaining the hope that all will be well tomorrow, we run away from the present moment and in doing so negate the force that supports our drive to create or to make the radical changes needed to make life something we want to engage with.

Let's say I am feeling bored, unfulfilled, alone. I am desperate to get away from these feelings and feel powerless. I don't want to sit with the feelings engendered in that experience, so I think of ways to run. I consider a holiday, I spend time planning it, in doing so I am mentally in the future, imagining a better time. The holiday is 3 months away. During the three months I spend many hours thinking about it, how good it is going to be and how much better I will feel. All that time spent daydreaming is time I am no longer in this moment. Thinking about the future is acting as a painkiller. I am no longer experiencing my discomfort at my current circumstances.

The discomfort, now deadened or minimized, is no longer motivating me to change my situation, I have deadened it. I continue meandering through daily life, then go on my holiday. Unfortunately, it was a bit stressful, the pool was dirty, the food wasn't as good as I had hoped, everything was more expensive than advertised. I felt stressed flying because my flight was delayed, and the trains were not running on time. There were good bits, but honestly it wasn't as good as the expectation I had built in my daydreams, so I feel disappointed, and I am back in my previous reality, the one I was running from; one I have made no attempt to change while I was daydreaming about a hopeful other existence. Expectations, tend to be fantasy, and often lead superficially at least to frustration, whereas hope of this sort, is an opiate which prevents action to create a better now.

Perhaps this is why Pandora left hope in the jar, it being the greatest plague on man, robbing him of present awareness through distracting thoughts about what might be and continue in the face of other woes. If you look beyond the hope, you will see there is a desire, something you need to fulfil. This desire may be a required part of your authentic self, struggling to be known, or it may be born of expectation which renders it pointless.

Ironically hope is often seen as a virtue, the optimists' refuge, seeking to assuage feelings of despair, yet it prolongs despair by putting it on hold and leads us down blind alleys in our search for that holy grail, escape from the present moment. Yet this present moment is where we exist, this is all we have, no amount of fantasising will change that. Hope is something often offered by religions all over the world. Hope in eternal life, hope in salvation, hope in a better tomorrow. But it seems to me a hope offered through fiction, when we inhabit reality.

Giving up Our Power

That sense of despair is often negated through religion by the introduction of God's grace and giving all our power up to him. Instead of saying I make a choice, it's far easier to say this is God's will. Instead of saying that something about sex and sensuality scares me, I can say it is forbidden, God has said so, it's a sin, therefore I can avoid it. To have contactful consensual sex we must make ourselves vulnerable, and at the same time we must engage with parts of us we do not fully accept, we must take what we need as well as give so that the other gets what they need. All parties involved must in some form make themselves both vulnerable and be ruthless enough to reach satisfaction. It requires contact with self and contact with others as well as a temporary confluence.

In most cases, religion asks us to give up our own power and become subject to the whims of a supernatural entity. The part where we make choices, the part where we allow our desires and enjoy contact with the world, we live in. The moment when we take responsibility for our actions and engage with life to the full is given up as we allow ourselves to be subsumed into the religious structure and conform to its dogma and edicts. Wherever there is a choice we can and must take responsibility for it. We must engage with our choices and the consequences, or we risk not engaging in life, this life, the only life we know for sure we have.

One of the shackles which enable the prevention of contact with self is the religious concept of sin. The shame and guilt-induced prevent full contact with parts of self which may require the forbidden. If the forbidden has been made unavailable by a pointless imaginary line drawn in the sand by people who are out of contact with themselves and the world; or by people who lived thousands of years before us, who had no concept of this world as we now do. Then if we follow it blindly without question or recourse to our authentic self, where will we find authentic contact?

Choice and Engaging

In the novel Grendel (1989), John Gardner uses the phrase "Everything fades: alternatives exclude." I first read this when reading Irvin Yalom's, *Staring at the Sun* (2008, 93), then went off and read the novel. This statement is for me a great truth, if there is such a thing as truth. I often say beliefs only find themselves, but once or twice I have found a truth which holds water so well, I am reluctant to let it go. Alternatives do indeed exclude. The word "choice" always suggests another possibility, that there are at least two options, and I might choose one of them. At the very least I can choose to act or not to act, to make a choice or not to make a choice. Given that there are always a minimum of two options, if I choose one, I negate or eliminate the other. I must therefore take responsibility for my choices, for the path I choose and the refusal of the other. I would also add that even if that choice is not to act, not to choose, that inaction is itself a choice.

Not everyone will take responsibility, some are so wrapped up in their fantasies of how others perceive them, that they become unable to see responsibility for what it is. The perceived judgement of others creates a fog to contact with responsibility. The projection of one's own internal critic onto others makes this perception seem even more real. This psychological group will admit fault or poor judgement to themselves readily, but often avoid responsibility and ownership for fear of this external judge. This behaviour makes authentic contact impossible and the burden of guilt greater.

Many religions advocate the abdication of responsibility for the self and giving it to a higher power. The 12 step recovery programs do the same. But when the illusory being, the great and powerful Wizard of Oz is revealed as the charlatan he is, we are inevitably thrown back upon ourselves and forced to take responsibility again. I have seen in my practice that recovery from mental health issues requires taking responsibility, building awareness of self, of our motives and drives. Taking responsibility for engaging in life and accepting our inevitable limits.

Taking responsibility for the choice means accepting from the outset that once chosen the opposite action is excluded. If I am sitting looking at a menu I must choose, but as soon as I do, I have excluded all the other options. If I see another possible meal arrive for another patron after I have placed my order, I may look with sorrow at the sumptuous feast and wonder if I have made the right choice. In a small measure, there will be a degree of anxiety, produced by the question "have I made the right decision?" Acceptance of responsibility, no matter the outcome, prevents us from becoming embroiled in the impasse of choice.

Some choices require us to push our courage to our perceived limits, it doesn't matter much if I pick a sub-par meal in a restaurant, I'll get over it and there will be other opportunities. Something important like choosing a life partner, choosing to have children, big life-changing choices, to engage contactfully with these and take responsibility takes courage; an acceptance of vulnerability and intimacy, to face the inevitable end. As a result, many people make these choices in total denial of the ontological self or awareness of what authentic contact with people would be like.

Take Courage

Religion stultifies. Loss of mystery is the deadness of religion. More often than not conformity to religious maxims replace the courage to be in the moment and take responsibility for self. We pick up others' rules and apply them fastidiously in order to deaden the parts of us we are afraid to express.

Courage is the driver behind our virtues. It requires that we trust our authentic selves, our own awareness of our potentiality and allow it without dismissal. This is what is required to take our place in the greater whole: to act, to create, to be. You cannot love without courage, to accept making yourself vulnerable to others, to the pain of sadness, grief and loss which is inevitable if you love. Without courage fidelity becomes conformity, anger resentment, love becomes submission. Creating takes courage, to put your original idea out there into the world where others are affected by it takes courage, to stand and say this is me, I am what I am and you don't have to like it, and that's okay; this takes courage. A courage religion sadly saps, leeching will and promoting conformity, removing the mystery and instilling contrition. To deny your original ideas and accept the contradicting messages of a holy text. Accepting religion instead of your authentic, organic self is to betray yourself and smother it in layers of roles and bind it with shame.

Anyone familiar with religious belief knows the impact of shame. Don't feel excited, it's not of God, don't fancy this person or that person, don't have sex outside of marriage, don't do this don't do that; if you do, you're dirty, you're bad, evil, shameful. The shame is poured in to replace courage, it covers the organic self in a miasmic haze. For people held in this place, looking within provokes such feelings of shame, it is as though we live an apology for self rather than a celebration. As courage backed up all our virtues, now shame backs them. This unholy alliance is not a match made in heaven, far from it. Courage is a positive expansive force, enabling expression outward into the world; shame drives our feelings underground, never to see the light of day.

Shame

Unfortunately, shame is one emotional response we see pretty much daily in therapy. Often experienced directly during the exchange. It is so all-pervasive that as therapists we must learn to work with it, if we attempted to avoid it, we would have no clients. It is such a powerful response that just naming our shame can invoke the feeling of shame. As it is such a difficult topic for most people to approach, let alone talk about. Most people will reflexively choose not to, it will be hidden from awareness and expressed in other ways. Avoided via mind-bogglingly creative adaptations, hidden behind masks and layers. Often shame is the last layer of the onion, it can take months before it is supported enough to be workable.

The exception to this is when I work with a recent trauma. There is frequently a shame response alongside PTSD and to traumatic events in general. Often a negative thread of blame has developed for the client which attaches shame as a response. The client may feel they were somehow responsible, for example, a recent client who was caught in a house fire, despite no one being hurt, despite re-entering the burning building to make sure a friend was out and being assured by the fire reports that it was an electrical fault which started the blaze, still, as a result of the PTSD managed to blame themselves and experienced shame as a result. Once the PTSD was resolved and the self-blame undone, the shame also evaporated. I know this link between trauma and shame exists for relational trauma too and have seen it played out as a result of complex PTSD built up over years of abuse. Though the PTSD symptoms may or may not be present where trauma is, shame frequently resides with PTSD and trauma.

Understanding Shame

The sense I am not enough and will never be enough underpins shame. Often stemming from childhood desires for affection, adoration or positive attention which were never met. The child develops a sense that it is somehow their fault rather than a lack on the part of the caregiver. In doing so an internal system is created, which turns the responsibility in upon the self, thus creating shame. The neurotic creative adaptations that arise usually centre on ways in which the inner child can engineer meaningful contact. The failure to get what is required becomes a sense that It's my fault, if I was enough, I would be getting what I need, I must not be enough. For whatever reason the caregiver was unable to respond in an attuned manner, unable to monitor and appropriately react to the signals expressed by the child.

Chronic shame tends then to appear in clients who experienced this rejection time and again, imbuing them with the sure knowledge that they are themselves not loveable and often a feeling they do not deserve to exist, should be punished and in some cases, suicidal ideation becomes the norm. I do not deserve to exist so I will end it all. Experiencing these events over and over, these moments of disconnection are akin to trauma, and our response to it can be very similar.

Shame is a uniquely isolating emotional response, it is something we experience separate from those we are related to, yet it is precisely because we wish to have closer relationships. We wish to be accepted, but shame appears when we are not. Shame then is often born of non-acceptance and experienced in isolation.

Culture of Shame and Original Sin

In the west, we have a culture of shame. We have grown into a society which shames people at every opportunity. Primarily we have learned this from the Christian Church, but this is not the only source. In the west, the church has been quick to use shame as a motivator for subservience. The entire idea that you are so abhorrently sinful, born sinful no less, that God himself had to kill his own son to pay for your sin. That in itself is shame-inducing (though how God concluded that he couldn't just forgive everyone is beyond me. particularly after admonishing everyone to not kill.) The entire religion seems predicated upon shame. All this pointing at your natural desires or inadequacies and calling them sin is not to build you up, it is to keep you low and subservient. A person experiencing shame is blaming themselves, turning the hurt inward. It is quite unlikely that such a person will rebel against the shamer, more likely they will rebel against the organic self and turn all their anger inward in masochistic, ritualised subservience. Or as we will see in some cases that frustrated angry self, will leak out in the guise of righteous anger and judgement of others. It's a twisted version of humanity, moulded by a toxic combination of blaming and shame.

Shame is so embedded in our society that we use it as everyday language, "Shame on him/her for....." for what? Pretty much any expression of self which others deem to be counter to the given society's norms. We name and shame people publicly, in the newspapers, on tv. And not just for outrageous acts against humanity, often for the simplest acts of self-expression. I remember when a famous footballer was paraded around the newspapers for seeing a prostitute, but that wasn't his true crime, other footballers were doing that. Yet this one was paraded for months because he was seeing an older prostitute rather than choosing a younger model. It was like a crooked weird open tribunal, in which no one seemed to be asking the right questions, judgement was made and poured out in a torrent. His true crime of course was to be famous, wealthy, and expressing part of the self that others could not accept. I'm not saying he was right or wrong. I think we as a society should not be shaming or causing psychological harm by public humiliation. Perhaps we as a society should be looking at our judgements of age and beauty rather than attacking people who act outside of our preconceived ideas of such.

Shame then is a vehicle society uses to make people toe the line. If public shaming has any use it is to persuade people who witness others' shame not to act upon their natural desires and do this thing, we have deemed to be terrible. Whatever that thing may be. Through shame, society instructs people in the art of playing a role, hide away your real self, play the role and we won't have to shame you. Personal wellbeing' on the other hand, requires an integrated self, the neurotic roles we play are a result of parts of self not being accepted and their non-integration, non-expression. These roles we are asked to play in order to hide our true, authentic selves prevent integration, The integration of the self and interaction with others through appropriate contact.

Those who experience shame often talk of feeling disintegrated, split, broken into many pieces. A sense of self as a cohesive whole feels impossible to achieve, the parts feel separate. As shame is predominately about feeling separate, not being part of the group in the way one wished to be as a child it is hardly surprising this is how we experience our shame. The religious group might seem a viable substitute, it has a father figure, the vicar, pastor, padre, father or the holy mother. And it offers siblings with whom to commune. When shame is the vehicle for social compliance, splits in self are inevitable. The intolerable sense of isolation is therefore never addressed once the person has become confluent with a religious body. Shame in this situation is used to both keep the shame alive as a frightening thing to flee from; while paradoxically offering hope its relief can be found in the congregation of the church. Yet it is the religion which perpetuates the shame now, and the church which perpetuates the inability to be truly cognisant of self through its restrictive practices. Therefore, it prevents the healing of shame.

Shame is such a powerful force in the ego that it is debilitating, particularly when chronic, it is greeted with such fear that any means to eradicate its effect will be sought. Even if that means at some level perpetuating the shame. Bear in mind also that the masochistic tendency to blame and seek punishment for the self which was not enough to evoke a loving response is also likely to be triggered. The shame is not only tolerated it is expected as the person feels unworthy of anything else. Within this framework, conventional religious attitudes can be seen as manipulating people by shame into social compliance. Within the Christian context, adding the shame of original sin to the already shame laden personality it creates of the self a slave, powerless and fearful, fearful of isolation, fearful of real contact, as it is through contact the real self may be seen. Religion also offers a solution through a fantasy relationship with a fictional entity, which being fictional is never enough and often perpetuates the shame it professes to salve. Unconsciously at least you will be aware of the lack, and be unsatisfied, always seeking something to fill the hole.

The roles played then cover the true self from the eyes of others but leave the damage and shame intact; only when alone, away from the distractions of religious life will the shame be noticed, and anxiety provoked. Only in isolation is the shame truly experienced.

Shame is at the heart of negative self-image and self-loathing. When religion hijacks the negative image, it invokes shame. Like it or not religion manipulates people through psychological means to feel shame. When religion teaches that you are not enough as you are, that you must be reborn anew, or you must be burned in the crucible and all the dross removed. When religion uses metaphors such as these it is essentially saying, "You are not acceptable as you are." This is the core of shame; this is the essential point which lies behind fear of isolation. If I am unacceptable as I am I will become isolated, for someone who already experiences shame for the self this is a powerful statement, which will inevitably lead to unhealthy consequences. Once enmeshed within a system which supports your shame, it is extraordinarily difficult to free yourself. If you feel the need to apologise for your existence, to be told by an authoritative other you should apologise for your existence is a seductive trap. In *Understanding and Treating Chronic Shame* (2015), Patricia De Young asks:

> If shame is, indeed, an experience of one's felt sense of self
> disintegrating in relation to a dysregulating other, then in each
> kind of shame the same three conditions should apply, albeit
> in different ways and at different intensities: a sense of self is
> disintegrating, the self is in immediate (real or imagined)
> ruptured relation to another person, and that person is
> experienced as "dysregulating," or a threat to self-cohesion.
> (Young, 2015)

This being the case, as I suspect all therapists will have seen this within their practice, no matter what their expertise, shame will always be present in some form; the dysregulating other we are discussing here is religion, the fictional God which cannot respond as you desire, or the religious body, the group, the society. The other does not have to be a person singular, it can be the imagined personification. It does not have to be real in any sense of a present physical form, the dysregulating other can be a fiction, an imagined threat or person, particularly an imposed fictional supernatural entity.

The original dysregulating other of course was likely to be a primary caregiver unable to attune to the expressed needs of the child's self. Now that role has been taken by a religious grouping or leader, the poor parental role is transferred. Shame is a profoundly isolating emotion to experience. It seems to occur when our emotional connection to a significant other is interrupted. Separation in the physical sense does not in my experience play a major role. For example, of those adults I have worked with who were evacuated during the war. Those that have an experience of shame do not cite that physical separation as the cause. It is more usually the felt sense that my emotional self is not seen, understood or accepted. Of those clients, the ones who experience shame as a core condition of their mental health problem were more likely to focus on the lack of response from a parent or caregiver on return from the evacuation, not the evacuation itself. This seems to support the premise that shame is relational or interpersonal, as a dynamic response to an unattuned relationship.

All the self must be accepted and integrated in order to shift shame from the core self. If the self remains a collection of disconnected parts the whole cannot function for healthy contact. In therapy, this is achieved through re-attunement, within a supportive environment. The relational self, explores what it is like to be within a relationship where the self is accepted and indeed encouraged to be, to grow. The acceptance of the authentic, organic self however must ultimately come from the client. No matter how attuned I am, if they cannot allow emergence and explore parts of self, the integration will not take place and some shame for the unintegrated parts of self will always exist. Key to this is isolation, as an existential concern, we must address our ultimate isolation and see it for what it is in order that we may be more fully connected to both self and others.

Later in chapter 14, I will also look briefly at sadism and masochism in religious idioms. At the core of both is self-disgust, self-loathing, which in turn is linked to the avoidance of chronic shame. The shame is masked either by punishing oneself for being unworthy or punishing others in order to feel powerful, thus negating the sense of powerlessness over one's environment and the shame of our apparently inadequate self.

Chapter 7

Expectations and How They May Hinder Contact with Self and Others,
How They Become the Basis for Feelings of Entitlement.

> Why do we harp on about original sin, it wasn't on its account
> we were expelled from paradise, but because of the tree of life,
> lest we eat of its fruit. Kafka (*Zurau Aphorisms of Franz
> Kafka*, Michael Hofmann, 2006)

Religion and the Cult of Doing

The adage that we are human beings, not human doings holds much water. My experience of religious life has been that of doing. Asked to do, involved in doing, be in the band, prayer meeting, prayer walks, raise funds for the homeless, sing praise, etc. Some of this doing, of course, leads to noble ends and is useful, as we already touched on earlier. But always to do, do, do and very little, if any, actual being is a sorry way to run a spiritual life. The doing gets in the way of being and in my opinion impedes spiritual experience.

Doing can be viewed as similar to the level of cliche in the five layers theory. It's a role. I am aware that we can also "be" while doing, and some tasks can be meditative, and we can be mindful in all things. We must do; as humans, if we didn't do, we would never eat. I am not suggesting we all stop everything we do. I am suggesting that much of the stuff of doing is cliche, surface level, marking time, filling space, a distraction from engagement rather than truly engaging in a contactful and meaningful way. By not engaging below the level of doing, of cliché. Head one step below the level of cliche and suddenly contact is possible.

Doing is, of course, necessary, and I would never speak against the raising of funds to house the homeless or feed the impoverished. That's all good, and one of the vital roles religions have played throughout history. Though it is not alone, and it has not been the sole cause of humanitarian altruism. I would add too that it is not necessary to be part of a religious group in order to be altruistic either, it is nonsensical to believe that without religion mankind would devolve into a brutalist monster incapable of empathy and care for his fellow man.

Constantly doing is a distraction. We feel good and full of pride because we have done something useful, which might be the case, and yet this constant clamour for doing is usually a distraction from the difficult existential truths we all face. As long as I am doing, I am distracted and feel relieved. If you allow yourself to stop what happens in the silence?

If we live in distraction we cannot live in contact. Part of our ontological self must be shunned or hushed. The trouble with distraction is it ignores our need to deal with and face our existential angst. Erich Fromm on doing:

> The state of anxiety, the feeling of powerlessness and insignificance, and especially the doubt concerning one's future after death, represents a state of mind which is practically unbearable for anybody. Almost no one stricken with this fear would be able to relax, enjoy life, and be indifferent as to what happened afterwards. One possible way to escape this unbearable state of uncertainty and paralyzing feeling of one's own insignificance is the very trait which became prominent in Calvinism: the development of a frantic activity and striving to do something. Activity in this sense assumes a compulsory quality... *The Fear of Freedom* (1942, 78).

I disagree only with the point about it being practically unbearable. We imagine it to be so, yet after we allow ourselves to be with the concepts of isolation, meaning, freedom, responsibility and death, with all their implications; once explored, examined and accepted, fear is not only displaced as the overriding emotional response, but it has also been replaced by inquisitive contact and the possibility of creative living. We must first make contact with ourselves and what these immutable aspects of life mean for us before we can safely say we are free to live a contactful life. It is through the life of intra and inter-relational contact we discover contentment, and through contact with self and our environment, we find meaning for ourselves.

Courage to Be Wrong

Can we be courageously committed and yet aware of our possible wrongness? There lies the paradox of courage. "Have the courage of your convictions," we are admonished. Yet simultaneously we must hold to the knowledge that we may be wrong, that we may need to let go of what we believe. We must hold our beliefs like sand in our hands, letting it fall through our fingers should it no longer be useful. It takes courage, of course, to admit we are wrong, or that we might be wrong, had I lived my whole life as a Christian then at the end of my days, in the stillness of imminent death, the smoke clears, the mirrors removed, I realise it was all myths and magic. It would take enormous courage then to let go of a belief I had held my entire life, to admit that I had lived my days dancing to another's tune instead of composing my own ditty. Far harder now that there is no longer time for me to start composing.

I think that religious hold over society continues to restrict progress toward personal freedom, be that progress of thought, morals, science or art. It used to drive art, in the renaissance religious concepts were the mainstay of the great masters, where would we be without the religiously inspired music from Beethoven's Missa Solemnis to the tribal chanting of Native Americans or Buddhist monks. There is no area of art which has not been touched or coloured by religions, or by moral judgement inspired by religion. Be that in the form of commission or censorship.

The church in various forms has sought to divest individuals of their sensuality and entomb them in the drab life of the monastic. It might have once felt useful to limit people's sexuality, even when the reasons are based as they were in historical documents of dubious renown. The restrictions handed down to us, in many cases by iron age peasants, are still surreptitiously restraining our societies. Telling us what we can think and what we should do. We know now, through the study of the genes of attraction, that the people you are or are not attracted to have almost nothing to do with choice and everything to do with your parents' genetic material, plus some nature/nurture influence. So, it is abundantly clear you have no choice as to which, if any, sex you are attracted to. Thus, if we allow ourselves to see, if we allow ourselves to dip a toe into a little knowledge beyond our restricted limits imposed by doctrine; it becomes clear that being one sexuality or another, no matter our gender has no relation to choice. I didn't wake one morning and decide I was going to be one orientation or another, I always was the orientation I am.

If there is no choice then it cannot be inherently evil can it? Even the most short-sighted, dogmatic, religious fundamentalist must surely see this. Still, religious people attempt to limit the horizons of people they don't even know. I have worked with Alzheimer's patients who have changed their sexuality because the dominant part of their brain which was functioning to make them fit their original sexual preference has now been destroyed by the disease. Are they evil then? Are they wrong? Of course not; it would be illogical to suggest such a thing. It is incomprehensible to me that anyone can imagine how this judgemental religious position is supportable. If the only excuse for the denial of medical fact is religious dogma, then it is high time the dogma went, and we instead deal with the void left behind for those individuals supporting the dogma.

Courage is required to let go of our ingrained ideas given by some significant other, to accept another as they are. Allowing a dawning realisation, we have no right to tell anyone what they can and can't be. To accept the feelings others may provoke within us as ours, without expecting their change; the courage to allow contact without the expectation that another will become like me or acquiesce to my desire for them to be a certain way. Courage to accept we have no control. We can have no clear contact where expectations intervene on the boundary between I and thou, those expectations make thou an object to be manipulated or destroyed, not accepted in a creative expression of contact, which might even be described as love.

Throughout history, it has been our artists, thinkers, composers who have been given prominence in the annals of fame. When we consider the famous men and women who went before, it is the music, the art, the provocative painters and thinkers who stand out, they are the crowd when we think of lasting fame. Every one of them took the courage to create, to think beyond the accepted idioms, to make their mark and say this is me, this is my thought, this is my creation. Every one of them allowed themselves to be, and almost every one of them was shunned or excluded, laughed at or ridiculed or feared, even killed, for thinking so differently and putting the status quo at risk. Courage was required to allow those creative expressions, and those expressions rippled on through the successive generations, and eventually, their thoughts and masterpieces became revered as ground-breaking. Not just that but foundational for the next generation to build upon. How much courage was required by every one of those people to be, and allow their authentic being expression?

In allowing their expression of the self, the creative endeavours then bestow limited immortality to the originator. The artists are dead of course so know nothing of the legacy and its rippling through future generations, or how long indeed those ripples will last. Will we ever forget Michael Angelo? Or Sigmund Freud? They achieved some semblance of immortality by allowing creative endeavours. Ironically it was for fear that man might eat of the tree of life that Adam was thrown out of the garden of Eden in the Genesis myth. Lest he eat of the tree of life and become like the gods.

Expectations as a hindrance to contact.

The "Gestalt prayer":

I do my thing and you do your thing.
I am not in this world to live up to your expectations,
And you are not in this world to live up to mine.
You are you, and I am I,
and if by chance we find each other, it's beautiful.
If not, it can't be helped.

(Fritz Perls *Gestalt Therapy Verbatim*, 1969, 1992).

Expectations, you may not be surprised to hear by now, are a block to contact. You can say to yourself "I expect to be respected." but you can in no way demand it. It is a desire on your part, a want, or need, not a certainty. You cannot 'expect' it. I suspect that expectations are also at the root of objectification.

Cultural and religious expectations can get in the way of contact with both self and other, usually simultaneously. If I meet someone for the first time, I am the ambassador for my culture, be that geographic, religious, familial or any other grouping which is different from one's own. I cannot expect other people to be like me or want to be like me. If I hold to an expectation that someone will see my way as the right way, which is frequently the case with fundamentally held religious ideologies, that expectation will get between me and the other, obscuring genuine contact. The expectation becomes like a veil through which we see a limited version of others. I was born and raised in Essex in the UK, but I can't expect everyone to behave as though they had the same upbringing in the same area or to understand what it was like for me as a child to become a young man in that specific environment. This is particularly true of people brought up many miles from my home. My local culture is specifically local and understood in the context of people who lived in it at that time.

Religious fundamentalists of all persuasions fall into this category of being in contact only with expectations created from their own beliefs, but let's not forget, in many ways we all do this in our personal lives too, we all hold expectations of others. If all I see is someone to convert to my faith or a heathen who doesn't understand, a person to be bent and moulded, persuaded, evangelised until they believe what I believe then I never really see the other person, or indeed my own insecurity which is driving me; I only ever see what I expect them to become or do, and I am likely to experience frustrated irritation by their lack of compliance.

Expectation as a basis for offence

This is the basis of offence, when people say "I am offended" ordinarily you will find an expectation behind the offence which says, this is wrong, or this is not what I believe, or more commonly you should be like this. When a behaviour is not as expected, offence is taken. It is a failure to see the other and only be held in contact with my expectations. If I hold the belief that a particular group of letters is a swear word, when someone else utters that word, I will hear it as swearing and if I also hold the expectation that people won't use this word, I will more than likely use that as an excuse to feel self-righteous and become offended. Ideally, according to my expectation, I will want to limit the other person's use of language and judge them as sinful reprobates. The entire offence though is brought about by my expectation. If I do not expect others to behave the way I believe we should, I would not have any offence. It is a closed system, a fixed Gestalt. If I have that specific belief as an introject and hold the expectation that others should believe as I do I will never have good contact with people who swear. However, I might if I allow myself to feel it, experience a short burst of joy at others' free expression. The delight is a minor response to that part of myself which feels constrained and would really like to swear from time to time, the excitement quickly converted to irritation through retroflection. This delight represents the authentic self, popping up from wherever we have been keeping it hidden.

The use of apparently crude language, or the use of the word "God" is a common cause of offence to many religious people. If I have been told that this type of language is somehow wrong, that it is forbidden, ungodly, the mark of the weak-willed, the last resort of less intelligent people, and these are all genuine things people have said to me about swearing, it's all bollocks of course. These sayings if swallowed, believed, internalised without being digested. This forms the basis of an expectation that people who swear are somehow bad, I am not bad because I do not swear, therefore I can now feel offended by anyone who uses the word cunt, but also, I can swell with pride because I am a good person for not using this word. It is also the introject which prevents me from fully engaging with language and self-expression, limiting my vocabulary and potential points of contact.

It is this expectation that everyone else must be a 'good' person like me, that gets in the way of me making contact with them, and my authentic self, as soon as I hear the swearing; it's not the language used, it's my expectation that that person must be a bad person if they use these terms in this manner. In this case, it is clearly derived from an introjected belief. As a therapist, I want to be able to challenge that belief because I sincerely think it is more harmful than any amount of swearing. If you don't want to swear then fine, it matters not one jot, but that behaviour should never get in the way of contact with those that do. The issue comes when someone says, that's part of my religion, therefore, I am offended, now you modify your behaviour, so I don't have to contend with the feelings it evokes.

This is where it gets difficult, because this idea that we should not challenge religious belief has created within the therapist, an expectation, an introject if you will, that we won't challenge personal belief full stop. Even though religion is just an idea, its man-made and ideas are meant to be challenged, they are not immutable realities. Therefore, I honestly believe that expectation is hindering dialogue and ultimately contact within the therapeutic community.

Contrastingly if I meet a person I have never met before without expectation that he should be like me or become like me; now we have the possibility of actual contact, and that contact will be clear and offer creative possibilities at the point where our authentic selves meet. Even if we have diametrically opposed views there is the chance of creative exchange of ideas and excitement if we both hold no expectation of the other. Perhaps I will become interested in him, or how he lives or how his difference works, perhaps I can explore what that difference would be like for myself. There is no expectation, just a meeting of two people, two cultures and the possibility of creative conflict.

This means if we can become aware of and let go of our expectation there lies the possibility of contact, but as soon as I expect you to be something you are not, or do something just because I want it done, then I am no longer seeing you, I am seeing my expectation unmet, and disharmony will arise.

Expectation and Entitlement

If I hold on to my expectation, it comes across as a sense of entitlement, I should be getting this, you should behave like that, this is my due. How many times have we heard "I work hard all week, so on Saturday I want this or that and I never get it." You may feel frustrated, unseen, unsupported and many other things, yet your expectation of getting these things will always result in limited contact with others when you see them as objects to fulfil your expectations. Your sense of entitlement resulting from the expectation will foster irritation and conflict, not contact. Your frustration may also prevent you from recognising what you really want or need and making that explicit, as you will be in contact with your frustration derived from expectation, not in contact with your original need. Your frustration, in turn, prevents you from clearly conveying what you need within the conflicting demands of your environment or taking responsibility for getting those needs met yourself. In letting go of the expectation, perhaps we can see the other, perhaps we can negotiate how we get some of our needs met, and in doing so increase our contact with others and our authentic selves.

Over the longer term, if I have been explicit about what I need, and if we are still not meeting despite the removal of expectations; If still there is no fulfilment of something I want from my environment and I don't feel I want to go without that missing something. In this position, it is my responsibility to do something creative and change me or my environment. If I back my needs with courage, I can move toward an environment which is healthier and gives me more of what I need in order to be. The key here is simply that it is my need and my responsibility, I cannot expect another to provide it or do it for me, I must be the catalyst for change as it is my needs which call to be met. Taking responsibility for oneself and one's actions, for one's life, is one of the founding principles of existential psychotherapy. It is hard to take responsibility if your contact with self and others is clouded by expectations.

In religious arenas and terminology, we see the negating of responsibility all the time. By giving things to God to change if it/he/she wills it, I am giving away my responsibility and power to change. I deny the little agency I have. There must be a payoff for that behaviour because that seems an immense thing to give up. My experience and that of some of my clients has been that people are willing to give up their power to change in order that they do not have to take responsibility. If I give it all to God and nothing happens, I have something else to blame, either it wasn't his will or I'm not praying the right way. Either way, I don't take responsibility for making a choice or not making one. I leave it to fate or God or some other fictional accident of rite. I avoid contact with actual responsibility and choice.

By making a choice of course we cannot ignore that it always means ruling out something. If I am at a crossroads in life, faced with 3 choices. I can't go back and change the route I have travelled to come this far, but I have roads ahead, I must choose to take one of these paths or become stuck where I am. In choosing a path I am saying no to the other paths, I can never come back and say, yes ok now I will take this path; because even if I do try to, I am not the same person I was when making the new choice, I have been irrevocably changed by the awareness of the choice.

Tempting then, to sit at the crossroads and ask a fictional entity to give me guidance. I know that guidance will never come. Thus, I never make the choice, I am forever stuck; maybe stuck-ness is preferable to the cost of making a choice and taking personal responsibility. But it's not living, I am forever engaged in asking God for direction and waiting instead of being in contactful engagement with my choice and the world of possibilities it opens. In giving up my responsibility and power I give up the pain of making the wrong choice and negating the choices I didn't make. The concept of God and its religious trappings then becomes a way to justify passive acceptance and renunciation of my agency to be.

Expectations and Acceptance of Others

Separate to religion but related to religion via expectations is the issue of our angry youth. We see in the West lots of angry children, youths angry with parents and those parents at a loss to explain it because they have given everything for their kids and live a relatively affluent life.

Adults in the west tend to see their children as objects they "should" mould into who/what the child "should" be; rarely are children accepted as they are, without the parents' expectation that they are something other than what they are. It is assumed they will become or do something else and rarely is that a function of the child's organic self. We saw that at play in the case study Angela in chapter 1. Much of it is the imposed thoughts and prejudice of the parent. Much of these expectations are religious in nature or formed from a culture which has been created by religion. The weight of parental expectation creates frustration in the child which is released as anger; often the youth concerned is totally unaware of what they are angry with, but the anger exists, all the same, it is directed toward the source of frustration, the parent, and must be expressed.

The parent might say things along the lines of, "I only want the best for him." "He would be happier if only he would do this." "I wish he would apply himself to his studies..." Even an overprotective attitude to parenting can create within a child a sense of not being allowed to be themselves, to go and explore spontaneously. This attitude might have been born of the desire to protect, yet it has become the tool of stifling overcompensation. Gradually then, frustrations build in the youth and if there is no outlet, no safe form of expression another is created. The frustrations will more than likely be expressed or retroflected as depression, eating disorders, self-harm etc.

This idea that my child must become like me, must behave the way I dictate, must become the person I wish, is detrimental to authentic self-expression; the child no longer behaves in an organic manner and denies those aspects of themselves they feel their parents would disapprove of. Those parts of self become unavailable in young life and later in adult life too. In many ways we can see religion as this overbearing critical parent that wants the best for the child so gives it a million rules and tells him/her not to be themselves. The child suffocates under the weight of expectation.

We want what is best for our children, of course, we do. However, the overprotective fussing or sheltering can be stifling to a child who may lose their sense of self as an agent in the environment. This loss of agency may be expressed as dependence on the parental figure, or a lack of spontaneity, a lack of engagement with the world, or a lashing out against the world in order to express that frustrated desire to be what we authentically are. This is also the picture created by religion as overseers of humanity. The majority of humanity takes the role of the oppressed child but is unable to see where its anger arises from.

Expectations and Tolerance

Acceptance of others without expectations is not just about religious tolerance. For centuries religion has played a role in suppressing a variety of behaviours commonly felt as natural. This is again founded on the premise that if you are not like me there is something wrong with you, the expectation that others will conform and become like me. Coupled with the entitled view that I, as a religious person, can dictate to others how they "should" behave. The word "tolerance" itself denotes exception; you are tolerated not accepted. My expectation also allows me as a religious ambassador to be offended by that which I have been told is unclean, or wrong, or any other introject supporting my fantastic view of reality.

No one can justifiably expect anything of another, no one has any right to ask another to deny the way they are, especially if that part of themselves has a demonstrably immutable source. We cannot expect another to be something just because it might be easier for us, in the same way, I cannot expect my wife to clean the house, or have sex with me whenever I want it. If she chooses one of these options then fine, but I cannot expect them, my desire cannot become an entitlement.

When I work with couples, I often look at their expectations of one another, because we all have them. Yet I cannot find a single expectation that stands. I want my wife to respect me, yet I cannot expect it because I may not be worthy of respect. In short, if you or I do something because it is expected we will inevitably feel resentment. I either do the decorating because I want to live in a better environment or because I enjoy it, or we find another solution, it cannot be expected because I am "the man of the house" or because of any other gender stereotype. If any behaviour is expected it always engenders conflict.

Chapter 8

Case study 2, John.

....even the worst person remains human and is entitled to our compassion. Erich Fromm, *The Anatomy of Human Destructiveness* (1973)

JOHN

This case I am presenting in considerable detail as it gives an interesting perspective on religious belief vs mental health. On the one hand, this man, John, has been diagnosed with Generalised Anxiety Disorder and Obsessive-Compulsive Disorder, which is driven by religious belief and what might be described as maladjusted thinking. His ability to mentalise, observe his state of being and evaluate himself as a self with a sense of agency in the moment, is severely hampered by the introjects born of difficult early relationships combined with religious schooling.

When John first came to me, he was unable to work because of his OCD and GAD. He has had a couple of jobs in the last 4-5 years but struggled to maintain them for more than 2-3 months. These jobs are mostly supermarket based, low level and unchallenging. John presents as highly intelligent with very low self-esteem and a frequent lack of engagement, so it is hardly surprising that the supermarket does not offer enough challenge for his intellect or support for his mental health condition. The co-morbidity might have been misdiagnosed as depression in the past, but I don't feel the issue is depression, more an unwillingness to make contact, a holding back. Married to a woman with bipolar or unstable personality disorder for which she is under the community mental health team, still awaiting a clear diagnosis, John says they are a perfect team because they both have mental health issues so they can't really moan at or attack the other for having them. In this way, they find a peculiarly companionable support for each other, but I do not see much in the way of positive purposeful support from either beyond a sense of vague understanding and tolerance.

There is a complexity in his condition which seems from the outset to be supported by religious belief; his OCD and GAD have deeper roots, particularly in his attachment style developed through his early relationship with a mother who was not only an ardent catholic but also anxious much of the time. His first relationship and experience of attunement, or lack of, was with a female who could not tolerate his emotional needs due to her own anxiety and feeling of impotence. Instead of attuning and supporting with appropriate soothing comfort and support of independent actions such as creativity and exploration, his mother opted to dismiss him and his feelings with intolerance and used religious dogma as a means to manipulate him into compliance. This was essentially a reaction to her own emotional experience, and in projecting her anxiety onto him, in order that she might not be afraid. As a result, he has learned to fall back on religious dogma when faced with difficult emotions, as though this will please his mother; he learned to dismiss his own feelings as they were perceived as a source of trouble and distress for others, something to be mistrusted, they are a cause of anxiety for others and as such should be avoided. In doing so he learned to become dismissive of other peoples feelings too, if his feelings are intolerable then so are everyone else's.

John's father was rarely home, a military man, he figured little in John's life. When John's father was home, he seemed frustrated and unable to fit into family life. John describes his early memories of his dad as like being with a stranger, never looking forward to seeing him and not developing a strong bond even in periods of leave. John's father died when he was 6, John thinks it was cancer, but has never really discussed it with his mum that he remembers and was never particularly interested in finding out.

John came to me after he realised his approach to his feelings wasn't working anymore, fighting them just seemed to make them worse. His approach to life just wasn't working as a system and his heightened anxiety was to him evidence that something was wrong. His relationships were all breaking up, he has been divorced once and might be heading for a second. John struggles to accept his daughter's feelings in much the same way his mother had difficulty accepting his. His own feelings of helplessness conflict with his desire to help his daughter and to feel close to her when she is expressing emotional distress.

Having never been shown that he can move toward, to soothe and comfort and support; he experiences a distance, a moving away from, and an increase in OCD, GAD symptoms relating to the resultant anxiety caused by unexpressed emotions of his own. Possibly the realisation that he wants for her what he never had, but being unable to be angry with his mother for using religion as a shield against him. That said, he is aware that "Something is wrong" and "This does not feel right, it's like I know I should be doing something else but all I feel is a growing distance." Looking at this issue in therapy, questioning his own and his mother's reactions, feels to him as though he is devaluing his mother and because Catholic dogma is also mixed into the same pot, he is committing a sinful act by doing so.

His denial of self is also connected to the idea that there is heaven and hell, and he must be good to avoid hell. Even questioning the rightness of his internal experience leaves him feeling shamed and brings on an increased frequency and heightened level of anxiety and OCD urges.

John also describes how when his daughter was born, he had a sudden increase in all symptoms and now feels guilty that something which "should have been a positive" is in his eyes a negative, that the birth of his daughter has been a negative influence serving only to increase his intolerable feelings and OCD urges. This is a form of existential guilt which has a convoluted path to understanding through awareness. I discuss existential guilt in more detail as a separate entity in chapter 12.

The birth of the first child is often a pivotal point for people as they come to terms with the evolution from being responsible only for self, to responsible for self and dependent others. Anxiety and phobia disorders often seem to start at this point in people's lives. I suspect the underlying issue is present far longer, as a nascent neurotic construct but becomes focused or a heightened figure through the emotional impact of having a child. I myself developed a fear of heights soon after the birth of my first child, which is only improving now he is an adult. My fears of being responsible for him and his possible death were transformed as it were into a generalised fear of heights. When people develop fears soon after the birth of a child it is often linked to the renewed responsibility for dependent others and the fear of death; the fear of one's own death projected onto the child and the fear of permanent separation from the child.

John's OCD always takes on a religious quality. For him, it is not a contamination issue so much as control. He must count as though counting the rosary beads, in order to make situations more tolerable. While counting he imagines the rosary in his mind, counting off the worry beads. Genuflecting is his second most common response, in magically warding off intolerable feelings by making the sign of the cross and counting how many times this is done. In many ways, his religion has taken on an OCD form, the ritualistic elements building upon his urges to relieve his anxiety, his expectation of its intolerable nature and his organic need to be soothed by another, retroflected to create a form of shame. Looking to God to be the parent and take his fears away with some magical/supernatural intervention. It's interesting that he shows none of the compassionate elements of his religion. He has, I think, never experienced that aspect, and as such has only introjected the harsher more critical aspects of Catholicism.

John has suicidal thoughts, but he suggests that the only thing stopping him from carrying them out is a belief in heaven and hell. That suicide is against his religion, and he will probably end up in hell for taking his own life. Upon further exploration, he does not seem to have a belief that God exists. His belief is clearly a construct created out of others' beliefs, his mothers, the priest, his father, auntie etc. He personally says he does not know if God exists, but he feels certain there is an after-life and a hell. John does not seem at all disturbed by the inherent incongruence of this missing element. Although I never actually asked John about this I did wonder if his lack of Godhead represented the lack of a father in his life. The inability to imagine an idealised father looking on or looking after because he never had one, so instead he has a vacant god who isn't there.

The concept of heaven used to assuage the fear of death and thoughts of one's own demise is discussed elsewhere in this paper. I want to highlight here how the polarities between rival concepts of heaven and hell can be used to control. The heaven/hell dichotomy has been used to create a punish-ment/shame-based driver for conformity throughout societies all over the globe. In John's case, it has helped establish or enforce distance from his emotional reality. John does not even talk of heaven as being a reward, it's just something to strive for and only figures in his thinking as the opposite of hell, his focus being first and foremost on the punishment to be avoided, not the respite to be gained in a heavenly realm.

Removing this belief might result in him choosing death, some might say this is a positive effect of religious schooling, that it is keeping him alive by preventing his suicide; it becomes a justification for upholding the belief and affirming it. I initially experienced comments like this from my therapist peers as obstructive, as though they were so afraid of John's response that they felt the need to ask me not to explore this aspect too deeply. John also presented in such a way that I felt him saying "We shouldn't go down this path because I will have no reason to not kill myself if we do." He didn't use those actual words; this was just the sense I had when we approached the subject of heaven and hell. It is a little like saying this far and no further. Part of him knows this is the route he might need to take in order to rid himself of the effects of religion and mother's anxiety-laden early ineffectual bonding, there is resistance, and ultimately it must be his choice.

That aspect of John is unaware at this stage but aware enough to be voiced in vague terms. I have already said I am not in the habit of challenging religious belief directly, so I allowed the client to take his own path. My feeling of immobilisation or dis-empowerment when the subject was raised is an important one. This is how the client describes himself in his relationship with others, and it is how his descriptions portray his mother's interactions with him. This is essentially a counter-transference, I was experiencing at this moment, in part, what he experienced as a child. I held this in my awareness and later in the therapeutic exchange came back to it as a point of reference. As is always the case though, the felt reaction was mine. It is the monitoring of this internal reaction which we use as a tool and in some ways a map in the therapeutic exchange. It tells us about our own experience but also a likely reaction of others the client has contact with.

The Work

I believe in this case my role as a therapist is to offer an alternative model of attunement. That he can learn through his relationship with me that his feelings are not only tolerable but useful and could possibly be encouraged. This includes me explaining or allowing expression of my own experience resulting from what I see as counter=transference. Through this interchange, I envisage he will eventually see that he is acceptable as he is, whatever he is feeling. If I do not become overly anxious and dismissive as his mother did, whenever he is anxious, perhaps he can start to experience some of that attunement he didn't experience as a child. In turn, he may, from this place of the novel encounter, move toward accepting other people's emotional reactions rather than becoming embedded in his own reaction to them.

This was alien to John at the outset, and it should be expected that novelty will induce some anxiety, particularly at the outset. John can begin to accept others' feelings initially by experimentally mirroring my behaviour. I initiate this by introducing safe emergencies. These are short exercises carried out within the relative safety of the therapeutic exchange. Essentially just short contact exercises made up on the fly, relevant to the current conversation; during which John is encouraged to explore his reaction to me and his feelings, while I, in turn, express what I experience in response. Gradually through this process, we begin to experience moments of authentic contact. The acceptance of self within the authentic exchange then begins the process of rewriting John's internal map. That is a short description of a very long process.

The more insidious nature of religion within his diagnosis will always be a challenge to this process. Partly because there is an expectation that therapists let people have personal religious beliefs and leave them alone. Some aspects of John's religious beliefs must be challenged if he is ever to be free of his disorders. He will always fall back on the spectre of divine punishment if he maintains his Catholic view of heaven and hell. His fear of committing the unforgivable sin, denouncing the holy spirit or questioning its existence holds him back from challenging his beliefs at all. The fact that this is also a disconnected behavioural thought process, not attached to a belief in a personal God, serves only to discombobulate. Often the thoughts of challenging his mother are confused with the concept of original sin, as though she somehow embodies the holy spirit or perhaps the Madonna. The guilt and shame attached to questioning her behaviours past was palpable.

Although I have no personal investment for him to believe there is no God or that Catholicism is unhealthy for him, I do not expect him to become like me and join me in my atheist camp. I am okay with him being what he needs to be. What I would desire for him is a life without OCD and GAD, a life where he can be more authentically himself and engage without the fear of God's judgment looming like the Sword of Damocles over his head. In his case, what he is, is troubled because of his avoidant attunement style and the supporting introjected belief system. I can't see these anxiety effects diminishing significantly until he relinquishes the glue of Catholic dogma, he has introjected from the moment he could understand his mother.

3 Months On...

After 3 months of weekly therapy, John moved to a more open position in our relationship. Experimenting to some degree with being vulnerable in measured doses and allowing his anxiety within the meetings. We established some trust in us as a working pair. He began to experiment, through safe emergencies, with the idea that his feelings were not going to overwhelm me, that I am responsible for me and my reactions, and he is only responsible for his feelings. Part of his own overwhelmed state derives from his fear that his anxiety would be too much for me to handle, as it was for his mother; can be eliminated when he realises, he is not the cause of the anxiety of the other. In remaining in contact with him and being supportive without "freaking out," as he described it, he learned that he can be himself with some people and they won't fold. In short, he was no longer adding the second fear of my being affected by his anxiety to his original anxiety. This meant his anxiety was diminished at least to a limited extent. At one point he even expressed delight that he could be distressed, and I did not need to retreat, his anxiety momentarily becoming excitement of a different order, though a confusing mix initially. It took a long time, maybe 8 months, for him to experience being with me and to allow himself to not create distance for himself, or to catch it very early and decide to stay with me. He threw himself into the therapy and began a dramatic shift when he started telling me every time he began to feel himself pulling away during the session. I in turn reflected every time I felt him retreating from contact.

The exploration of the theme of retreat in the interchange at those moments proved ripe ground for his understanding of how he disengages. One exercise I asked him to attend to every day was a night-time breathing meditation. It helps people get to sleep while also developing the ability to monitor, regulate and mentalise emotional reactions and thoughts. Essentially you just lie down, be aware of your breath. Allow it, don't force it. When your mind wanders from your breath, notice where your thoughts have gone to, then gently, without giving yourself a hard time, bring your awareness back to your breath. Rinse and repeat for as long as you wish or until you fall asleep. It is essential in this process to come to terms with us as the observer. We are not the thoughts themselves, we are the one observing, as we observe the breath and the flight from breath to thoughts, and back again.

Much of the therapeutic work was done by reflection on the present moment and current somatic experience. His awareness of himself as a feeling person separate from me increased. His observational self-learned to watch and monitor this during trigger moments. He learned to allow and tolerate his distress, to breathe into his felt emotional being and thus, through experiencing his emotions in a supported environment he was able to explore parts of himself hitherto disparate or lost to awareness.

As the therapist, I offered containment for his chaos and supportive reflection on the present moment as well as a description of countertransference feelings when they arose. It is important to note that at no point would I ever have implied these feelings definitely were countertransference. I just allowed them and if they were useful, we explored them, if not we let them go. I say that because sometimes we as therapists can enter the therapeutic alliance with expectations too, the expectation that these are always countertransference feelings would also prevent clear contact in that moment. Had they been something else my insistence would have derailed the work.

Throughout this process, the largest hindering factor was the sudden shutting down in contact by John, caused in the main by religious thoughts, an introjected law or saying, and followed by the desire to genuflect, which was the taught ritual. During these moments I could feel his retreat from contact and ask him where he was going. This intervention encouraged him to stay with what he was feeling, even if it was a felt sense of retreating, he gained more experience of how and eventually saw more clearly the mechanism of his retreat from contact. In doing so he was able to see that part of him, an increasingly larger part, desired to be in contact, that the pulling away was not what he wanted; indeed, this was what brought him to therapy all those months ago, and now his behaviour was becoming a source of frustration. Consider this as the third layer in the Gestalt 5 layers of neurosis theory. John was experiencing an awareness of the role he was playing, he also experienced the fear of contact and started to retreat. Now the impasse began to focus from his wanting to relinquish his role; in feeling the pull of contact at the same time as the desire to retreat from contact. He was beginning to allow more contact but not having the emotional skills or experience to do so was struggling to stay with it.

It was around this time he realised without prompting that the dogma he had learned from his mother was not his. His light bulb moment, or as pearls would say, mini satori, came when he said through tears, "She didn't know what else to do, I don't think she knew how to be a mother. She couldn't do it, she should never of been a mum." As he contacted his compassion for his mother, he simultaneously acknowledged her failure and allowed the idealised image of her to dissolve momentarily. He had just challenged her without the shame of feeling he was badmouthing her or running her down. The religious edict that he must always honour his mother lessened its grip. In this moment he not only allowed compassion for her but began allowing compassion for that part of himself she had reacted to.

I suspect in part this came about because he had engaged with compassion for the woman, she was rather than his expectation that she would be something that she was not. She was never going to be the mother he needed, and she was not the idealised fantasy mother/Madonna; he could relax his grip on that expectation and allow her to be her. This, in turn, requires an understanding to coalesce, of his separation from her and the realisation of his existential isolation.

At that moment John was, of course, contacting that same part of himself, that he could be distressed and would survive, that he could be upset and seen, even held by contact with another though not his mother. It was in his words, "A confusing mix of joy, hope, disappointment and excitement." I picked up on the lack of anxiety in his statement. John realised with a laugh that he was not experiencing anxiety in this moment at all. "I thought if I said she was a bad mother I would feel anxious, ashamed. I always felt so guilty about that; But I don't, she wasn't a good mother, maybe she did the best she could?" The second part was inflected as a question, so I replied, "That sounds like a question, are you asking me if your mother was a good mother?" John laughed. "No, no, she wasn't."

It is a common semantic trick to turn the thing we wish to say into a question, in order to get another to express it for us. Particularly when it is something we might be ashamed of expressing. It can be useful to request the client converts the question to a statement, in order to bring the immediacy of the message home.

A year on and John still has no abiding belief in a personal God, but has a sense that a God of some sort must exist, "Or else, where would all this of come from?" Gesturing to the world around us with his arms. I made no effort to dissuade him of this. His image of what God might be has changed. He no longer holds to most of the beliefs he had picked up from his mother and isn't afraid to explore them anymore. What's more, he is learning to engage with others in a more contactful way, specifically through noticing his desire to retreat and engage with his self-compassion for the part of himself he is protecting. The part which was unacceptable to Mother and reflexively withdrawn from a position of vulnerability.

John's religious ritualistic behaviour is melting away and with it the shame and constriction. He will more than likely never abandon it entirely, he has challenged many of the introjects but there are so many that have become so second nature to him that it is unlikely, though not impossible, that he will ever relinquish them all.

John still gets OCD urges when anxious but has learned that an urge is an urge and will go away if he pays attention to his anxiety and breathes into it instead of trying to run from it or soothe it with ritual. Though he also recognised this means he must accept feeling vulnerable and taking responsibility. His mantra, in mentally talking to his urges, has become, "Thank you for letting me know I am anxious." It doesn't tell the urge to go away, and it accepts his anxiety. Then he tries to deal with the source of his anxiety if possible. The key aspect is breathing while maintaining awareness and not running or fighting anxiety. That alone feels like a massive shift for John.

He would no longer be eligible for the GAD diagnosis but has a long way to go before he can say he is comfortable with allowing his distress, but then who is? His attunement issues, we dealt with in part by mirroring and specifically directed mindfulness practice. We both think he has made enormous strides in a healthy direction, though I am not certain we ever entirely undo the damage of mis-attunement, it is diminished to the point where John can live without constant anxiety. He is learning to override his initial instinctual response to run away and distance himself and is instead practising mirroring others in order to get understanding. He has also started to ask more, "What do you need, can I help and if so, how?" Or derivations of those questions, and to accept that he is not the cause or solution for others emotional wellbeing, yet he may be able to help if they can give him guidance in how to support them. Ultimately, he has accepted that his moving closer to others is for him a better solution than dissociating and pulling away, though it still feels alien, and yet exciting. Maybe one day he will give up on the Catholic idea of heaven and hell entirely. That part is not my job.

Chapter 9

Religious Behaviour and Attachment.
The hi-jacking of the Familial Self

I'm not a fascist. I'm a priest. Fascists dress up in black and tell
people what to do. Whereas priests...
("Father Ted", Series 3, Ep 1, 1998)

Attachment Styles and Religious Behaviour

Problematic attachment and attunement were a significant aspect of
John's early interpersonal and intrapersonal development. His own attachment
style has been undoubtedly affected by the lack of effective accurate attunement experienced from his mother in particular; as well as his almost entirely
absent father.

Attachment styles fall into several basic categories and subcategories,
across which there is overlap and some diversity. The four general groups for
attachment descriptors are insecure: ambivalent, avoidant, disorganised, and
finally secure attachment. I don't intend to give an overview of all possible
styles and interplays. You are better served reading one of the hundreds of

books dedicated to the subject, however, I am going to outline the areas of concern I see most commonly in people who have become embedded in religion and ended up in therapy. I realise I am deriving this from anecdotal evidence, that I am only considering those people I have either worked with or had relationships with, therefore it is a narrow field. I include those who have also had a religious belief in a supernatural deity and follow a religious doctrine based around such. I also recognise that many of these people have come to me because they have underlying mental health conditions and are not necessarily representative of the entire religious population group; my concern is chiefly with those people who presented needing support for mental health issues

I might see well attached functional human beings for personal development, but it is rare that these come to me from a religious background while still maintaining a religion, especially monotheistic in nature. In these instances, people probably seek personal development within the religious community. I cannot, therefore, say with certainty this snapshot I present is totally representative of the wider community. I am however convinced that religion has a limiting effect on attachment development, in young and old alike, as it restricts contact with self and promotes deflection, retroflection, projection and transference. There are few instances where the large, organised religions encourage attunement of the kinds required for developing better attachment styles or understanding and awareness of our own.

Predominantly I see leanings toward anxiety and dependency. Attachment patterns tend to be more fluid than the descriptors suggest. Although I might use a term like ambivalent attachment style, that does not mean that someone will always behave in the described manner. People may be a little avoidant and show ambivalent traits for example. It's not important to put people in one box or another. That may, in fact, limit our contact by expecting only the associated behaviours to manifest. It's only useful for us as clinicians to have a rough framework telling us about the likely reasons for this or that reaction. Bear in mind also that much of the behaviour is only evident in novel situations, the restriction of novelty by religion may be useful in diminishing presentation of affect derived from attachment disorders for some people, though in doing so also limits awareness and possible growth toward healthier attachment and attunement.

Ambivalent Attachment Style

The ambivalent style is marked by swinging between clinging behaviour and aggressively resistant behaviour, or the counter experience of extreme passivity. These clients often report being experienced by friends and family as difficult to comfort; they are likely to have more than usual anxiety and have considerable difficulty navigating any novel encounter. The anxiety experienced is caused by others' lack of attention, either to detailed planning or attention to the individual experiencing the anxiety. Blame is shifted and responsibility for one's own feelings is neglected. They would more than likely have been doggedly obsessive about their primary caregiver's location, always wanting to make sure that he/she was available. In adult relationships, they are frequently jealous and controlling. This person will not have developed the skills required to explore situations, particularly novel ones with any degree of security. Their internal map of the world is too limited to safely predict the interactions; thus, these clients will become ambivalent to contact in order to prevent feeling the insecurity of their psychological position. This includes self-exploration, which is frequently restricted to simple, safe, known paths. New exploration is discouraged and avoided.

Prone to responding passively to authority, clients of this grouping tend to prefer to be in groups led by charismatic, present individuals who seem very clear of their path, people they can follow without question. Though they may at times be resentful and angry about the imposition of being expected to do things; in religious groups, this is frequently retroflected and becomes transformed into guilt. The passive stance to authority will be a hindrance to accepting one's own will or critical exploration of one's own agency. The frustration created by negation of the authentic self will more than likely be projected onto an authority figure, that might be a religious leader or spouse.

Avoidant Attachment Style

Often linked with dismissive behaviours, avoidant attachment is characterised by a lack of resourcefulness and an inability to remain flexible during moments of change. The reaction to novelty would likely be to avoid attachment to others. The inflexibility expressed in the inability to move between the novel situation and the attachment figure. The usually expected expression of emotions is restricted to the point you might think nothing was being felt. Indeed, the adult in this stance may say he feels nothing whatever. We find these individuals to be stoic. However, the felt reality will still be going on within, even if not in awareness or expressed. This is particularly the case with the expression of emotions relating to attachment and separation.

An interesting aspect of this attachment style and the associated avoidant behaviours is the tendency to idealise as a means to not feel. For example, if I idealise my father, I may not have to feel my despondency at any perceived failures on his part. During periods of separation, I can hold him as ideal within my mind, within this fantasy realm I am protecting myself from experiencing the pain of separation or disappointment, avoiding feelings of distress or vulnerability.

Monotheistic religions tend to engender transferential familial notions. Specifically, with terms such as "God the father" or "the holy mother of God." The idealised godhead becomes the replacement for the parents that lacked the ability to respond to the infant who developed an avoidant attachment style. The fantasy of the omnipresent idealised father who can respond to my every need fulfils the unconscious desire to be met fully and contactfully by our primary caregiver, through the medium of attunement and with appropriate levels of attention. The desire to be supported, held, looked after, during moments of threat is part of an evolutionary back story that helps us seek refuge in the face of danger. In the avoidant adult, it has become unawares, but it is still working behind the scenes. The lack of response from the God in question is dealt with in the same way as the original unresponsive parent.

In the therapeutic dialogue, we might expect these clients to disown their own vulnerability and need for support or comfort from another. More usually we experience them projecting their own vulnerability and need onto others. The need in others is judged to be a weakness or fault in those we might otherwise have a loving supportive relationship with. It might also be coupled with an inflated sense of self- importance and perceived inequality between the client and their acquaintances.

Disorganised Attachment Style

With the disorganised attachment scenario, clients may experience dissociation. This where the current felt experience is filtered, as though it is happening to someone else, or in extreme cases, clients may experience an out of body experience or what might be considered a split in the personality; where some aspects of experience are only experienced by one part of a person's self, while disregarded or not felt, possibly even entirely forgotten by other parts of the personality. It is an attachment style we often find associated with clients who had a traumatic or frightening childhood. When familiar events, sounds or smells present in the current time frame, the client may revert to the childlike state of trauma or overwhelming fear. Dissociation is then a way to minimise the impact, the effect and affect will be seen as happening to someone else rather than to the actual person. This client might at times behave in ways which seem contradictory, bizarre or paradoxical. Imagine if one of your parents was the only source of comfort while simultaneously being a figure to be feared. It is hardly surprising then that this person might be conflicted about attachment and contact.

In my experience, people with a disorganised attachment style are likely to be prone to catastrophic thinking, and will react with potent, emotional expression at seemingly innocuous suggestions. Discussion of simple everyday separations may result in considerable distress. It has often been the case that disturbing life events have neither been understood nor processed in a manner which would lead to a good internal map for future events. Remapping of the past events may be required before the client can begin to process the here and now experience, they find overwhelming.

The disowned experiences remain a disturbing factor even though they have been disowned, they may be out of awareness, but they are known to at least some part of the personality construct. Though just out of awareness they will occasionally be triggered as partial or full recollections by sights, sounds and smells. These triggered recollection events are at least as traumatic as the original, having lost none of the emotive potency and frequently adding the fear of repetition, knowing what is coming, to the original trauma.

Contactful behaviour for these individuals is disorganised, often momentary and frequently provokes anxiety. All contact creates a felt response in the individual, this carries the possibility of triggering one of these experiences and provoking an emotional torrent.

In my experience when clients with this attachment style are involved in religion, religious behaviour is used as a proxy contact. Stuck in the realm of cliche, playing the role of the good parishioner, pastor, minister, priest, nun, etc. provides enough superficial contact to fit into a life that does not require full participation. Events that might be threatening are distanced and disowned aspects of self can be hidden behind edicts and labelled as undesirable. Religion then becomes a firewall through which contact with self and other is mediated and restricted to ensure safety and mask disorientation. A further complication may be found in this group as they may exhibit some schizoid behavioural traits. Though this is varied it often results in swings between isolation and merging, both these states can be experienced as terrifying. When clients of mine have spoken about hearing the voice of demons, God, angels they usually fall within the disorganised attachment patterns.

Secure Attachment Style

The ability to explore contact, moving in and out of contact with otherness, self and environment without undue anxiety is the hallmark of this attachment style. Most of us can achieve this to some degree. A contactful individual will also be able to remain with the changing flow of the emotional continuum during contact. This requires the ability to maintain awareness of self, to mentalise what is happening internally while also paying attention to external influence in an ever-changing environment. All this without becoming embedded in the experience. The mindful observant stance is an essential aspect of the aware state required to be in contact and not to feel overwhelmed by the experience. People with a secure attachment style are far closer to and more likely to be able to learn these skills.

Secure attachment does not mean a lack of conflict. Conflict will be accepted as an integral aspect of living in contact with others; tolerated as a disagreeable necessity. Where two boundaries meet there will always be the possibility of conflict, however in the securely attached individual this is often experienced not as a negative but as a creative positive. The possibility for growth and development are recognised as a probable outcome for well-managed conflict. Contact is, in essence, allowing creative exploration and possible integration of the new, while allowing for the possible disintegration of the old.

Confluence

I want to mention confluence here as it is often mistaken for secure attachment by people who are confluent. People who show a tendency toward confluence often consider themselves securely attached but are blissfully unaware of the confluent state. Confluence is a merging of the boundaries between self and other. In the confluent position, with no clear separation, clarity of observable self is lost, the sense of containment or security is really an illusion, as two have momentarily become one. If the sense of self is lost in the exchange, then the attachment is likely to be unhealthy.

In the therapeutic exchange, confluence results in areas of potential conflict for the therapist not being explored in the client. As a simple obvious example, I might smoke, in which case I might not challenge your smoking or even see it as an issue. It can be a complicated mode to see enacted in self. In essence, the therapist won't necessarily see any area in the client which is a blind spot for themselves. Or they may not engage fully in the discussion of difficult areas if they themselves have not fully engaged with their own processes around the same concept.

If you are angry with your mother and I am angry with my mother, I will be less likely to challenge you to explore your anger as it relates to your mother. In actuality, I will probably enable a tacit agreement that the anger is appropriate without ever exploring it. It may well be appropriate, but it may also be far from. The lack of exploration because of the blind spot is the issue. The therapist and client have effectively become merged, the separation and differentiation at the contact boundary that usually exists, and that is vital for good healthy therapeutic contact is lost. Joseph Zinker said in *Creative Process in Gestalt Therapy* (1977);

> The therapist's greatest enemy is that state in which he finds himself deeply identified with his client, embedded in the other's psychological skin. The psychological boundaries — what we call contact boundaries — begin to merge. This State is called confluence: The loss of differentiation between two people. The characteristic result is that they can no longer rub up against each other. Creative conflict, or simply good contact, is sacrificed for routine interactions which are flat, static and safe.(46)

In therapy we must be able to take risks, we must create enough tension for the client to gain awareness of their discomfort in order to address the source and make a choice about how to be in the future. Without this creative conflict, without a clear differentiation of boundaries, this process is impossible.

Confluence is the process through which an individual loses himself in society. By going along with trends, such as fashion, the individual becomes confluent and gives up responsibility for personal choice, it's also a means to feel connected, though at the expense of merging. It's obvious to even the most casual observer that religion requires confluence in order to gloss over all the restrictions and contradictions that interfere with authentic expression. Confluent behaviour removes the rubbing up against each other and the creative conflict that arises from the contact, it also removes the need for personal responsibility for choice. Therefore, if you are confluent with your environment, you will not challenge your religious leaders, or the ideals expounded. We can become confluent with our society, no longer challenging norms, or even seeing them.

Confluence becomes the unwritten contract between the self and society. It's unwritten as it is also unnegotiated, it is assumed. We follow the rules, we toe the line, moderate our behaviours, our thoughts, we limit what we challenge and tolerate much we would otherwise despise. In return, we expect to be looked after by society, to be part of the whole, to be able to make a living and live well enough. Isolation is limited because we are part of the group, responsibility is negated as the society tells us what to do and expect, even how to behave. Confluence then makes for a stable but dull existence, living without really living, existing but with limited opportunity for good contact.

Understanding Another's Environment

The effects of environment on self and development can never be fully comprehended by any other than the person experiencing it, though if confluent they may well be blind to its effects. I could never explain my environment to you in such a way that you could fully comprehend its impact on me. I will leave out my blind spots, I will colour aspects to tint them in ways

I think you want them to be perceived, I will lie to myself and to you, and all out of my awareness. My being is co-created within the framework in which I live, my perception of the environment is tainted by my introjects and my objectivity limited by my experience and its influence on the now. These are filters to my reality which you do not possess, they are uniquely mine.

As therapists, we attempt to understand, and work within or shape our interventions to help meet the demands of the psyche presented before us. Much of the time we might admit we have no idea how the client perceives reality or if our interventions are likely to have an effect. We creatively adapt, we explore with experiments created on the fly that take in all our perceptions of the client and their presented world view. We run through theoretical frameworks while making sense of others' described experience. We attempt to make contact through experimentation and safe emergencies and hope that within that contact the client will have a moment of clarity about themselves and how they interact with us and the world.

It is useful in this setting to be honest with ourselves about our limitations as human beings and as therapists. There is nothing we can ultimately do to give us a perfect picture. Always, we are seeing another's world through a tinted mirror. We can polish the mirror a little, but it is always a reflection of the original. The only person equipped to know what they are experiencing is the person experiencing it. We are privileged to be witness to, but do not experience directly. We must then let the client teach us about them and not assume we know, no matter how similar we imagine their experience of life is to other encounters we have witnessed.

Chapter 10

Heroes and Myth, Is the Truth Really All That Important?

> We hunger for heroes as role models, as standards of action,
> as ethics in flesh and bones like our own, A hero is a myth in
> action. Rollo May, *The Cry for Myth* (1991, 54)

Importance of Heroes

I am a big fan of the Greek myths, maybe that started by watching the 'Harryhausen' movies. The stories these myths convey through metaphor and archetypes are an important aspect of developing a mental map of humanity, how humanity works and, in some way, where we fit into it all. The fickle all too human gods and the heroes struggling under the yoke of favour, which often seemed a curse rather than a blessing, encapsulate the essence of human endeavour and struggle for existence and meaning. I too had heroes growing up. Unlikely space-faring heroes with very dodgy parents. I also fell in love with the Tolkienian world of Middle Earth and the many heroes, often flawed, struggling to overcome trial and tribulation, the temptation to power in the fight for good vs evil. I loved that people so small and unobtrusive could be the main players in a drama played for the most part by big people that overlooked them. Mostly I loved the expression of courage and audacity in the face of horror after horror, that and the fantastic world they inhabited, it was an escape.

The stories of *Star Wars*, *The Hobbit* and *Lord of the Rings* are also myths of a sort. They contain many of the archetypal psychological constructs we recognise in older myths. The messiah figures. The one who sacrifices all for his/her friends. The hero fights to save the beleaguered female, who is in no way helpless anyway. The search for who am I, who is my father, my mother, where do I come from? What am I? Is played out in so many characters in both these worlds. I'm sure some of that is planned, and some of it just serendipitously happens through unconscious processes of the writer seeking to explore the unconscious urge to know. Jung, throughout his writings, expressed that writers, poets and artists tapped into the collective unconscious and drew out narratives common to all. I'm not sure about that collective unconscious theory, it doesn't sit well with me, but I do have a sense that we are all connected by myth and stories. Stories give us inklings about how to be, often they give us messages that are unhealthy. They can be the source of moral codes, but also tales of rebellion, standing up against the tyrannical world and tyrannical parents, be they Darth Vader or Zeus.

Growing up without myths would create a void. A space in the narrative that makes up our mental map. We know we create our own moral codes based on empathy and our own needs. Left to their own devices people would do that as a natural aspect of human development. We would build our own code of behaviour irrespective of religious input, but myths, myths strike something perhaps more primal. Myths help us work out who we are, where we come from, and held within those tales is an essence of what might bring meaning to our lives. This meaning is usually just a cover, a hiding place for our feelings of meaninglessness, but it is nonetheless an integral and important aspect of storytelling.

By way of example, the myth of the hero is often picked up by leaders at times of war and crisis. It sometimes gets in the way of contactful, creative approaches as the leader becomes more in contact with playing the hero than in being the leader we need. When one takes on an archetypal mantle described by a myth it becomes hard to step aside and make choices which do not fall within the parameters of the myth. It is possible that people begin to feel they are the hero or must be seen as the hero.

For the majority, it is through myth that we share our heritage, our sense of where we come from and what we are, at the very least the tale of our ancestry. It can be good and bad, healthy or unhealthy, and these definitions will be fluid also, changing from one generation to another, though the myth remains the same. If you believe in the myth of the superman, the Aryan dream, or fundamentalist nationalism it is likely to lead you down a dark path. But the belief in another myth like Karma might conceivably require that you try to be a better person. It is not the myth that is important, but how you allow said myth to impact upon you. It's how you employ it in enabling behaviour moving forward. Bear in mind also there is no way to know that the myth of Karma isn't harmful at times too. If you live your entire life suppressing and denying aspects of yourself in order to be something other, if you play the role presented by the good karma narrative; you are likely to end up lacking contact in some areas of life. Outwardly you will appear to be doing no harm to others, which is a noble endeavour, but it may be at considerable cost to your psychological self.

Myths are frequently the description of a journey, a wish for something lost or the push toward the reconciliation or reconstruction of a utopian ideal; the Biblical Garden of Eden being a good example of a paradise lost through our own ineptitude coupled with the desire to usher in the kingdom of heaven, a second paradise to replace the first. A journey which is inherently moral in nature, and a myth which has been coupled to human ingenuity in order to drive our cultural dependence on one religion or another, for example, the Abrahamic religions all have the garden myth as a starting point.

Another interpretation of this Garden of Eden myth is that it describes the birth of the human ego. At first, we are born innocent, knowing nothing, then we learn to recognise good and bad. We were commanded not to eat the apple, we did not need to work, we needed to make no choices, we had no responsibility other than that given by the authority figure God/parents. Once the choice is made to eat the apple we have gone against the initial familial authority and learned what it is to take responsibility. We have learned the difference between good and evil, in short, we have begun to think for ourselves, we begin to become independent. We start to experience our sensuality and start to cover parts of ourselves because of shame of exposure we didn't have as children. It is a myth about becoming a thinking, acting adult, about growing up and leaving the familial home, the comfort and ease of Eden, in order to make our way in the world.

Yet the myth continues, we long for the state of innocence, youth, and a return to the idyllic heavenly garden of our uncorrupted state but remain an adult and must take responsibility for ourselves. We want to give that responsibility up to authority, we long for someone else to take control and for us to return to Eden, but we can neither become a child again or undo what has been done. So instead of living, we search for a way to return to innocence, a state which, like youth, can never be attained once lost.

Religion is by its very nature replete with myth. One reason people are drawn to it is a desire for meaning in a life which otherwise feels stale or vacant. Religion is also full of archetypal heroes, be it David taking on Goliath or Arjuna as portrayed in the Mahabharata. The archetypes relayed by these myths form the basis of personality types and modes of being, from the underdog to the all-conquering Casanova.

It is important that we have these snapshots into humanity. To read about David is to read about a low man brought up, who won against the odds and against scorn from his siblings and through action, his own bravery and courage. The shepherd boy that became king, how seductive might that tale be to an impoverished man with no sense of personal agency or power. We can well imagine him taking a story like that and use it as motivation for personal change. If the boy can become king, I can get out of my demeaning situation. It becomes more than a story, it becomes a map, a motivation toward personal change.

Equally, we see time and again, people in the therapy chair who say they will never match the ideals of society. Myth has been subverted, far from a motivational factor it has left them with a greater sense of nonbeing and impotence. One of my clients said, "I can never match up to that, I can never be like Christ no matter how hard I try. I just make mistake after mistake." His sense of self, his perception of him as a human being was disfigured by the constant need to live to an ideal imposed by significant others of his youth, backed up by generations of God-fearing Christians. It was only in recognising where the ideal had come from, and that it was imposed not sought or naturally felt, that he was able in due course to give it up and begin to accept himself as he was without needing to become like Christ to be acceptable.

The effect of role models for good and ill can be seen throughout society. Heroic archetypes are useful vehicle for understanding heroic behaviours and expectations. Many problems with archetypes I have come across in therapy arise from the shoulds attached by religious belief and the adoption of myth as truth.

When told by authoritative people, "You should be like this" while they point to an unattainable heroic archetype such as Christ the Messiah.

What is implied is, "You are not enough as you are" you should in some way be different. Should, should, should... the age-old red flag marking the insertion of introject. The reality is starker, and indeed more dangerous: if I am given an unattainable goal, such as being like Christ, I will never feel satisfied as I am or indeed remain in contact with my true self as I will feel compelled to change what is into something it is not. I may feel moments of pride, but only when I successfully force myself to be something I am not. As a direct result, I can never rest because I have not reached the height, I am told I should be at. I then live in the grip of guilt, fear and shame brought about by my seemingly inadequate person. Yet, I am what I am, I am not Christ and never will be him, either in fact or fiction. Let me be me and let him be him. It is important to stress that if I am not accepted as I am, I will never experience contact with my accuser no matter how much I might long for it.

Myth as Truth

Perhaps as damaging to the collective psyche is the establishment of beliefs and myths as "fact" as "truth" when it is just a story for which we have no real evidence or basis beyond the expression of deeply held ideas. Even if there is a kernel of truth within the story, it is not only unimportant to establish this "truth" it is positively damaging to do so. Usually, mythic stories are told and retold to suit the day's needs, cherry-picked from a mass of other stories for its important message. However, this endowing myth with an aspect of truth leaves the listener no space to manoeuvre, imagination is disengaged, and creative reasoning disabled. Particularly if the listener or reader has never been taught to think critically, or if they are young and impressionable or of an age where it is hard to discern this tale may not be true.

Religious instruction is inherently introjective. Taught to swallow whole without recourse to critical faculties, and frequently enmeshed with transference toward the teacher, the Father, the Mother Superior, the Holy Father etc. our familial expectations of authority and patriarchal/matriarchal power struggles shores up and lends credence to their wishes that we accept all that is presented rather than challenge that which is taught.

The religious stories and myths we learn as children will then have a lasting impact upon us as we seek to become adults in a changing world. I grew up with some of the bible stories, some of them, if taken as myth, may be useful in giving me a blueprint to some interactions. However, most of them were written by and for nomadic iron age peasants. Their world is a far cry from mine. I'm not certain I need to give up pork, though I can understand how that might have been important in a culture that had no refrigeration. The first Buddha died from eating a piece of bad pork, maybe that's why the religion that grew up around him started advocating vegetarianism. Likewise, many of the rules laid down make little or no sense in today's world, and some of them are so far outgrown we baulk at the very thought of them. Yet we are instructed this is the truth, thus God's word creates a conflict between what I deem to be right for today's society and what I am expected to accept because it once fitted a distant culture 2, 3, 4000 years ago.

The mythical properties to the tales can still be important and still be interesting, even enlightening. But we do not have to prove that this or that happened for the myth to stand as a useful story. To do so in effect kills the message it portrays.

Importance of Critical Thought

If you were not taught to think critically, to chew up the information you are given, the story you are fed will remain unchallenged and swallowed whole. The life of the person taking on the myth as truth, is shaped by the belief that this myth happened. The vulnerable are enveloped in the superficial, all-powerful Father/Mother/Spirit who will take care of them. This is exactly what the vulnerable have wanted, someone else to take responsibility and remove all this pain. Our existential pain and confusion around taking responsibility for something we cannot truly control or understand can be momentarily soothed with the ointment of myth. It doesn't matter if it's a belief in a flat Earth, or that Elvis is alive and well and living in Slough, or that the Garden of Eden was a real place from which mankind was expelled by God or gods, depending on your religion. The given "truth" once delivered and accepted takes on the role of delusion, shaping behaviour and limiting contact with self and the world with all its possibilities. Perhaps the trade-off is of intrinsic value.

The mythical hero would be better served if never seen as an extant being, that was never the point. The story is a story, it gives you clues about life and its accompanying woes. To be told it is real, that it happened exactly this way, is to remove all the depth and mystery, and like any named thing, once labelled it has lost its novelty and we no longer seek to understand it. The denial of mystery is so often the deadness of religion. The attempt to hijack myth for the purpose of imposing sociological norms and collective control is detrimental to all, not least the people to whom conformity requires relinquishing joyful contact with otherness.

Modern advertising is also another form of religious attitude, whereby we are force-fed soundbites and factoids, which are meaningless for the most part; or seek to imbue meaning where there is none, in order to part us with money. You are buying a fiction; the advertising is attempting to persuade you of that fiction. In this realm we are encouraged not to think, we are stimulated and enticed but never asked to properly consider, to de-construct and digest. In the first part of this book when discussing freedom of will and choice I mentioned the use of makeup and reworded a well-known advertising slogan. We all know these jingles and enticing copy. But are you aware that they encourage you not to engage your critical faculties? Are you aware that they are encouraging you to entertain a helpless state of compliance? When an office full of beautiful women are lusting after a shirtless well-muscled man, you are not just being sold the drink its advertising, far from it, you are also being told that if you become a muscled well-toned man, you will have women lusting after you. You are being told you are not enough as you are and being given a complicated message about body image. It's insidious, and it's indoctrination. You are being encouraged to turn off your critical reasoning, and you are being force-fed ideas which are not your own and which will stay alien to your being as introjects. It's not being fit and healthy that is the issue; That should always be encouraged, it's the comparisons invited that cause harm today as we are bombarded with images of apparent perfection daily.

The Myth of Robin Hood

I want to take the tale of Robin Hood as an example. A mythical tale from olde England, which may or may not have elements of many historical figures woven into the rich tapestry of the story. The idealised myth is of a dispossessed lord, who seems to have somewhat socialist leanings. He is also a man of violence; he steals from the rich through banditry and gives to the poor. There is a sense in the stories that this was foisted upon him because the rich were taking so much from the poor and taxes were so harsh the poor were dying, or in other versions that his king took his lands or banished him from the kingdom. He is a hero to many simply because he is standing against the despotic overseer and on the side of the underdog. There is still the subtext that only someone from the world of nobility can set the world right and rescue the poor. But that aside it is a story of brave daring-do and rescue, replete with characters like Friar Tuck the religious man with a drinking habit and violent streak. Little John, the gentle giant etc. Any materially poor person reading it will be drawn to the story because of the perception of the Messiah we have learned from other myths. This is one man who can be seen as fighting for them, he embodies their own wishes to be powerful, to take wealth from the rich and have some lasting effect on their own life. It may also relieve the guilt of wanting to attack society to get what is needed, if it's ok for heroes it's ok for me.

It's just a story, with its many characters it encompasses many archetypes. Yet for some reason, some people have been determined to work out who the "real" Robin Hood was. Seeking facts where they are not needed, losing the mythical element and making it easier to explain and understand. I would suggest it is the mystery that helps its appeal, from within the mystery we can tease our own sense of understanding. Why remove mystery, why this drive to make it real? Why can we not just accept it at face value, as a myth that speaks about power, greed, violence and class imbalance? It is the loss of mystery that deadens experience. It doesn't matter if the tale of Robin Hood happened historically, that is not the purpose of myth, what matters is the significance to us personally, of the narrative and character archetypes expressed through the myth. If we thought The Iliad to be a true representation of past events it would lose its grand appeal. The heady tales of heroes and monsters are its glory and delight.

We all need some markers to steer by in order to feel psychologically safe. Myth plays a significant role in providing some of those markers. Myths help us form a moral code for ourselves from the chaos of crazy stories and mistakes written down by past wizards of the page.

The Hidden Dichotomy in Myth

Myth is one path to meaning and understanding of the human condition. We can learn about our clients by listening to the myths they present. "The problem of identity, as Erik Erikson has emphasised, is present in our clients and in all of us, and we can approach a solution through listening to the various myths the client may bring up." Rollo May in *The Cry for Myth* (1991, 33).

I am reminded of one of my very first clients, who came with an alcohol problem. He provided a stylised version of himself. His description of himself seemed full of lies, as he presented an idealised form. He even proclaimed that he had won the lottery. I remember in a supervision group being scoffed at because I had accepted his lies at face value. In truth, I had done no such thing. I felt he was telling me, through his lies, of the person he wanted to be. He was ashamed of who he was and presented another version of himself in order to cover his shame. His elaborate lies about the lottery were preposterous, but really, he was telling me, "I feel powerless, I want to be this other person, and the only way I can see to get my life in order is to win some vast sum of money." It's not an answer to his emotional distress or his lack of acceptance of his selves that were lost to alcohol. It is another myth we have all heard, that money and wealth will bring us happiness, it is a myth that fuels our frenetic running from angst. As to my client, yes, he lied constantly, but in doing so he also shared more of himself than he could know. If I had engaged with the lies and called them out that would have ended the therapeutic alliance. He already knew he was lying. There was little to be gained from pointing it out.

You could say this was a delusion, but at no point did I ever feel he believed these lies. There was always a sense of him presenting himself as a fantasy other, more than an entrenched belief that this was reality. We must trust the process, that clients will find their truth for themselves, and through awareness of their behaviour begin to allow a lessening of the grip on myth as fact. If we join the client where they are, in their psychological world, without becoming confluent, remaining as a conduit to other possible psychological realities, it is possible the client will feel accepted enough to explore other possibilities until the myth they have created is no longer needed. I had another client just a few months ago who after 6 months proclaimed that some things, he had talked about were lies. The conversation went something like this. "I am sorry, but I have to tell you something. I feel ashamed just saying it, but I lied, all the work we did about x.. it was all lies, it never happened. I realise I have been wasting your time and will have lost your trust, so completely understand if you feel we can no longer work together." We talked about the trust issue, we engaged with the reason behind the lies, we looked at what they covered, and we looked at how difficult it had been for him to bring his deceit to me and expose his truth in the process. We then went on to look at how he presents a mythical self to the world in order to cover his truth. It was the most contactful work we had done to date. We are still working together as I write these words.

As far as my feeling as though trust was broken, this was his assumption and expectation of how I would respond. I pointed out to him the number of times I had expressed concern over the lack of contact between us, as though something was not quite right, and how since his disclosure that had not been my experience. We explored how that lack of contact had been telling me he was not being authentic. For me, it was never about trust. If a client chooses to present a false self, they are wasting their time, I'm still there and still doing my job, it's all grist for the mill. When the client feels safe enough to be authentic, I won't be disappearing because they lied in the past.

The dichotomy inherent in myth is partially temporal. We read or hear about something that "happened" in the past, yet we experience our reaction now, in the present. The morals, ethics and other messages are transported through time by the narrative, but they are not ours. We can choose to pick them up if we wish or accept these were just something that people used to believe. It is not real, it is not now, it is a representation of ideas, but our reaction is real and now.

The other aspect of the dichotomy hidden in myth is that we need a sense of meaning, yet we must create our own, we cannot get it from external sources, yet we use myth in some measure to give meaning to our lives. When we read of the archetypes with which we resonate we are aware of the split between us and them in psychological time. If I read about a hero in the Greek Myths, I might empathise with this or that aspect of his/her personality. I may also recognise parts of myself, or my life played out in the myth. But recognising I am not that hero; I still must complete my journey. This split between myself and the archetype I am emotionally drawn to represents in no small measure my own feelings of impotence. The myth is not real in the historical sense, but I am in the present sense. My desire to be more than I am and my seeming lack of power to meaningfully impact my situation is brought to the fore by my connection to the myth as I understand it.

Here is an interesting idea. 'Ego', the 'authentic self', the 'id', the 'superego' etc. These too are myths. Myths in the sense that they are just fictions. Things we have created in order to understand the world. They are ideological constructs. We can say that Ego does not exist, and we would be correct. It is just a term for something we see in personalities. But it is not a real thing, you can wrap it up and put it on display and say here is an ego. These terms are like myths, in that they are used to impart meaning, to give structure and definition to psychological discussions. Without them it would be very hard to explore our psychological world, but they don't exist. I think the difference between this and religious fiction is that at no point will I be telling you "this is the truth, this thing exists." It is just an idea, and like all scientific ideas it is subject to exploration, examination and change.

Chapter 11

Case Study 3, Letting Go of Religion.

... Thus religion, according to Freud, is a repetition of the experience of the child. Man copes with threatening forces in the same manner in which, as a child, he learned to cope with his own insecurity by relying on and admiring and fearing his father... Erich Fromm *Psychoanalysis and Religion* (1995, 11)

Letting Go of Our Parents' Religion

Rolo May in his book, *The Discovery of Being* (1983), describes clearly the interaction with a client who went through extraordinary emotional distress at giving up her parent's faith and joining another. This wasn't even a case of giving up the idea of God, just moving from one type of church to another. However, the experience was so extreme that she would have fainting fits, described as grasping at oblivion. As though if she was somehow not conscious, she would no longer have to take responsibility for her conscious decision to change. Later in the book he adds this after the client asked if this was likely to lead to psychosis

"I asked whether her fear of going psychotic was not rather her anxiety coming out of her standing against her parents, as though genuinely being herself, she felt to be tantamount to going crazy. I have, it may be remarked, several times noted this anxiety at being oneself experienced by patients as tantamount to psychosis. This is not surprising as consciousness of one's own desires and affirming them involves accepting one's originality and uniqueness, and it implies the one must be prepared to be isolated not only from those parental figures upon whom one has been dependent, but also at that instant to stand alone in the entire psychic universe as well." (32)

What Rollo May has described here, the moving from dependency and subjugation to a sense of self and choice is the move toward personal responsibility. No longer bound to the sense of duty to parental influence; the sense of isolation is inevitable because we realise, we and we alone are responsible for ourselves, our feelings, wants and desires, and once seen those wants and desires are ours and ours alone, we can no longer easily project them or shift the blame for them onto another for in each instance our awareness will make them a figure once more.

To a confluent person it provokes anxiety as the realisation I am me, this is me, I am my own person, I am responsible for me alone; helps to remove the illusion of parental support. That they will always be there for me, that if I behave like them all will be well. However it is couched, removal of that particular blinker, either through realisation or death, will likely produce anxiety because it is a novel situation, and a situation we have avoided seeing. I put death in there because this very state is often found in those who have recently lost one, or more commonly, the last parent. It's as though they finally realise, I am next, no one else stands between me and death, existential isolation is finally realised.

We can see this anxiety as a reaction to the novelty, but also a reaction to death itself and the sense of not knowing what to do with this realisation. Supporting the person to stay with it and breathe into it and explore it, helps foster the knowledge that they will not fall apart, disappear, crumble or any of the other catastrophic imaginings we are presented with. They may be distressed for a time, but it will pass as they offer themselves support with breath for the feelings. In my experience when you breathe into your anxiety it transforms into something else. In this situation there may be many complicated interlinked feelings which have been suppressed, which now push for expression.

Case study 3 – Jimmy

Jimmy was a 54-year-old male, he had always felt he would follow in his father's footsteps. This was backed by the myriad of "should" originating with his parents. He should do this, he should do that, they chose his subjects at university so he could pick up as a partner in his father's business, he followed the stern parent's advice and became like his dad. He even developed the same dislike for dogs his father had. It was a form of confluence so pronounced that the two men were sometimes mistaken for one another.

When Jimmy lost his mother at 49, he was not overly affected, he described his grieving as "a little sad, though not to the point of tears." Following his father's lead, he put on a brave face and kept his sadness hidden, even from himself. That was the done thing, to be strong for others according to the family rules. Which we all know for the lie it is. Then, at 53 when his father died, Jimmy was suddenly struck by overwhelming anxiety. Something which had never troubled him before. It was his anxiety which eventually brought him to therapy as the anti-depressants he was prescribed did nothing to help.

Jimmy took a month to warm to therapy, he was initially sceptical and dismissive. This pattern often occurs, it's a warming process, a building of trust. It can also become a role clients play to cover fear of intimacy or vulnerability, to hide the question, "What if?" If I engage with therapy, I must take responsibility for myself and allow my vulnerability.

Jimmy had become aware that he was next to die, but in his keeping it light in order not to tax me, he pronounced that he was not overly troubled by the prospect as he had faith in the Presbyterian God of his father. Jimmy described it like that "the Presbyterian God of my father" not my god, not my personal deity, no relationship at all. This was his father's god. I pointed out this incongruity and asked about the adoption element in his statement. Jimmy batted it aside as it had nothing whatever to do with his anxiety. "I have come here to deal with my anxiety not to talk about God." I also challenged his need to keep it light to look after me. This was also dismissed as "it's what I've always done, I can't change that, it's part of who I am." It may be what he has always done but he was still projecting his need to keep it light to avoid distress onto me, converting it into a need to look after me.

Jimmy came initially with the expectation I would cure him or give him some trope to manage his feelings. He would regularly dismiss my efforts; frequently I felt he would remove my claws with hostile quips, resisting interventions left, right and centre. I would respond by pointing out how many interventions he dismissed and the hostile tone but never pushed him to accept. It took a good few sessions before Jimmy would consider this, "Breathing into his anxiety nonsense." I must admit I laughed when Jimmy described it as that. However, when Jimmy came to a session after a night of bad dreams, anxiety attacks and almost no sleep he finally found enough courage, or maybe was desperate enough to try anything. He breathed, for a long time that was all we did, just breathe, and I asked him to notice this movement or pay attention to that area of his body; promoting awareness of various aspects of his body and the felt response. Jimmy found his anxiety gradually changed or shifted. But he didn't like what he found. Initially, it moved around, as though trying to escape his internal glare. When he made contact with the sensation, at that moment he primarily found he was deeply sad, he was unable to see the root of his sadness. I asked him to be aware of his physical sensation, which at this point was an ache in his chest. Then on asking him to ask it (his sensation) what it was for Jimmy was surprised to find the answer, his mother's death, which had been several years before.

Jimmy was totally bemused as to why because it had all seemed so simple at the time, not much sadness at all. The rest of that session he alternately cried and felt ashamed for crying in front of me, apologising for every tear. I kept responding with something along the lines of, just breathe, or who are you apologising to? After a few similar statements he woke up, stopped, sat up straight and looked directly at me and said, "No, I don't need to apologise to you." I asked him whom he might be apologising to. Eventually, he came back with a very quiet, "Mum and Dad." Then followed at least a minutes silence, then "FUCK." Jimmy didn't swear previously, that was the first, but not the last time he swore in a session.

That was the beginning of taking responsibility, realising these were his feelings to do with what he wants, and he doesn't have to do it the way his father wanted him to. The anxiety though, at dropping the game and challenging the script he had followed for his entire life seemed extraordinary. Every step he found he was not that man, that he wanted something else, but was scared to be the other as it was so contrary to his upbringing. So used to being what others had expected him to be, he no longer knew how to just be. He was discovering who he was; and who he was not. Jimmy likened it to being mad, "Nothing makes sense at the moment, it's all nuts, I don't even know how I like my eggs anymore!" He had always eaten them boiled, with a little salt, the way his father had.

It was a journey of personal discovery, punctuated by anxiety and fear of isolation and responsibility. Coupled to this he was experiencing an awakening sense of loss of meaning, his meaning had been to be like his father, yet now he was letting go of that like a snake shedding a skin. It's a journey far too many people never make. Every step was marked by painful transitions. Profound levels of guilt followed by the realisation of the resentment behind it, which once expressed opened the way for a sense of Jimmy to come to the fore.

In the months we worked together Jimmy gradually removed one rule after another and replaced them with something that felt okay for him. Sometimes he kept the rules or modified them slightly. He always fell into the trap of apologising for his tears, so ingrained was the lesson. As time went on, he became more adept at catching it and letting it go, but it was always there.

A tough part for Jimmy, toward the end of therapy; was realising he never really thought about God before, he was a Christian because his parents were, because they, and their church, had said God existed. He started to challenge his idea of God and God's existence. Jimmy realised with some horror that his idea of God was exactly like his image of his own father. He started looking at his beliefs and concluded they were not his. Looking further at the tales he had been presented with as evidence he soon found scant indication of anything but coercion. This realisation initially provoked anxiety, but once Jimmy breathed into it, he found the anxiety soon transformed and became anger.

Jimmy was initially fearful but eventually triumphant. It was the last step in his journey with me, many other foundational stones had been replaced already, the yoke of his parent's disapproval had been put down, though with the occasional picking up to try it on again. The God part wasn't too hard to shed, in as much as, after much effort and digging into his beliefs the shedding happened quickly. He was left with tremendous resentment at the rules he had followed which had limited his interactions and existence, their instigation and the dominance of his parents' needs over his. The often, "Puritanical insanity" as Jimmy described it, rules to limit and control his every thought and feeling.

Overall, for Jimmy, the hardest part of letting go of God was letting go of the idea of heaven. The realisation he would not live forever in some eternal, comforting realm other than this existence, and that he may have wasted so much time not really living. He did realise he had used the concept of heaven to cushion the prospect of death. In this way, the discussion of death marked the conclusion of therapy. Accepting death as a reality, an end to be faced not ignored or hidden beneath comforting myths. The end of therapy is an apt place to explore moving on and how to approach endings, including future endings.

Anxiety was down to "normal" levels, whatever that means, tolerable perhaps; and in this titanic struggle, Jimmy had found a route to himself hidden away under the expectations of his parents and the church. He was still searching for meaning, and aware of his existential guilt and losing so much time covering his authentic potentialities with others rules for living. Yet Jimmy was starting to wake up and live, he had to grieve not just his parents, but also the time he felt he had wasted on his adult life, following ideals that were not his own. The last session was 8 months after we started. Jimmy brought me pictures of his new dog. Jimmy likes dogs, 'Who would have known?'

Following Ancestral Beliefs

We all know that humans tend to follow the beliefs of their parents or the local environment. If you grow up in what is designated a Christian country you will more than likely become a Christian, Muslim, Muslim, Hindu, Hindu, so on and so forth. We know this is not because of the excellent properties of one religion over another, it is simply because of the education of children by parents and state. Familiarity. Our environment establishes within us these basic concepts, then suggests that if we don't follow them, it may not end well for us. It is indoctrination, and as such removes the principle of critical thought and exploration. If you grow up being told you don't need facts you need faith, it's faith that makes you a great man/woman. If you trust the person telling you this or look up to them, if they are an authority figure, it stands to reason that you will take on their words and swallow them whole. Without challenging them or the message contained you won't be able to decide for yourself, challenging them later in life as Jimmy did is tough. There was an old Jesuit saying, "Give me the boy until he is 5 and I will give you the man."

It seems cruel when spoken plainly, to take away someone's reason, to prohibit critical thought, often reframing such activity as pious. I can still remember a friend telling me I shouldn't listen to Simon and Garfunkel, that it was not of God. I do remember thinking they were slightly cranky, but still the message was there, an attempt to control my behaviour was made. Or maybe an effort to hide their own fears.

Letting go of our parents' religious belief then is likely to be a momentous challenge, temporarily confronting us with a threat to our foundational beliefs. These are the kinds of pivotal beliefs we feel make us who we are, though in reality they are just a role we have collected from a significant other. One of our cornerstones as it were. It matters little that they are built on myths and conflicting ideas, essentially, they are one of the pillars supporting our personality. They offer us a limited sense of meaning and are a map of our existence. As therapists, we want to challenge the delusions, but we cannot just remove a supporting pillar and expect the remaining structure to stand. The dogmatic autonomic behaviours enshrined in religious belief may be limiting to human behaviour, but they also offer security, surety. "This is how the world is and God has it all in hand." How comforting to have such certainty. I can well see why so many would give up freedoms in order to feel so contained. Religion can be seen then as a salve against existential angst, though not a cure. Therefore, working through these concepts in therapy can feel a little like one is going mad, having a psychotic episode. Leaving behind all you thought was real and embracing something very different, shaking your foundation and seeing what is left standing! That takes courage.

Chapter 12

Meaning and meaninglessness, isolation, freedom and responsibility.

Man cannot endure his own littleness unless he can translate it into meaningfulness on the largest possible level. Ernest Becker, *The Denial of Death* (1973)

Meaning

Isolation and meaninglessness are two of the major existential issues we all face during our lifetime. The realisation of the reality that we are alone. Once separated from our mothers at birth we are always separate, and in the end when we die, we do it alone, even if people are about us. When all is said and done, we are responsible for us and our wellbeing and we will always remain separate from, though not uninfluenced by, our immediate environment.

Religious groups are of course an obvious way to feel part of something, to avoid immediate isolation and to develop a sense of meaning.

Often, they organise people, volunteers and paid workers to reach into the community. Unfortunately, that is all too often evangelism dressed as good deeds. Despite this, I don't wish to deride the efforts made, religious groups are often full of people who want to have a positive impact on the environment. These groups can do a tremendous amount of good because they meet regularly and have a common goal. Also, if we take an example like the Christian Church, as they have the underlying code of ethics and the layers of guilt and shame built in to aid compliance, these kinds of groups are very likely to seek to do good for the fellow man because they have been "commanded" by God or the church to do good deeds.

The act of doing good is at least partially separated from them, in some cases even foisted upon followers. It is a rare thing to do something for someone else, mostly even when helping others it is in order to feel something about ourselves or to be perceived in a certain light. In the religious context, the moral code and ethical bias for good works has been created elsewhere and inserted as a series of introjects. Adherence to the code removes contact with the act itself. By following an introject there is less real meaning because the urge to help is at least partially generated by another's command. It will require considerable mental gymnastics on the part of the congregation in order not to experience resentment at the imposition. All too often this resentment is turned inward and becomes guilty feelings, guilt about not being or doing enough to please God or the minister. Alternatively, the resentment is turned outward toward the non-believer or the person who is different and expressed in less than favourable conduct justified by righteous anger. Besides the unhealthy context, this process is still a way to create a sense of meaning where previously there was none. Everyone needs to feel as though their life has meaning because otherwise, well, what's the point of it all? It might as well be 42.

We are just a minute animal life form on a massive ball of rock hurtling through space, we imagine we are important, that our life has meaning, that we are the centre of the universe. That is one of the reasons it is so hard to imagine ourselves dead. Facing the reality of death means realising our lives have no meaning beyond the now. The brutal fact is nature is totally impartial, it does not care if we live or die, it has no awareness of my existence and will kill me if I don't take care. The difficulty we have conceiving our own deaths is a common source of religious ideas. In part, we must believe that our lives have meaning, and filling them with religion seems to provide a meaning of a sort, even if it is a fictional reality.

Irvin Yalom in his book *Staring at the Sun* (2008), gives a wonderful name to a process which might in some ways help us achieve a sense of meaning, in some small measure at least. Irvin calls it rippling. The rock thrown into the lake breaks the surface with an explosion of water, but then sinks. The ripples from the impact continue to expand across the surface until they reach the edge.

Everything we do and say ripples through society from one person to another. In some ways, it's a little like a religious belief, excepting that there are no rules, just awareness of impact. I think back through my life and see mistakes that will ripple after my death, these I am not happy with obviously, they bring me no great joy, but they do act as a reminder not to do that again. Likewise, I love the idea that even after death some of my more usefully employed words, thoughts or actions might be passed along to others. That one of my more grateful clients might have a better life, or even something mundane like teaching someone else how to cope with panic might promote a fuller contact for someone which influences someone beyond them as they pass it on. I hope in part that this book will give food for thought and change some minds, perhaps encourage a search for greater contact.

Now, I am aware of my effect on others, I live in a social collective, not in isolation, everything I do has an effect for good or ill. We co-create our environment and each of us develops our personality in combination with others. The judgement of good and ill is of course a changeable entity and through the course of history, it will no doubt change again. In the same way, we look back at the Spanish inquisition and see barbarism where they previously saw piety and salvation. Perhaps in two hundred years, the people of the day will look back at us therapists and, having moved on, will regard us as barbaric torturers of the self, lacking the ability to heal and condemn us as cruel. Unlikely from my standpoint, but hey, no one expects the Spanish inquisition.

> The problem with meaning. The dilemma facing us is that two propositions, both true, seem unalterably opposed. 1. The human being seems to require meaning. To live without meaning, goals, values, or ideals seems to provoke, as we have seen, considerable distress.... 2. Yet the existential concept of freedom.... Posits that the only true absolute is that there are no absolutes. An existential position holds that the world is contingent-that is, everything that is could as well have been otherwise; that human beings constitute their world, and their situation within that world; that there exists no "meaning," no grand design in the universe. Irvin *Yalom Existential Psychotherapy* (1980, 422)

We all need meaning, but as we co-create our world it appears there is no meaning to be had beyond that which we create for ourselves. Religion, through a little mental sleight of hand, gives its devotees a sense of meaning, whether they are missionaries or just followers doing the deities' will within the community. Even daily devotions can be seen as a way of offering meaning to an otherwise meaningless existence. The act of devotion itself gives meaning, even if the devotion is to a fictional supernatural entity. It is therefore supremely seductive to those that wrestle with the unconscious realisation that there is no actual meaning.

By way of example, for millennia the judo-Christian worldview has insisted on the concept of humanity being part of a divine plan. This alone seemingly offers meaning, you were meant to be here, it was planned, we are following God's will etc. It is not lost to me that this also removes responsibility for co-creating a sense of meaning or acceptance of living within the lack of meaning from the devotee. Meaninglessness is a constant theme in the therapeutic exchange. People come because they feel their life has no meaning, or because they are doing the same repetitive drudgery day in and day out. If it feels meaningless there will be no contentment derived from it. Therapy is a form of unflinching self-exploration and as such we will always explore our meaning within our co-created environmental framework.

Finding Meaning

Though we might struggle to find a sense of meaning in life, we can co-create some semblance of meaning. At the very least we can consider how our interactions with others affect those around us, finding meaning in those interactions, in the experience of contact; particularly when that contact is healthy for both and creates a shared positive experience. We need purpose too, separate from meaning; for me establishing and maintaining healthy contact is purpose. Working with people to establish better contact is the purpose, helping explore disparate aspects of self is the purpose.

I have already discussed how religion provides some sense of meaning, and that meaning based on fiction is inherently delusional. I also touched on how there is no meaning by design, life is random, we just happen to be. Meaning cannot be derived from random happenings. I suspect then that It is important for us as individuals or as a contingent co-created cooperative to find meaning which works for us. Once we relinquish the set, bound, goal-orientated meaning established by religion, we can experience autonomy and create meaning for ourselves. Meaning which fits us, rather than meaning we have been fit into, or meaning that was handed down from previous generations.

For some, it will be enough to live with dignity, in the face of the absurdity of a random life in a universe indifferent to their needs. Others may need more purpose to feel fulfilled. If that purpose were to co-create a world, even a microcosm in which people can reach their full potential, we might all benefit. There are many ways to create meaning, it does not have to be inherited.

I shall add here the creative path, as an exploration of meaning, I can think of no brighter path. In therapy, the moments that stick with me are the moments of creativity, where we are open to experiencing our creative selves. When we meet and the contact produces a creative spark which moves us forward momentously. But also, when thinking about existentialism, creativity has been the hallmark of its thinkers. As I mentioned earlier the great names of people, we remember through history are mainly of an artistic nature. I think these people had and still have meaning because of the impact they had then and still have now. Even beyond death, an impact on those experiencing the art, music, ideas or literature. Their purpose may have been to express thoughts, feelings, concepts etc. but they have meaning because they have an impact on people around them. In science, it is the creative leap, the intuitive thinkers who make great strides forward and change our understanding of the universe we inhabit.

Throughout this book, I have been talking about clients who are enmeshed within religious ideals which are not their own. Who, with frequent regularity suffer distress because of religion. As such I have concentrated my description of how they have become trapped and given pointers for how they may come to self-expression. However, I have also maintained that this is done in contact with other humans. I have discussed contact as a tool in therapy, but also as a prerequisite for healthy relationships. If a person becomes too introspective and separate from his environment by looking in, it will be harder for him to derive meaning from his interactions. The flow of contact will be stifled by introspection. It is vital to meaningful living that a person, once free of bondage, establishes a connection with otherness and other people with whom interaction is not just possible but also healthy. Introspection is useful sometimes, but not as a mode of total being. Mindful compassionate connection to others is likely to create a greater sense of contentment and meaning for all parties.

Meaninglessness and Depression

People who arrive in therapy with a description of depressive symptoms, often experience a lack of meaning. It has a different quality to depression derived from retroflected anger, infused with hopelessness. A childlike ego stance is often the role enacted by clients in this condition. You can give them as many options as you like, and they will just throw them back like a bored toddler. In my experience, it's best not to engage with that game. Meaning must be found, not given. I can find my meaning but cannot give meaning to another. Though we may, together, co-create meaning where we contactfully interact.

If meaninglessness is a cause of depression, or at minimum an antecedent position if not a causal link, should we be removing religion from the equation? As I said previously, we don't need to remove religion from those who don't wish to relinquish it. I have had at least 3 clients who described having a "spiritual" depression. They envisaged some spiritual interference from the devil or some such external supernatural agent causing this depression. How that view fits with seeing a therapist I have not the slightest clue, I don't have supernatural powers to remove the influence of the devil. In every case, this concept of the personal attack from a personification of evil, or in one case a curse, were a cover for a sense of meaninglessness. In each case the client once reengaged with meaningful activity, recovered from the depression. Two of the clients went back to a religious lifestyle and engaged with community work related to their churches. The other struggled more. It became clear after a short time she was already questioning, "What is this all about? Is God real?" It was a far longer process, but ultimately, she needed to find meaning in a system which seemed meaningless. Distraction was no longer enough. In these cases, a re-owning of agency is important as clients take responsibility for creating meaning which works for them. This also often means accepting other existential elements such as isolation and death.

The psychological state of meaning, or indeed the phenomenological state of meaninglessness are both important to the psyche and to psychotherapy. There is another related issue, our disconnection from the natural world. I have spoken a little about diversion and distraction, specifically our modern tendency to distract ourselves through mediums which promote limited contact. The restricted version of contact we promote in our society also promotes a disconnect from the natural world. We seem to be a generation of screen watchers, with many spending 8 hours working as screens only to come home and watch a screen. We find little or no meaning through such distraction. We are losing our identity, partly through our ignorance of our necessary interconnected states. We interact with computers, with TV, and much of our communication is via screens. Most of our experience is filtered through screens. This filtering of experience removes immediacy from contact and promotes interpersonal distance.

Our distance from the natural world harms our sense of identity as part of the co-created whole. Our sense of meaning is limited by the separation from the world we inhabit. We have given our time, our lives, to the pursuit of money and material gain; in doing so we have severed our connection with the natural wonder that supports us all. We are no longer grounded, many of us take almost no interest in the world around us, even the walk to work, should it exist, is spent in thoughts of work, or money or holidays or a million other vaporous obscuring fictions, none of which provide meaning. Our lack of intimacy with the natural world is also connected with, if not a source of depression. It is not a glib statement. Depressed people frequently feel they have no meaning, and often do little which brings them in contact with the natural world. Loneliness and isolation are linked to meaning. This is not just about interpersonal interaction but also the separation from the natural world. Experiencing self as an interrelated part of the natural world, as well as interpersonal relatedness, creates a sense of being within and a creative field on which to experience self. Thus, a sense of meaning can evolve from being with and allowing contact with the natural world and the beings which inhabit it. We are not created as separate selves in this regard, we are co-created within this field, within the entirety of our existence.

For meaning to be created there must be contact, with the world as a natural entity, with the self as an interdependent co-created being and with others, through whom we can experience contact and fulfilment. Feeling connected to nature, allowing our contact with and experiencing the phenomenological response associated with a dawning realisation of the enormity of our natural world and our connection to it, usually engenders a healthy response to external concerns. Much of which provides a basis for getting to grips with meaning. There is a healthy fear or respect of nature which can be experienced only while immersed within it. That experience of connected understanding can help support the development of meaning for the individual as he gains a greater sense of himself as part of something bigger than he. He is at once separate from, dependent upon and interconnected with the world in its totality, including all humans that share it.

Isolation

We don't have to face our own individuality and isolation if we are constantly in a wider community of people with the same belief, we are always part of the group, and always will be if that includes an after-life. Of all the things religion does well it is creating large gatherings of people and giving them a sense of something to belong to. Humans long for interconnected relational exchange. It is a source of contentment to many and a comfort to the existential fear of isolation.

I talked in the section above on meaning, of our need to be interconnected and how depression frequently results from disconnection with self or others. The self is not a fixed entity as such, it is a fluid state. Changing minutely with every interaction. It exists as a continuum of experience. We experience ourselves in connection with others, be that with objects or another self. The interactions will be meaningful if contact is allowed to exist without hindrance. Isolation is inevitable, each of us must experience it, and in turn, each will respond in a unique way. There are three types of isolation to consider, intrapersonal, interpersonal and existential. In the main, I will be discussing existential isolation, but as therapists, isolation in all its forms is a common theme we deal with almost daily.

Intrapersonal Isolation

Intrapersonal isolation is a complex matter, it involves the isolation of parts of the self. I have already discussed in various places throughout the book, how aspects of the self can be hidden or become unaware through the adoption of religious thoughts and behaviours. If we are disconnected from, or parts of us are isolated from other parts, there will be a discontinuity within the psyche. In its most extreme forms, we will find schizoid personality disorders, such as schizoaffective disorder or schizophrenia. More commonly a person will experience part of themselves as not desirable. Often within a religious context parts of the authentic self are described as undesirable, sinful or to be managed away. inevitably this leads to intrapersonal isolation and conflict within the psyche.

Interpersonal Isolation

Isolation from others, or interpersonal isolation, is more usually experienced as loneliness. There are many reasons for it and solutions too. More complex versions arise when this form of isolation is married with personality disorders such as schizoid types. Often these personality types tend to swing between the terror of isolation and the terror of merger with others as the sense of self as a cohesive separate entity is difficult to maintain when the self is split into disparate parts. More commonly though, people will come to therapy because they are experiencing loneliness, often through enforced separation. A death, divorce or children leaving home are common themes of separation we encounter. Alternatively, people attend therapy because they long for and/or fear intimacy.

Existential Isolation

Existential isolation is often an underlying factor in the above two states of isolation. When we examine closely the nature of isolation, we often find it masks a fear of existential isolation. Which is to say an awareness that ultimately, we are alone. We are a separate being, we are responsible for ourselves, and eventually, we will die. This is something that we can only do alone, we cannot take others with us at that moment of death, no matter how much we wish to. It is the realisation that despite our interconnectedness, despite our desire to be in contact with otherness and despite the contentment we gain from said contact, we are ultimately separate.

Interestingly I have had many clients describe a feeling of dread overcome them when they entered the bathroom. The second most common space to affect them is the bedroom. There is a good reason for this which I will elaborate on in the following paragraph. With the bathroom, there were various stages apparent during which each would experience a dread, often profound enough to inhibit them for the rest of the day. In every case, the root of the experience was a sudden realisation of loneliness and isolation. The dread experienced was that of oblivion and death, which will be explored more in a later section.

This dread fear seems to have been brought about by several connected triggers. The first is physical isolation. The bathroom is often the only room in the house where we lock ourselves away from others, the second room where locks are used being the bedroom. This locking ourselves away seems to awaken a metaphorical realisation that we are isolated from the world. An awareness of our existential isolation forms, if only momentarily, and the client experiences this as dread. The second trigger in the sequence is undressing. In the exposure of the physical body, we are allowing vulnerability. We are exposing that which is usually covered. The armour of our clothing is shed to reveal our defenceless physical form. Defencelessness against physical and psychic pain are experienced simultaneously.

The third trigger is the shower or less commonly the bath. The thought of entering the shower seems to awaken a fear of defenceless isolation. I am unable to defend myself while in the shower. While in the shower I am entirely cut off from the rest of the world, I cannot even hear noise from outside due to the noise of the water. I will have to close my eyes against the water and soap. All these actions bring to awareness my fear and dread of death, my sense of isolation and vulnerability as I am forced to disengage my senses from the world.

There are similar effects felt in the bedroom, though in my experience, this location is reported less often. In the bedroom we may lock the door. We will at times be naked, and we will more than likely face issues of intimacy, or the lack thereof. The onset of sleep may also be a trigger. The moment of falling to sleep is sometimes described as a sort of mini death. A rehearsal for the main event. Many clients have told me how they don't like falling asleep, they feel vulnerable and wonder if they will wake again, or just die in the night.

Existential isolation then is inexorably connected with meaning, responsibility and death. Religion frequently offers a fictional trope to soothe away such fears as isolation. "God is always with us," might seem a bit unpleasant to those who are averse to voyeurism, but to those who feel isolated and alone, the thought that an invisible entity is omnipresent and omnipotent can seem a comfort. However, as I have no doubt made clear in other parts of the book. The soothing of these feelings is not the goal. The loneliness we experience, if contacted and allowed, becomes a motivational force which stimulates action. This action will move us toward contact with life, not death. If pursued further, eventual satisfaction or contentment. Soothing away difficult emotions with religious constructs does nothing to solve the actual, real-world problem, it just provides a convenient smokescreen through which we don't quite see our experience of the world.

Introjected behaviours of a religious bias will frequently move us away from meaningful contact with people and with life. This contact is where we create meaning for ourselves and derive contentment. The imposed restraints of conduct tend to limit horizons and outlook making us less likely to see beyond the beliefs instilled. The resultant lack of contact may drive us further into religious solutions which in turn mean we never fully contact the world or allow a contingent aware experience of contact.

The existential isolation we are all subject to is concealed below the layers of distraction. Be those ritualistic, escapist or materialist in nature. The true reality of our existential isolation is still there beyond all the veils of hopeful distraction. Eventually, we will have to face them, and hopefully, we will at that point have enough self-support to allow contact with it, in order to comprehend its substance, via comprehension, our understanding will relieve some anxiety. Specifically, with the realisation that although it is what it is, we are no less human because of it. The existential isolation serves to remind us that although life is short, if lived in awareness we can find contentment in contact with self and others for this finite period. Although we are separate beings, the dichotomy is that we are also interrelated, and we co-create our experiential reality. It is possible for us to accept our separateness without seeking to cover it with fictional models of the universe or ourselves. We can use it to motivate us toward experiencing fulfilment through the I-thou of contactful engagement.

Responsibility and Freedom

"Your task is not to seek for love, but merely to seek and find the barriers within yourself that you have built against it." Rumi (Essential Rumi, Jalāl ad-Dīn Muhammad Balkhī, 1995)

I have covered responsibility to some small degree in various places throughout this missive, particularly as it pertains to freedom of will and the imposition of automatic behaviour via the interrupting mechanism of introjected beliefs. I feel we, as a wider society, have lost sight of what freedom means. We have seen individuality as the solution and made ourselves more isolated in our search for freedom. Individualism gave us limited freedom but also enslaved us as we sought alternative bonds. It has ushered in an era in which man has become aware of his potential; to allow his self-expression means taking responsibility for them, this has been a step too far for most. By fleeing responsibility, we have sought other prisons. We think as individuals we are free, yet we cling haphazardly to ideologies which offer to disguise the need for responsibility and provide a facade of freedom. This trickery has enslaved many. We imagine we are free; we desire to be free, yet we are afraid of that freedom and thus cling like the dying man to the mirage. We will not be free if we cling to individualism any more than if we cling to religion. Man must take responsibility for his freedom, he must allow his expression of will, of sensuality, of joy. He must express his emotional and intellectual potential and in doing so take responsibility for it. It cannot be hidden beyond the past ideological religious forms, nor behind modern individualism.

Through individualism we have developed many apparent freedoms, we have the freedom to express religion, most have freedom to express their sexuality, though we have a long way to go before we can safely say gender or sexual preference discrimination has been eliminated. We are free to vote, for the most part. We are free to get an education, though there is still a class divide we need to overcome, we are free to travel, to live with whom we choose. Racism has decreased, but we still see it every day. We make great strides toward equality of gender yet have so far to go that the mountain is still looming tall before us. The battle to bring about external freedom is monumental and I would argue, must be continued. All these freedoms are important and the struggle to see them fulfilled has been an important part of individualism and its role in shaping modern society. Yet many of us have seen this external freedom as the goal, as all that is required. We have allowed ourselves to become blinkered, we have given up many internal freedoms again, in order to be part of the society of individuals. We have given up our responsibility for our authentic selves, and ironically, for our self-expression. Our authentic selves are shackled to the role of individuality which has left us isolated and impoverished.

Followers of ideologies take responsibility in part for being a good whatever their belief system says they are, this being a role engineered in part to suppress or inhibit aspects of self, society deems problematic. This behaviour is in fact a complex displacement of responsibility. As constituent members this group of individuals doesn't have to take so much responsibility for personal choices by virtue of the group norms. When talking about religious ideology the responsibility is usually projected onto the fictional supernatural entity perceived to be in charge. "It's God's will." "I'll pray about it and see what God tells me to do." I have had clients tell me God has told them they are called to do such and such, then a week later it's something else. It changes from week to week. Obviously, it's not God, they just can't make up their own minds.

These clients have an idea that they might like to do or try something, but not wishing to take responsibility for the actions required, they project the desire onto the deity. When they discover they can't heal people after all, or become a great artist overnight, or travel to some isolated part of the world to help the heathens find God; then in giving it up and choosing another plan they can again give away responsibility for the perceived failure, for giving up, for finding it too challenging, for not having the concerted effort to study, in short, for avoiding contact. Each of these is avoided by saying God has now called me to something else. It never occurs to followers that God has a very changeable mind, or how odd it would be for him to be giving conflicting directions from one week to the next.

Personal responsibility is key to good mental health. We must accept responsibility for ourselves if we are to continue growing, exploring ourselves as human beings; and living a healthy, contingent, contactful life. "Nietzsche asserts that, "joy does not come from submission and abnegation, but from assertion." May, Power and Innocence (1972, 119). Indeed, it is through the assertion that contact is made and maintained, this is the essence of being, this is how we are co-created within our familial sociological environment, without it there would be little joy.

It takes enormous courage to see and allow another's truth. Much of the time we wish to run from it in fear. "Error (the belief in the ideal) is not blindness; error is cowardice. Every conquest, every step forward in knowledge is the outcome of courage, of hardness towards one's self; of cleanliness towards one's self." Nietzsche, Ecce homo (1908). It's not the education or facts that are lacking but our willingness to accept them or even explore them. Our willingness to make ourselves vulnerable and accept that what we assume to be true may in fact be erroneous. In chewing over our beliefs and thoughts we can, through interrogation, destruction and reintegration, make them ours or throw them away. It requires the courage to admit those we have admired may have been wrong in their assertions, and to admit that what we have believed in the past was spurious.

More important than getting simple facts to the point of understanding is to get to grips with what this ideal or belief did or does for me. How I used it to shield myself from contact with certain aspects of myself or my environment, specifically my interpersonal connectedness. It doesn't matter if it is a belief in a personal god or the belief men shouldn't cry, any belief held must be explored. If I can ascertain the nature of my introject and its source, I can also define its effect and decide, is this good for me? Do I still need or want this? Perhaps I might be better served with something else, to let go of what I thought was truth and allow a new one to form. In taking responsibility for the exploration and digestion of our introjects we give ourselves greater choice and freedom over how we behave.

We see this giving up of responsibility in the language used throughout society. A client of mine just this morning said, "Well you feel angry don't you." when I asked her to repeat the statement replacing you with I she was forced to accept she was angry not me. What's more, in taking ownership of the anger, the taking responsibility for her words and making it less projective, the experience of her anger became more immediate and pronounced. This awareness in turn brought her to the point of expression and clarity.

Personal responsibility is reduced by depersonalisation through terms such as "it." "It was an awkward silence," sounds like a valid statement, but it is less immediate and imparts less impact than "I felt awkward with the silence." which immediately promotes the questions relating to the origin of my awkwardness. By taking back our projective or depersonalising use of language and owning the statements with I, we can begin to establish responsibility for phenomena we have conveniently dismissed with deflection or projectively blamed on others or objects. Personal responsibility is attenuated with the use of a deflective or projective language.

In considering working with personal responsibility, long term therapy is often essential simply because it can be a period of months before clients are able to begin to take responsibility. Giving up the security of relinquishment can be a long and difficult process. The first steps are often linked to the change in the language used and the awareness aroused by the change. In taking responsibility we must include all aspects of human personality. It doesn't matter that I have dyslexia for example, but it is important I have owned it, taken steps to minimise its impact. I acknowledge my limits and its immutability; I know, for example, if I am stressed words will be harder to read and are more likely to move from one sentence to another. From this place of knowledge and acceptance, of the effects and my limitations I can be secure enough to be, and if I need support, such as finding a good editor for this book, I can do so. Equally if I ignore any aspect of myself, it will likely become a blind spot. This is particularly crucial when dealing with clients. I have met many therapists who proclaim how odd it is that "insert ego state or content here" never gets discussed by clients. In my experience it is because the therapist is not comfortable with it, hasn't explored and owned their relationship to the subjective state. In these cases, the client more than likely picks up nonverbal clues and doesn't bring it to the fore as it won't be safe to do so. Or the therapist will un-awaredly ignore all paths that might lead down that route, blocking the way for future exploration. This is one of the reasons I see being in therapy as such an important aspect of being a therapist.

We can assume that if you accept responsibility for yourself, you will simultaneously experience existential isolation. You will become aware it is you and you alone on whom the responsibility rests. It is a cosy comforter that religion provides in masking both isolation and responsibility. Our task in psychotherapy is to bring awareness of how one gives up responsibility and introduces the process of reintegration. "The concept of responsibility is crucial to psychotherapy -- and it is pragmatically true, it "works": acceptance of it enables the individual to achieve autonomy and his or her full potential." Irvin Yalom, *Existential Psychotherapy* (1980).

Our own agency and will, cannot be ours unless we engage responsibility for our actions and affect, both internal and external. Without contact with the source of our motivations and action, we have no will of our own beyond basic instinct. Will and responsibility are linked; we cannot remove the one from the other without diminishing contact. Our attitude toward our situation is what makes us human. We cannot remove the effect of genetics, environment or chance. What we can do is take responsibility for our response and reaction within the given circumstance. We alone are responsible for our reaction to adversity, a contactful approach offers the chance to learn from the situation rather than just be a victim of it. Even with something as complex as PTSD, which is a response to situational trauma over which we have no control. Even then we can be responsive to ourselves, seeking support and taking responsibility to find a therapy which works for us, while learning to treat ourselves with compassion in the face of horrifically difficult symptoms.

Freedom is not just the absence of external constraints, which is perhaps its most easily relatable aspect. It is also the ability to respond in any given situation according to our authentic self and our needs. If I am bound by constraints of a religious or moralistic nature, which have been appropriated from others without contactful awareness or discernment then I am not free to be myself. When discussing this, people have often become quite angry with me and suggested that the alternative is some form of orgiastic hedonism. I think it ridiculous to suggest that the only alternative to living a constrained life is to head straight to what most people consider depravity. To do so would entirely miss the point that in contact with self and others, the contact itself would posit joy and contentment. For most people hedonism would not be required and for those that want it, it would no longer be taboo as a choice.

All of this also suggests people who jump to these conclusions still want to be telling other people how to live their lives, rather than allowing them to take responsibility for themselves. They also avoid taking responsibility for the feelings that arise in themselves when they hear of hedonistic behaviour.

-218-

Freedom and Authoritarianism

Freedom and authoritarianism appear to be two sides of the same coin too. The two cannot be separated in thought or action, just as man longs for freedom, and often jumps at what appears to be freedom but, is just another form of slavery, such as materialism, individualism, etc. Counter to freedom man also longs for submission. We long to give up responsibility to an authority figure and we long to have choices made by another so that we do not have to accept responsibility for them. It is a longing to return to the child state where the parent assumed responsibility and ego was submissive, a longing to return to Eden.

There are plenty of people who would also like to take an authoritarian approach by limiting others freedom and plenty that do so in order to gain a modicum of self-worth or the illusion of control. I suspect much of our current swing toward the far right in the west is down to people wanting or taking an authoritarian stance in the absence of real freedom, or perhaps a lack of understanding of what freedom is. Currently, it seems mostly to be a chance to blame others for our lack, then to extend that guilt as authoritarian limitations on the perceived problem areas in society, be that immigrants, refugees, the poor, the mentally ill, just pick your minority group and add them to the list.

We are seeing petty dictators attempt to coerce society to their way of thinking, and all too often they are getting a grand following. Blatant lies are ignored in order to express hatred, even when those lies are plastered on the side of a bus. All this to exert power or control over people. The hatred expressed is all too often a projection of hatred for self, because they have been unable to achieve what was required to express the authentic self, or because of some other perceived shortcoming. Either way, the self-hatred is projected out onto a group in society who are unable to defend themselves and become the scapegoat. The projection of hatred might be a dynamic adaptation to circumstance, yet it is as damaging as it is irrational.

Political Power and Freedom to Be

I will briefly mention that man's submission to authority at the expense of self often comes as a result of penury. All human beings have basic needs, the wide base of Maslow's triangle (see: A Theory of Human Motivation, 1943, A. H. Maslow) We all require sustenance and shelter, we all require support for our physical well-being. This is a primary need, our basic drive for survival is governed by the lack or abundance of these basic elements. We will sublimate ourselves into a system we neither like nor want in order to meet these needs. Frequently people work for less than they deserve or are worth, fulfilling jobs they are neither interested in nor care about to any great degree. In order to receive a regular wage: interest and creativity are dampened, boredom and frustration accepted. Our physiological requirements are not our only needs, though they are primary, so they take precedence. We also strive to avoid isolation from our fellow man. Be that via actual contact, or via a shared value system.

"The kind of relatedness to the world may be noble or trivial, but even being related to the basest kind of pattern is immensely preferable to being alone. Religion and nationalism, as well as any custom and any belief, however absurd or degrading, if it only connects the individual with others, are refuges from what man most dreads, isolation." Eric Fromm, The Fear of Freedom (1941).

I have already stated that we are co-created, we do not exist in isolation, despite the reality that we are isolated within society. In the same way, we must feel a connection to other humans, animals, and the natural world. Our lack of awareness of this drive for connection will likely lead us to join in actions which would not ordinarily be congruent with our desires. We would not think to ourselves as we woke up. Ah, what a beautiful morning. I will go and work in a factory for 10 hours and come home in the dark, that seems like a good way to spend this day. We must meet our basic needs and will submit in order to do so, we must feel connected and will submit in order to do so, we will likely feel frustrated as a result, as neither outcome is what we want. The expression of this frustration will likely be projected as rage or hatred or internalised as self-loathing and/or experienced as existential guilt. Ultimately if left unresolved it is likely to become a root for depression.

When political power is lacking, and we are feeling isolated, unable to take responsibility for ourselves, or as though we have no power to change our situation, turning to the absurd can seem like a useful solution, frequently religion or superstition becomes the perfect substitute. As I discussed earlier, from this position of sublimation, people forget about the lack of political power they experience, they forget personal responsibility for what is actual and assume responsibility for a fiction, commonly the soul. A community is joined, masking the true isolation in a cliche level interactive environment, responsibility is projected onto the supernatural deity and the self-hatred is either subsumed into the religious character structure and expressed as purges and torment of self, or it is projected out once again onto the external group who don't fit our fictional representation of how life "should" be.

Freedom is lost when we become embodied within an organisational structure which does not allow for our ontological self; the concept and understanding of freedom are closely tied to isolation, responsibility and meaning as we have seen. Diving into authoritarian structures is just the other side of the coin and helps the individual justify feelings of helplessness. You will also notice that where religion is concerned freedom is expressed in negative terms, freedom from this or that urge, gaining freedom from the desires of the self. Whereas in psychotherapy we are primarily concerned with freedom to be as you are. As in, developing enough self-support in order to allow yourself to be what you need to be for each contactful interaction rather than freedom from the urges which promote contact.

Freedom to Be Confluent

In the brief look at confluence in chapter 5, we can see that the perceived freedom to follow our religion is, for the most part, the freedom to be confluent. The loss of self, in merging with the subject community renders actual freedom impossible as awareness is lost to the confluent boundaries. Freedom in this sense has very little if any meaning, it is given up in order to negate personal responsibility and isolation. Faith, as a virtue, while in this confluent state has two possible effects: the first is an expression of relatedness to the fellow man, such as having faith that so and so will see the light and be saved, the second is a conciliatory expression which rises from the realisation we are isolated. It may be experienced as a feeling of doubt which is quickly squashed by religious thought, through the study of scripture for example. I do not personally believe this sense of doubt arising from isolation can ever be resolved by intoning religious liturgies. In order to address the doubt, we must examine our isolation and accept it and its effects. This then will enable us to move to greater contact, not confluence. Freedom then is the freedom to be, but also the freedom of the self to accept our existential being and act according to the self and its needs. Freedom cannot be known from a confluent stance. Within that position, we can only experience the merged self and will be unaware that we are merged. Freedom requires acceptance of our separation and isolation.

Responsibility and Existential Guilt

Existential guilt tends also to go hand in hand with responsibility. We cannot work with one, without touching on the other. They are like the celestial twins Kastor and Polydeukes alternating between life and death and ever-present during moments of danger. I make the distinction between guilt feelings, usually derived from retroflected resentment, and remorse, which is a healthy response to causing harm and guilt as may be established in a court of law. Taking responsibility frequently means adding accountability. When we talk of existential guilt we are talking about this sense of remorse, plus the added dimension of transgression against the self. Guilt at having harmed the self in some form. For example, if I have, through a neurotic need to placate, relentlessly subdued my own feelings of anger; if I become aware of this process, this role I have played, I will also become aware of the harm I have caused myself through the acting out of said role. This harm may be in the form of psychosomatic tensions such as headaches or IBS, or it may just be a realisation of wasted years with diminished contact with the world. This existential guilt is often hard to differentiate as somatically it is like remorse and neurotic guilt.

There is also the close link between guilt feelings and resentment to consider. In this instance existential guilt may initially be played out as anger toward self, the resentment expressed toward the self for having harmed the self through the enactment of the role. This resentment, however, is more likely to be healthily expressed as resentment toward those from whom we learned the role; or for whom we felt we must take on this mantle in order to placate. We are in essence guilty of not being true to our organic, authentic selves, the self that would be if allowed to live without the expectations of society. This is what Rollo May referred to as "the individual's unrealised repressed potential" in Existential Psychology (1969).

If we can be with our existential guilt, it can be a solid motivator toward change. It might feel unpleasant and is frequently run from, but if tolerated and explored it becomes a driving force for change, to never be that way again lest we revisit this unpleasant guilt feeling. If the client moves through being angry with others and resolved that it was his choice to pick up the mantle, he can at this point, in taking responsibility, forgive himself and move toward greater contact with himself via compassion, and then toward others from a more grounded stable centre.

That religious teachings tend to undermine this process means we see time and again people in therapy, who, having had a strict religious upbringing, are burdened by guilt and have no idea about what they feel guilty about. This untangling of the different aspects of guilt is key to recovery, and an integral part of supporting a client to take personal responsibility for himself. Not to be confused with the desire to retake responsibility for things we have been instructed are wrong.

Personal responsibility then is the crux upon which existentialism and useful therapy balance. It is a clear area of conflict with organised religion and the entropic belief systems which diminish personal responsibility.

Chapter 13

Case Study 4 and 5, an Exploration of
Death and Death Anxiety.

"Time is too large, it can't be filled up. Everything you plunge
into it is stretched and disintegrates." Jean-Paul Sartre

Death

Death is something most people have some anxiety about if they allow
themselves to consider it fully. I am writing this paragraph in the UK during
the COVID 19 virus outbreak of 2020-21. Many of my clients are experiencing
greater than usual terror at the rising death toll. Essentially though they are
terrified that they may be next. For people who already have a tendency toward
anxiety, it is a time of great stress and emotional complexity. Coupled with the
enforced isolation we are seeing an increase in existential fears.

It is interesting that of those clients, the ones with religion are
seemingly more out of contact, and at times are bordering on dangerously
laissez-faire. The belief that God has this all in hand, or that there is a heaven
to be translated to if they die has taken on an almost manic, ungrounded

aspect. As soon as the subject of death or the virus comes up, the religious quotes, comments and liturgies are expounded automatically. I feel as though they are used as a magical device to ward off not just death itself, but also the feelings it ordinarily invokes. Unsurprisingly none of these people is comfortable talking about the afterlife now that the afterlife is looming closer than ever. It seems to me as though the veneer of religion and superstition is at its most fragile when people are faced with a real crisis from which they cannot hide.

Those that are unashamedly putting the responsibility into God's hands and taking no precautions, even continuing prayer meetings etc. This group is, for the most part, seem to be the most out of contact of all my clients and acquaintances. None seem to fathom the risk to self and to others, none are taking responsibility. In this case, any accountability has been safely projected onto God with comments like, "If God wills it" or, "God is looking down and looking after us all." All of which means nothing and does nothing to consider what actual death might mean, or any other consequences of meeting without safety measures. Simultaneously I am hearing reports that some Christian schools are remaining open, I sincerely hope none of their pupils are hurt as a result. Whoever made that decision must surely be out of contact with reality and allow their religious thoughts to supersede any rational internal examination or analysis. To go against the advice of medical professionals because, "God will protect us," seems irrational in the extreme. It's not the first time and won't be the last either.

Life and death are two sides of the same coin since none of us is immortal. We all live, and we all die. Even if that life is brief. As death is present for us all we can not entirely ignore it. Death is usually less of an issue for those who believe they never really die. At the very least it puts the fear off until the moment of death is known. It's a convenient device to suspend the inevitable, but it seems to work less well once the spectre of death is close at hand. Fear of death remains just below the surface and is never far from our experience of life. It takes little to awaken this fear and consideration of obliteration or oblivion. We are surrounded by it, not just during a crisis like this; Generally speaking, every day we are given reminders of death, whether it's seeing roadkill as we drive, or hearing of friends and relatives who have lost or nearly lost people recently. The funeral processions and the graveyards we walk past, a child stepping off the curb without looking; even autumn, when the trees are dying back and leaves are carpeting the ground, this too is a reminder that everything has its time, and eventually we too will enter our autumn years, assuming we don't fall off the tree before, through ill health or accident. It is an ever-present spectre, haunting us with constant reminders.

As soon as the facade presented by a religious belief begins to dissolve, we are faced with all the existential questions and all the unruly emotions they provoke. It is not comforting or pleasant, it's a hard truth and difficult to face or imagine. It's hardly surprising then, that so many people choose to give up freedom in order to be so wrapped in comforting words. Even if that is at the cost of so many restrictions.

As therapists, we are, in many ways, restricted to the clients' presenting symptoms or concerns. We must proceed with caution and at the behest of the client. In Jimmy's case described previously I never directly challenged Jimmy on his religion. I did support him while the elements standing in the way of his awareness dissolved though, and attempted through discussion, attunement and modelling to offer an alternative way of being. The choice to explore must always come from the client, we cannot force our views, opinions or agendas on them. To do so is no better than the religious indoctrination of old. We accept the person, not the things they do and believe. We meet our clients without the expectation they will change or become like us. As we saw earlier expectations always lead to a loss of contact and the improbability of seeing others as they truly are.

Avoiding Thoughts of Death

By not fully engaging with the life we have, we avoid having to contemplate separation and death. The mode of denial under scrutiny in this book is religion, in this regard religion would be seen as a maladaptive denial strategy. Living through religion in order to maintain a distant form of contact can also be viewed as a sort of death. The death of the ontological self. If I do not fully contact life, if I restrict my interactions with joyful existence, I am dying a small death by living a small life. Much of this restricted contact is a way to not feel my fear of death. If I am not fully alive, if I never allow myself to be fully awakened to joy or contact with others, I am not reminded at that moment that the joy and contact will end; or that ultimately, we will all die and this moment, aside from this contact, is meaningless.

We cannot afford to leave death to the dying, in order to live we must accept its undeniable presence. Acceptance of death, of ending, will enable us to be more present to the now. In essence, by accepting the inevitability of death we become more aware of life. Death then in this instance becomes a positive contrasting element to life. Like light and dark, you cannot fully comprehend the light without shadow being its contrast; similarly, joy would lose its meaning if we never experienced sorrow. Life becomes fuller and more knowable with the knowledge that death will end it.

In religious thought, the soul has been the mediator between self and other, between self and God. It has become the transient element which moves between realms and for which we have been asked to take responsibility. As both God and soul are fictions this was always an unstable proposition. Now we have replaced soul with Ego, and God is dead. Ego is our representation of the co-created self; we now take responsibility for ego and our contact with the world through it. Ego has replaced the soul, at the very least, in a scientific sense. Ego is also a concept, an idea, but a concept we can apply to actual knowable aspects of self and other.

Death is often present in the therapy room. Clients discuss their fears of their grief over and their desire for death. In a very real sense, it can be a positive motivator in the therapeutic encounter and in life. I have seen people who after making a suicide attempt and failing, suddenly become full of life, as though the realisation of what death is and the near-miss or a much-lauded second chance revitalised them toward greater contact. Similarly, a near-death experience can bring people to a totally different level of being. After Surviving what was imagined to be the end, what remains might be cherished, and previous fears are often explored and relinquished in order to live life more fully.

Case study 4 — Penny

I had the privilege of working with a client called Penny. Penny was a client who struggled with personal identity, perceived judgement of others, body image and self-esteem. Penny came for about 3 months, during that time we looked mostly at how she projected her judgements of herself out onto others and assumed others saw her in the same light. I was aware Penny disliked gatherings and groups, as her sense of self was, as she put it, "Overwhelmed by other people's judgements." At about three months I tentatively suggested she join my personal development group, specifically because we can explore in the here and now her experience of others as judges, and perhaps re-own her projections. She said she would think about it and let me know. Then she disappeared for 2 months. I didn't hear from her and assumed I had scared her off by making the suggestion. I was a little dismayed because we had a good rapport and were making what I saw as progress, albeit slowly.

I sent a follow-up message as is usual when clients don't turn up for a session and waited for her response. I had just about given up on her returning when I received a call. Penny had been in an accident, she had broken one leg in two places and the other at the hip, she had been in the hospital for the best part of 4 weeks recovering. The car had rolled twice into a ditch landing on its roof; the driver was still in the hospital. Penny was by all accounts, lucky to come out so lightly damaged.

Penny came back to therapy, her first words to me, after a brief hello, were, "I thought I was going to die!" Accompanied by floods of tears. Her near-death experience was terrifying for her, but also proved to be liberating. Firstly, Penny began to talk about death, to talk about what it means to her, and the realisation she only has one life. Which, in her words, "I have been wasting wondering what others think about me, rather than just getting on with it." The brush with death left her marked physically, because of the scars from operations to insert pins, and the months of rehab/physio. It took her a long time to recover physically, but mentally she bounced back remarkably quickly, and not only bounced back but made more contact with disparate parts of herself than many clients achieve in six months' work.

Penny let go of her fears of being judged by others. She allowed the pettiness of the expectation of judgement to become apparent and decided it made not one jot of difference if others liked her or not, she was what she was and had to make the most of it. She realised quickly that it was her that judged herself and that this had arisen from criticism of others at school, people she neither likes nor sees any more.

Through this process she became more confident in herself, accepting her physical form and inhabiting her body more fully: contacting herself somatically, noticing the ways in which she collapsed her chest and rounded her shoulders. She took up yoga in order to explore and strengthen her posture. After a month it was like watching a different woman, gone were the rounded shoulders, soft voice and timid stance, replaced by an open demeanour, full sonorous voice which was accompanied by a realisation she had something worth saying. Though it took longer, mostly hampered by the physical recovery, her walk became a confident, purposeful stride. The transformation is remarkable and a testament to the power of a near-death experience and her dogged determination to face life and live it fully. Death in instances like this can become a positive motivator toward a greater life. Life's priorities become realigned when balanced against death.

Case Study 5 Ben

Ben was held up at gunpoint. He came to me because shortly afterwards he was suffering from Post-Traumatic Stress Disorder and could no longer drive or work. PTSD is unremittingly debilitating, often resulting in: loss of routine, insomnia, inability to work, suicidal thoughts, heightened awareness of danger, quite literally jumping at shadows, a feeling the personality has irrevocably changed, nightmares, night sweats, panic attacks and tremors. This is not an exhaustive list and if left untreated PTSD can limit lives to such an extent that people can barely live. PTSD is also relatively easy to treat in many cases, by easy I mean short term, 6-8 weeks. Mentally, emotionally it is exhausting and very tough for the individual in treatment. It requires enormous courage to go through the treatment.

Ben's PTSD was such that he could not function well at all. He was having suicidal thoughts and feeling as though his life was over as he couldn't face living with PTSD. Daily life was a struggle and he had not been at work for over a month. It took about 5 weeks to clear the PTSD symptoms and for Ben to finally get behind the wheel of the car and get back to work. Afterwards Ben continued to come to therapy. He was finding he had questions he had not faced before; significantly he was considering death. He had been staring down the barrel of a gun and had thought his life was about to end, and he had struggled with the thought of living with PTSD. In therapy, he explored death and his relationship to it. From possible death, Ben moved to look at the inevitable end of his life and how he is living now, the counterpoint to death.

Ben began to look at how isolated he is and how he maintains that isolation. He looked at separation and how he has been enmeshed with some family members, and how dissatisfied he is with that now. He began to look at his lack of anger and started to take responsibility for holding it back and then experimenting with assertive expression after some more cathartic experimentation within the confines of the therapeutic encounter. He began to explore his lack of relationship, how he keeps himself in a job he does not particularly enjoy, and which offers no stimulation. He even looked at his food choices and how he eats to exist rather than eating for delight and nourishment. He began to cook from scratch for the first time and started to seek advice on cooking. Ben's brush with death resulted in him questioning and re-evaluating everything relating to life. In this process, he has begun to move toward greater contact. Building awareness of how he limits his life by constricting himself or allowing himself to be enmeshed with others. He resolved to take responsibility to extend himself, change his job and find something more meaningful, learn to cook good food, to assert his anger more directly and stand back from the enmeshed relationship with a sibling. For a man in his early 20's he now faces a bright future where he can choose more contactful interaction with everything life has to offer.

Restricting Exploration of Death

The religious life in contrast, by avoiding thoughts of death, either by talking of an imaginary afterlife or by asking people to follow restrictive principles and edicts, prevents people from fully engaging in this life. Placating the need to hide from the inevitable end, keeps the person out of contact with what is an immutable aspect of living, disengaging the part of them that would be fulfilled in living with the engagement of the authentic self. Our ubiquitous terror of death is, in its commonality, a connective tissue we all share. If all else is missing or awry, this at least we will always share. We spend so much of our time avoiding death anxiety we often miss its importance in promoting greater connectivity with others and with our own existence. Following the myriad distractions offered by society, and any one of our major fictitious ideologies, be that mainstream religion or the belief in the myth of progress, leads us to perpetuate an impoverished life. Our motivational factors for joining religious movements are themselves self-sustaining distractors from joyful involvement with life. The obsession with living for tomorrow or what is to come, to have more; is perhaps incontrovertibly, in conflict with the premise of engaging with living today, in the here and now. Paradoxically, now is all we have, we have this moment and no other and paradoxically, exploration of death will likely enable greater fulfilment and engagement in life.

Death Anxiety Transformed

In the therapeutic exchange, we will rarely see death anxiety displayed naked before us. Almost without exception, the client will use some motif or circumlocution to disguise the original anxiety. If you are willing to explore these proxies beyond presented symptoms and see past surface anxieties to the hidden source, you will find death anxiety masked in many interactions. Clients bring it with frequent regularity. It often feels as though despite hiding it away, and attempting not to look at it, our fascination with death keeps bringing it back to the fore. It is like a recurring dream, which won't resolve until explored.

Death anxieties centre around three temporal aspects: the fear of things leading to death or pre-death anxieties, the fear of the actual moment of death and the fear of what will happen after death. The fear of things leading to death may be represented in many forms. Illness or accident seems common; hypochondria for example often masks a fear that one will be terminally struck down by illness. Perhaps persistent unhealthy behaviours such as smoking, which can be viewed as a slow suicide, may also be an attempt to explore death before death happens.

The fears pertaining to the actual moment of death are often concerned with pain, will it be painful to die, will I be aware of my death, what will the moment of body death be like? I had one client who had Cotard's syndrome, I never thought I would come across a case, as it is so rare. This client believed he was dead. An interesting paradox to be faced with. He was a danger to himself and others as he had no sense of danger; you cannot die if you are currently dead. As a delusionary defence, it was strikingly effective. No thoughts of death were going to worry him as he was already dead and couldn't die again. He had no concerns about what happens after, as he was already living the afterlife. The third aspect is, "What happens after I die, to my body, to my possessions and to any unfinished business, and to my essence, will I continue to exist?"

Primarily where religion is concerned, this is solved by the introduction of rebirth, reincarnation or the translocation to an afterlife of some description. In describing an integral part of the self, usually soul, as indestructible and eternal, death is temporarily negated. We discussed in an earlier chapter how this device is also used to engender passive obedience to political will by removing the need for personal agency. The concept of soul is frequently linked in monotheistic religions along with working for the afterlife while still in this one. The idea of building treasure in heaven rather than on earth. Which has led some to lead generous altruistic lives, yet as a construct, the idea has been instrumental in bringing about a subjugation narrative. Despite the possible good the person may do, the lack of focus on the now, the removal of personal responsibility for the self in the now and the imposition of fictional laws and the removal of personal political power has for most created a hindrance to and simultaneously blocked a vital route to contact. It has become so accepted and embedded in society that currently it is unfashionable to challenge religious belief as though it were as immutable as the colour of someone's skin rather than just a series of ideas.

I cannot have full contact with people who hold fundamentalist beliefs without being accused of racism, insensitivity or bigotry. The current social rules and norms prevent it. These introjects within the politically correct structures of society prevent the possibility of authentic contact. Unfortunately, though altered or masked, death anxiety does not disappear for people following religion. It might appear at times as though it no longer exists, but, it is often hiding just below the surface of these fictional escapes.

Often death anxiety is transmogrified into a variety of phobias. On the surface, a phobia may appear to be a genuine fear and is expressed as such. But phobia may well, and frequently do, represent a deeper fear of death of self. During the therapeutic exchange, a phobia is often unmasked as the surface layer covering death anxiety. Treating the symptom of the phobia is evidently not the answer, as the original fear remains, and it is likely a new phobia will present to cover the now exposed fear. Learning to manage your anxiety is not necessarily a long-term solution; though it may help you ease your discomfort from time to time. If you can find support, enough to tolerate your anxiety long enough to explore the underlying fear there is a greater chance of full recovery. By exploring the fear of death and accepting its inevitability you are closer to finding a lasting solution. Not to death, but to your fear. If you can allow this while maintaining awareness of your experience and our shared reality that none of us can be certain what it is like to experience fully; after all we take that part to the grave, then paradoxically many phobias can be cured by accepting the reality of death. I would argue that we have a need to address death, to understand it and its implications for us as extant beings; to make sense of our fear in order to live fully. By hiding our death anxiety away behind fictions, we risk never really living.

Suicidal Thoughts and Death

If we view suicidal thoughts as a retroreflective ego state, we find the desire for life as a counter to the desire to die. The desire for a fulfilling life turned inwards. On reversal 'I want a better life' becomes 'I don't want to live like this anymore.' These aspects are two ends of the life death polarity. One outward and expressive, "I want a fuller life, I want more life, a better life than I currently have." This is an outward moving expression of need, requiring motivation and action to increase what is desired and reduce what is not desired. Its reversal "My life is awful. I wish it were over." is an internalised action, a turning in of what could be an outward expression. Born from despair and powerlessness. In therapy it is the supportive discussion of death as the apparent solution, which can bring awareness of the alternative, 'I want a better life.' Once we realise, we want more not less, once we take responsibility for ourselves, what we are and need; from this position we can become aware of what we want and how to move toward. Usually, this requires greater contact with the environment and self, coupled with greater personal agency.

—An Exploration of Death and Death Anxiety—

It is not introspection alone, but also greater awareness or the skill of mentalizing, allowing greater observable contactful expression toward our environment. Movement from suicidal to life seeking is a reversal of the retroflection. Taking the energy turned inward and using it to move outward into the environment to create a better life.

I in chapter 9 spoke about religion negating personal agency, by removing the need for political will through the imposition of edicts and the concept of the soul. So, logically this means part of the solution is temporarily hidden by religious attitudes. Often religion circumvents the opportunity to discuss suicide by establishing a taboo. In pronouncing it forbidden, as a sin, or as a certain path to hell; the second layer of guilt is added to the psyche of a person already suffering enough angst to consider ending it all. Far from being supportive, this stance does more harm than good. With the expectation of adherence to religious ideals about suicidal thoughts and actions, the dialogue is limited as expectations diminish contact with the distressed person. The confrontation of these limitations is difficult for therapists as we are likely to be seen as being judgmental of others' religion.

I am suggesting it is the discussion of death which will bring its counterpart, life, to the fore. I suspect these religious idioms came about as a response to fear of death, certainly most superstitious behaviours relate to averting disaster, or perhaps stemming from the erroneous idea that if you talk about death with a suicidal person, they will be more likely to carry it out. Also, within the mental health field, there is an unhealthy overreaction toward those talking of suicide. I think it is the same fear being played out. Though in this instance through fear of litigation as much as concern for the client. The imposed procedure and fear of perceived failure of clinical staff when a patient kills themselves act as a barrier to contact with the client and in many cases prevents full exploration of underlying rationalisations for suicidal behaviours. The procedures imposed often act in the same way as the restrictive religious taboos, impeding contactful investigation of distress, leaving the client unsupported through psychological anguish. Often, I hear from new clients how they have felt hounded by the medical model but unsupported, given a medical Kosh and restrictive medication regime, watched and monitored but little or no meaningful conversation or talking therapy. Often discussion seems to have been limited to the discovery of suicidal thoughts, followed up with an exaggerated and overprotective, often infantilising approach to aftercare. I'm acutely aware of the similarity between this behaviour and the parental transference elements of religion.

Ontological Anxiety

Moments of contact with others experienced without expectation are momentary windows to the self, capable of stimulating reorientation and integration. It is during these periods we experience re-attunement and a refocus of experience which highlights the old, learned pattern and its inadequacy in expressing or realising what is required now to overcome ontological anxiety and allowing self to be. In contact we meet the other with self and know the self through that contact.

Religious precepts frequently interfere with the felt sense of self. Anxiety about our true states, being judged and seen warts and all, stands between us and contact. Ontological anxiety as provoked by judgmentalism, it is not grounded and will prevent full contact between self and others. The I-thou state is never realised, fulfilment is limited. As a result, this anxiety is likely to be diverted via neurotic means into unhealthy behaviours. Yet, contacting the root cause becomes more onerous as the religion in question puts ideals and expectations in the way and masks the ontological source, often enforcing the relinquishing of personal responsibility; or replacing the true motivational drive with guilt and shame.

In my practice, I am seeing a profound rise in young men and women who have anxiety. Chiefly described in the first interview as social anxiety. This anxiety is, on reflection, usually ontological in nature. The fear is not of society or being social, this is a superficial facade and convenient place to peg one's anxiety. It's a large target and as such unmanageable for the individual. Under the surface layer of social anxiety remains the angst about self which is projected out onto others in assumed judgements. People are increasingly anxious about being themselves, about their essential self being acceptable to others. The key component is the person's inability to accept themselves.

Part of the issue underlying these manifestations of anxiety is a sense in which people have become separate from the natural world, unable to be within or connected to the natural world as ontological self. Many of these clients describe an existence devoid of natural contact: they have limited social circles, communicate extensively through handheld devices such as smart-phones, they rarely go out except to go to work, food is ordered as takeaway and delivered to the door or bought as ready meals from supermarkets and clothing is ordered online. In the place where I live, we have a beach 3 miles long, and the town is shrouded by the South Downs, yet many of these people rarely if ever venture past the front door other than to work or shop and almost never visit the beach, woodlands or hills.

Individualism has become a trap through which estrangement from the world has become a norm. The existentialists' prediction that mankind would experience more existential angst in the coming generations because they were losing a sense of being, seems to be coming true. This generation seems to be lacking contact with self, with others or with the world as a natural entity and they are the product of my generation. This divergence has cleft a void. These people are despairing as they have no place, they have no sense of belonging to the world or a place with others, no sense of the world about them or how to approach it. Social media has become a second, and sometimes first home. Beset with judgement, expectations and comparisons they sit within a bubble of tormented reality in which they can neither be themselves nor attain the anticipated goals expected from others. Eventually they collapse under the weight of expectation from within and the perceived expectation from without and become isolated and despairing that they will ever be able to have a relationship with themselves or others. In touch with isolation but not understanding its portent, depression seems inevitable. Often other comforting behaviours such as eating and constant distractions become combined into an unhealthy lifestyle in order to cover the angst.

In the past, people were more readily removed from this felt sense of isolation by hiding behind the safe walls of religious dogma. Religion provided a sort of community within which one was forced to exist outside of the home, to be part of a wider community. Though it has held us back from experiencing this existential isolation and separation it cushioned us from some of its effects. We have been so contained by it we do not have the skills to deal with the isolation when it is no longer possible to run from it. Religion is losing its hold but as a society, we lack the concepts and abilities to deal with existential realities without the fictional constructs previously used to shore up the angst.

Within our ontological anxiety falls our perceived inability to reach or even be aware of our potentials. The lack of meaning, the lack of direction and lack of means to contact personal agency suggest a life stuck in indecision, blind to potential selves. In discussing this issue Rollo May states "We have stated that the condition of the individual when confronted with the issue of fulfilling his potentialities is anxiety. We now move on to state that when the person denies these potentialities, fails to fulfil them, his condition is guilt, that is to say guilt is also an ontological characteristic of human existence." *The Discovery of Being*, (1983).

I agree that the lack of fulfilment of potential will provoke ontological anxiety. However, there is a little more to be said about the source of that anxiety. "The condition of the individual when confronted with the issue of fulfilling his potentialities (may) be anxiety" but it is not a given. The state arising is also likely to be frustration or anger, experienced as boredom or disconnection. If unexpressed or unsupported that may in turn become anxiety, or as is more likely the case, feelings of guilt as anger is retroflected. This is as a consequence of not supporting resentment or anger; not always as a direct result of the failed potentialities.

There may be some anxiety about potentially novel experiences. Though this may also be complicated by existential guilt arising from the realisation of our missed opportunities, our unexpressed potential; I suspect this is a later state which usually comes after the awareness of anxiety has evolved; this is likely to result in existential guilt. It will likely be preceded by guilt resulting from the retroflection of resentment toward perceived imposed restrictions. This initial guilt may need to be worked through before we uncover the ontological anxiety.

Guilt is usually the counterpart of resentment as described in the previous section on existential guilt. I feel resentment but cannot express it, as a feeling which requires or promotes outward expression in order to be cleared; if I will instead retroflect the resentment back onto myself, it becomes guilt. For example, Mother tells me I should have been kinder to the boy I just spoke to. I was cross and honest with my feelings, but the expression of my anger is being criticised as bad or rude. I could feel resentful towards my mother for not supporting me and my feelings or for taking the other child's side, but to take this stance is dangerous for me. Instead, I learn to turn it inward and experience it as guilt for having done something wrong.

To say this is a complicated collection of interconnected feelings and responses is an understatement. In my own practice I see this lack of contact with society and with the natural order frequently described and expressed as social anxiety and isolation, yet all too often the root is resentment, feeling I cannot exist ontologically as I truly am. In some cases, this has become a tendency to apologise for one's own existence, which is more akin to shame than guilt and a likely path to suicidal thoughts.

If there is enough awareness to know that religion's dogmatic take on life is no longer going to mask my fear of death, my isolation and separation from others, or allow me to divert responsibility; I will at some stage experience existential guilt and ontological anxiety. I have come too far to allow this awareness to subside so masking it behind rules and judgments is unlikely to work again. I must find another way to experience life and express my authentic self-lest I fall into another pattern of neurotic response. Some might seek more restriction in another religion, and some may attempt to throw off the ties that have bound and begin to explore freedom.

Allowing Angst

Like all feelings, if we support it and express it rather than fight or run from it, allowing awareness of the somatic response along with the antecedent stimuli, then the feeling once expressed, transforms. It will either become less potent as we come to understand it or alternatively, it transforms into another felt response and through the movement from one emotional reaction to another, creates a deeper comprehension of our emotional continuity. Just yesterday I had the following exchange with a client:

C: I have a sense of dread, like a fear of death.

Me: Try to stay with it, see if you can allow your experience of dread for a moment...

C: (laughing, raised and excited, mock angry voice) God no... it feels shit, the last thing I want to do is feel it more!

It was a small excerpt from an hour of therapeutic work, and no, he never went back to his dread. However, it serves to highlight that the desire to run from, to salve our feelings and hide them away is an entrenched system which is automatically employed; I suspect a fixed Gestalt, formed from the influence of previous generations, as well as other environmental and social factors is culprit. Within this closed system, non-expression and denial were supported by religious dogma. Though in the above case it was a deflection employing laughter and joking behaviour to defuse tension.

Now we are seeing religions' epistemological grip slackened in many places, as their hold over well-educated people lessens, but we are not currently equipped as a society to deal with the fall out for we are still told not to feel. Our first instinct is to run from and distort the feelings that arise rather than experience and express.

Even mainstream spoken therapies see anxiety as something negative to manage or flee, rather than a feeling with an intrinsic value which is telling us something important about us and the world we inhabit. The being with, and expression of the anxiety by breathing, observation and expression, which is demonstrated in the mindful stance, allows this state of being to inform us of what is taking place within and without.

Breathing into my anxiety I will find it transformed into something else. I am afraid because something is frightening, or I am frightening myself with thoughts. More often we are taught, 'I am afraid and must run from my fear because it feels terrible.' This is a limiting option. If all we can do is run, we will end up running countless marathons, only to stop and find the angst has run along with us just waiting for us to stop.

In saying all this I do not wish to undermine people's efforts to live with anxiety or lessen the impact it has for many daily. I know from first-hand experience, from my own experience of PTSD that anxiety states are debilitating and limit our capacity to rationalise and feel fully present. Once experienced as a neurotic obsessive pathway, it is terrifying. I understand why people want to run from that state. I am not suggesting for one instance that we should accept panic attacks etc. I am proposing that by the acceptance of felt realities of any description, followed by contactful expression and exploration, those feelings will never need to become the horrific aspects of chronic anxiety if healthy contact and support can be maintained.

It is useful to remember that understanding reduces anxiety and fear to a tolerable level from which we can operate and experience our being without being overwhelmed with affect or embedded in an emotional response. Paradoxically, the process of remaining with feelings, for many people may itself prove anxiety-provoking simply because it is novel; maybe at times because it has been outlawed by others and we are doing something against the will of our imprinted societal patterns

Learning to stay present without becoming embedded within our emotional experiences, then through appropriate expression and contact with the environment is in my opinion key to being authentic and indeed the hallmark of good mental health. Being without the ontological angst we have described, to know that it matters not what others judge me to be if I am contactfully in tune with my authentic self. I am me, not your judgement. If

—An Exploration of Death and Death Anxiety—

I can accept my death, and my existential realities, I will inevitably relinquish the need to neurotically guard against them. Released from the neurotic patterns of defence I can experience contact with self, and from that secure base, contact with others too. Perhaps even occasionally an I-thou moment, though if you seek that it won't happen imagine trying to maintain happiness because you want it to last forever, it will just disappear in the effort. It's the same with the I-thou interaction, it either happens or it doesn't.

Chapter 14

Case study 6: Jacob

> "Let he who is without sin among you, let him cast the first stone." John 8v7

Jacob

Jacob, where to start with Jacob? A remarkable and beautiful human being, the kind of client I sit in wonder at how they have managed to survive with as much of their personality intact as they have. I guess it is important to say he has never had security, of any sort, but he longs for it. He is a man full of contradictions: wanting security yet never finding it, placid but full of rage, lonely, but afraid of connecting so never quite meeting.

His main presenting issue was the abuse at the hands of his parents. It's a heart wrenching tale, how does anyone survive that level of neglect and trauma? Occasionally people like this come through our door, and they are like a conundrum representing the best and worst humanity has to offer. It has been my absolute privilege to help him piece some parts of himself back together.

I will not go into a lengthy discussion of Jacobs' background here. It is horrific and could encompass the entire book. But there are two important aspects pertaining to religion which I want to highlight. The first is sadism at the hands of his parents and the second, sadism at the hands of a pastor at his local church.

I think we can all agree that parents who neglect their child to the point of near starvation, provide no nurture but instead physical torture and psychological humiliation are sadistic. When these same people go to church on Sunday and are considered upright members of the community it feels all the more incongruous. His father was a deacon, and his mother led the Sunday school, pillars of the religious community if you like. Children were routinely left in their care by members of the congregation. When people like this are torturing their children behind closed doors, one must wonder how religion has played a part, how the justification of this behaviour is even possible within the personal lived Christian context. This abuse, both physical and emotional, went on throughout his life, it was a daily humiliation on the physical and psychological level.

I will give a couple of brief examples, so you can understand the level of neglect and abuse. Jacob came home from school one afternoon, approximately 7 years old. His mother's reaction to him entering the house was to scream at him for being late. He has no recollection of being late, he had gone straight home. She forced him to stand in a wardrobe until his father came home. His father, on return several hours later, asked no questions, just got his belt, strapped him and then sent him to bed without dinner. His bed had no blanket, just a thin sheet because his parents thought he needed to toughen up. He was cold, his sleep interrupted by the chill and lack of food.

This sort of thing happens daily, often justified with comments about him being a terrible boy, naughty, a bad Christian or admonished to look at the distress he causes his mother and father etc., justifications along the lines of "we are doing this for your own good", "we are trying to make you into a good Christian."

At age 15, on discovering Jacob was attracted to men, his parents lost the collective plot. Calling him evil, thinking he was possessed, they took away his clothing, took away access to the phone or any other communication device. They locked him away in his room, where they brought him some food, but not much. They forced him to stay there and pray for forgiveness, and until his "filthy" desire was taken from him. This imprisonment went on for about 3 months. If his mother came and found him not on his knees, she would hit him with a bamboo cane from the garden. This went on until he finally convinced them he was now "healed." For the next few months, he was allowed to go out to church but that was his only freedom.

It didn't stop there. Age 19 Jacob ran away from home without telling his parents, in order to get away from the abuse. After leaving home, Jacob was desperately in need of community and consolation. He was needing to find answers to some big questions. Because he was never going to find them in his family when he left home and needed community, he turned to the church, the only other community he had known. He was isolated and looking for support. He was unloved and alone and looking for love of pretty much any description.

The pastor of the church took Jacob under his wing, and under the guise of 'counselling', I used the term loosely, as the pastor was not a registered or trained counsellor in the therapeutic sense of the word. He used the time to draw Jacob in, to ask him about his life to find out about him. The pastor seemed concerned and behaved as though he was. It was a manipulation designed to draw out more information, and Jacob, feeling supported, supplied it.

After the 4th session with the pastor Jacob was initially surprised and a little delighted to hear his name within the sermon one Sunday morning. His delight quickly turned to terror. The sermon continued for some 10-15 minutes longer, it was a humiliating verbal attack, people got up and moved away from Jacob, he was left to sit on his own in tears and eventually got up and fled before the end.

The pastor had taken the information which was given in confidence and was using it to attack Jacob publicly. You might wonder how this is possible, why would a pastor do this to such a vulnerable person? Well Jacob had confessed he was bisexual, and he admitted this to the pastor as something he was ashamed of. Primarily because people had in the past told him that gay sexual relations were wrong, dirty and evil. Jacob's struggle was one of guilt and shame about his desires. Jacob's sexuality was exposed, he was vilified for being bisexual, and openly condemned, by the pastor, to the entire congregation. Jacob left the church and soon after came to see me. All of this in the name of God, in the cause of rooting out evil.

Disguised Sadism

I wish this was an isolated incident, but I have heard this story in less potent terms many times before. Where religiously motivated parents or community members have attacked children they are supposed to be nurturing. Religious leaders have verbally attacked people, either privately or in public, exposing them, calling them evil, and dressing it all up as a loving concern for the soul. It seems, from the examples brought to therapy, almost exclusively to be centred around sexual desire, and always results in the religious leader or parental figure entering a campaign of sadistic attack upon the person concerned. I have mentioned in places through this book how sadistic behaviour is masked by religious thought. I want to look at it in more detail here.

Sadistic behaviours tend to come from a root of insecurity, where the sadist needs to bolster their flagging sense of self by imbuing it with power over others. This does nothing to support the self it spawns an unconscious realisation that this behaviour is required to feel good about oneself, and like many potentially addictive pleasurable expressions must be run again to experience the momentary pleasure or buff to the weakly inflated ego. Like many addictive pleasurable behaviours, it loses its effectiveness and must be employed more forcefully the more often it is employed as a defence. In the case of religious sadism, the harm to others is overlooked and justified by religious ideals as attack is suffused with virtue.

We see three varieties of sadistic behaviour played out through religious settings, each linked to this taking of power over another; though these are not limited to religious spheres, and you will see numerous examples by looking around society at large.

1: The tendency to desire others to submit to oneself. Which will be expressed as actions which create submission or enforce submission. In the worst cases, these characters will require absolute allegiance and submission in all things, frequently in Christian churches, this may be referred to as "heavy shepherding" and considered quite normal/acceptable to many. This may include Pastors telling parishioners how much money to give to the church, whom to marry, what to do with free time, what house to buy etc. You can well imagine this of cult leaders, and it is easy to see how it could lead to extreme results. For example, there have been religious leaders who require everyone to commit suicide at a given time.

2: The second is to take this control over people and to use it in extorting something from them. This is often financial coercion and results in the sale of prayers and mega-churches where financial tallies are worshipped almost as much as the gods espoused. Although it may also refer to emotional taking and coercion of a psychological nature, we might refer to that these days as gaslighting.

3: The third is a desire to see others suffer, either physical or mental harm. The desire is enough to engineer situations in which others are harmed or to preside over the harming. We might consider the minister who humiliated Jacob in this light. He manipulated Jacob into giving up sensitive information while pretending concern then used the information to inflict psychological harm upon him. All these forms of sadism are and have always been found within religious groups where containment has been sought by followers and sadistic people take advantage.

It does not help that these people are frequently followed by the people on the other side of the coin, that of masochistic leanings. If a person who derives "pleasure" (usually relief from psychological angst) from being humiliated or hurt joins a sadistic charismatic leader and it's all justified by religious teachings, the enmeshed behaviours that ensue are healthy for no-one.

The masochist is trying to deal with an unbearable sense of existential isolation. This drives them to make their psychological self-disappear, usually through belittling, humiliating behaviour. They make themselves smaller and insignificant. Thus, psychologically diminishing the part of themself that could be isolated. In merging with a sadistic religious grouping, the masochist loses yet more of themselves, they become confluent to the system which humiliates them. In doing so they also become part of a larger system, they are lost but the isolation is diminished. Ultimately, they will be looking to the Godhead to punish him, the greatest power available to make his lack of power ever more apparent. Their self has been surrendered in order to be subsumed into the larger whole. Within this larger system, some semblance of meaning is found. Or at least a proxy that is strong enough to mask the desire for meaning.

Remember also that the sadistic element can be internalised, when we are berating ourselves for failure or forgetfulness. Perhaps beating ourselves up mentally or physically for not being this or that trait, which is highly desirable, more intelligent, more good looking, younger, older, more sophisticated, fitter, thinner, fatter, taller, etc. the list of complaints we might have against oneself is limitless, and the internal attack frequently relentless. This is a sadistic trait played out internally, and the other part of self we are berating contains our masochistic self, both are disguised from the authentic self.

Both masochism and sadism then spring from the need to deal with existential isolation and meaning, from a diminished sense of self. Neither are inherently destructive though much destruction has arisen from both aspects. Both are attempts to understand and make sense of existential angst stemming from isolation. It is complicated by religious thought which often promotes sadistic and masochistic behaviours as pious.

Chapter 15

The End

No book can ever be finished. While working on it we learn just enough to find it immature the moment we turn away from it. Karl Popper

Endings

Karl was so right. But I must stop somewhere. It is fitting, in a discussion about inevitable ends that this book and the process of writing it comes to an end. For a long while I wondered if I would ever finish it, the temptation to continue editing and editing is relentless. My own contact with the process of writing has been an interesting personal journey; I have discovered parts of myself long hidden and began to undo introjects previously lost to my awareness. After 25 years of therapy, there is always more growth to encourage.

In conclusion, I will summarise, I propose that most religions, religious thought and superstitions are fiction, ideas we cling to which were developed over centuries via our neurological systems which evolved to protect us.

Certainly, I have seen no specific scientific evidence for the existence of an eternal supernatural deity. The beliefs are founded on delusional activity, which is neurotic in nature. The neurosis is there to mask our existential fears, to placate and smooth over what is not only immutable but also difficult to explore and understand. This exploration is one of the many goals of psychotherapy. In following religious belief, we give up our freedom and personal responsibility. We lose ourselves and give ourselves to the notions created by past societies. We become confluent with the norm of the religion or society we are born to, and because our critical thinking is hindered by our lack of contact with self and environment we fail to self-actualise. We never live, because we don't want to take responsibility for living or face the reality of our inevitable death. We fail to contact or engage with what it means to be human.

Psychotherapy then can be a tool to explore our existential realities. It is a craft. We can read endless books about therapy, like this one. We can discuss ideas and diagnostic tools, we can intellectually understand, direct and digest a million facts about psychology and behaviour; but none of this will make us a psychotherapist.

Imagine if you read 20 books about carpentry. Would you then be a carpenter? No, of course not. You must practice. You must handle the tools, get a feel for the chisel blade against the wood. You must learn to sense when the saw bites and when you have missed the mark. A good carpenter will look at a piece of timber and know, this grain won't work for this job, but it will work for this. A craft, like therapy, is best learned through experience.

Psychotherapy then is best learned in the company of others, hands-on, mistakes and all. We must learn to share our hard-earned wisdom, our sense of the client, our feeling for the process born from countless interactions. We can share this by being with and working with each other. To learn from each other through the sharing of experience. Through interactive experimentation, mentoring and immersion in psychotherapy as a way of being. I trust this book has supplied a little of this.

I believe the best books I have read about therapy are the ones which challenged me and made me rethink my assumptions about the world. Which is perhaps a mirror of therapy. In this book I have tried to accomplish just that. Religion is a pithy subject and understanding it will help us work with some of the toughest challenges we will face as therapists. It is my hope that you got as much from reading it as I did from writing it.

One last note of encouragement

There is no sure way to find peace, that doesn't sound as encouraging as I intended it to be. Let's try again, you will never find in one book a list of commandments which give a framework which is perfect for you and helps you in all things be content. Not this book or any other. This is something only you can achieve, by being in contact without the hindrance of expectation. In contact with yourself and your environment. With others as they are, not as you expect them to be. In allowing the full expression of your love, to love and be loved; to be self-directing, always following the desire of your authentic self in contact with others. Finally, by understanding and being understood, being able to make yourself understood. If you can do these things, you will find joy. By allowing full expression of your emotional world, engaging with your sadness, anger and fear, being human, allowing your authentic self to be, without hindrance and without resorting to abusive endeavours. In this, you may find contentment. In the clarity of contact, when I and thou meet, when we truly see each other and accept ourselves and the other; in the knowledge that this will inevitably end. When we experience that awe, that spiritual connection, here we may find contentment, here we may find joy and sometimes even peace. But this path is different for all. My path is not yours, though perhaps one day they may collide, if only for a moment.

Have courage.

Courage

The greatest virtue, all others pale beside;
All backed and driven,
As though without they fail, guttering half-hearted light
struggling to reach even the brightest eyes.
Love then without courage behind its veil? All dependency.
Great love in contact, through vulnerability, must accept the end
　　　　writ large
In days to come, to tear with rending tears your thou from your heart.
For if you love, with courage, inevitable ends;
Will create for you a void of unimaginable pain,
yet fill before your moments with contentment so rich,
your breast cannot contain.

A poem by Steven Eserin 2019

Appendice

An explanatory overview of the main psychological theories used in this book.

"The teacher may call a pupil good if he is obedient, does not cause trouble, and is a credit to him. In much the same way a child may be called good if he is docile and obedient. The "good" child may be frightened, and insecure, wanting only to please his parents by submitting to their will, while the "bad" child may have a will of his own and genuine interests but ones which do not please his parents." Erich Fromm, *Man for Himself* (1947)

The theory which I outline below describes "role" as the surface layer of neurotic behaviour. It can be more thoroughly explored by those interested in this model of neurotic behaviour in *Ego Hunger and Aggression* (Fritz Perls, 1941) as well as *Gestalt Therapy: Excitement and Growth in the Human Personality* (Perls Hefferline and Goodman, 1951).

The following theory is a model of the path taken when neurotic behaviour is broken down. It has often been overlooked, despite giving a very clear map of likely passage through neurosis to contact.

"A lot of attention has been given to the Cleveland contact cycle, in contrast to the relative lack of attention given to the model of neurosis described by Perls (1969, 1991)

Perls model is not, and was never attempting to be, a model of human functioning. However, it is a model of working through neurosis: through the layers that form like a scab over authentic functioning." Peter Phillipson, *British Gestalt Journal* (1998 vol7, 5).

Although I will talk about the contact cycle later, I wish to be clear it is only connected to the five layers theory in as much as it describes the usual process through contact which is interrupted by neurotic behaviour.

In the main body of this book I have given consideration to religion as a neurotic function, or the foundation of neurotic behaviours. This descriptor of neurotic behaviour should give a little more insight into how we use religion to mask fears. The five layers is Fritz Perls theory of the phases people ordinarily move through to undo automatic neurotic behaviour.

The five layers of Neurosis:
- Role, cliché or phoney
- Phobic or fear
- Impasse
- Implosive
- Explosive

Cliche or phoney (role)

The cliché or phoney layer includes roles we play in life in order to represent ourselves as something we consider more presentable than our judgement of ourselves. It is a role because we are playing at being something we are not, presenting a self that is not our authentic self. We usually employ a role because we do not accept part of the self or have never been given enough support by our environment to be what we are, or perhaps need to be.

We play these roles instead of allowing our true organic/authentic selves to be given free expression. To be authentic often requires being vulnerable or accepting conflict; therefore, instead of allowing vulnerability, we create a role we play in order to appear to be strong or implacable. It is neurotic as we are mostly unaware of this behaviour, and because it is an adaptation or creative solution which masks the real self. I use the term playing a role several times during this book when describing religious behaviour. We eventually believe the role is really us. This layer of cliché, or the phoney layer, prevents us from experiencing rejection and isolation. If I play the role of an unsympathetic autocrat, I do not have to show the part of me that is sympathetic. The latter quality may not have been supported by my early environmental experience, so I don't make use of them and represent myself in other ways which are not really me but may have been more acceptable in my infancy. Having played the role of autocrat for so long I will now do it automatically, without awareness.

In group settings such as religious gatherings we commonly see examples of cliche interaction; people placating instead of risk conflict via contact between selves, or attacking in order to hide hurt, though attacks are often, but not always, reserved for people outside the group. Bringing awareness to alternative behaviours, and especially looking at the polarities of behaviours can reap hefty rewards as far as new interaction and expression of untried feelings. All neurotic behaviours stem from our inability to find an organic balance between ourselves and the environment, the cliché layer is just another example of an attempt to create balance misfiring and producing neurotic interaction instead.

Phobic (or Fear)

As awareness of the phoney layer or awareness of the role we play instead of allowing contact with the authentic self evolves, we will develop an understanding of the fear sitting just under the surface, the role is a mask to cover the fear. This fear may also be experienced as shame, a very deep-rooted sense that the real me is not enough. If we become aware of the real nature of self under the role, we will directly experience fear, hence the term 'phobic'. This might be immediately transformed into a desire to avoid, to deflect the new/alternative behaviour, we might imagine catastrophic consequences if we allow genuine behaviour. For example, "if I start crying, I will fall apart, therefore I will put on a brave face" is the kind of fantasy people use to prevent making genuine contact with sadness, even though that sadness may be an integral aspect of their authentic self. The fear of one's vulnerability, particularly around emotional interactions and affects which were not supported by our developmental environment, is a powerful deterrent to further exploration.

Impasse

Below the phobic layer, if we have allowed ourselves to experience the fear and sat with our somatic response, we will reach an impasse. In the 'Impasse', we are caught between not knowing what to do and how this new experimental behaviour will affect us; we might hold ourselves still, or become silent, or we might attempt all manner of distraction techniques. We have hit a wall we do not know how to get over or through. It's common for people to flit between the impasse and the phobic layer as fear of going through the impasse grows. The new experience and related feelings and expressions are novel. All can be a source of anxiety if not supported by breath or if unsupported by the environment. All new behaviours are likely to be noticed by others we know, as they are unexpected, they may not be welcomed, they may even be opposed.

Implosion

Beyond the impasse is implosion. This is the point at which we turn our energy in on ourselves, often expressed in grief, or attacking ourselves for the wasted time; Or possibly existential guilt for the lost opportunity, for "all the years I've been allowing myself to hold this in." In short, whatever the form it takes, we implode as we come to a better realisation of how we have constricted ourselves. This implosion is a drawing in of somatic resources too, which once gathered will enable the next phase.

Explosion

In this phase, previously unused, pent-up energies are released in an explosion of expression, this might be a cathartic expression, it might be a new behaviour or a creative outpouring. There is no one descriptor for what happens except that it is internal forces poured out into the environment. The energy that was trapped by the neurotic behaviour now has an avenue for expression. The release of the energy enables contact; with the previously hidden part of self, contact with the constructs which enabled its submission or subjugation, the environment into which the expression is poured, contact with our self, our organic, authentic self, the self that would be if it had been supported or left without interference from the outside world. The self as expressed without neurosis.

Top-dog and Under Dog

This might be a good time to introduce the concept of 'top-dog' and 'underdog' dichotomy, as this is an integral part of neurotic behaviour. Usually, this appears as an internal process or dialogue while we are enacting the roles existing in the phoney layer. Here you have two elements of the self at constant war with each other, and the battling results in stagnation and frustration.

Consider the top-dog to be a little like Freud's concept of the superego, it's the part of you that wants control, it's bossy, it uses terms like "you should ", it's authoritarian and will punish you for not fulfilling its wishes. It is that part of you that bullies the other parts of you into submission. The top dog tries to enforce "good" behaviour. This is an internal psychological construct brimming with introjects. Neurotic behaviours always include aspects of the top dog/underdog, it is a psychological position we all know well. When you told yourself "I shouldn't have this chocolate", that was the top dog. Whereas the part that responded with, "shame to waste it though, I can start my diet tomorrow." or words to that effect, that was the underdog responding.

The underdog is the bullied part of self, the part that submits, but it also tends to avoid doing the top dogs bidding by evading, frustrating or undermining. "I'll do it tomorrow," "ok I need to do that, but it can wait until I've watched this TV program." It uses words and phrases like "yes but," or "I'll do it when I am not so tired." etc. The underdog invariably wins long term by frustrating the top-dog with agreement and inaction. One intention of therapy is to integrate these two warring factions and by getting the two aspects of self to converse with each other, to unify them. Whenever someone is playing a role the top-dog and underdog will be present as the authentic self and the role are likely to be opposites.

The Contact Cycle and Figure Formation

A brief description of figure formation is important to understanding contact. Figure formation is pivotal to the concepts of awareness and allowing contact with our experience of our surroundings and our interactions with others.

Figure Formation

A figure can be described as that which you are most aware of at any given moment, the brightest most interesting phenomenon within your current experience. Figure formation is important in as much as every contact cycle starts with the development of a figure. This does not equate sensation with the figure as such, the figure can start to form at any point in the cycle. Rather it is something we become aware of, and as we focus upon it, it becomes clear and distinct from everything else; everything else being the field surrounding it. The field is our entire environment but includes our internal landscape. By way of simple explanation.

Imagine you are out shopping for shoes, you like shoes, but more than that you have lost a pair you use for walking, so you actually need some new ones. Your need for new shoes was your original figure, and since you became aware you needed shoes you have made plans toward getting more.

Right now, you are out in the town, you are aware of your environment, the people, the noise, the bustle, litter, smells etc. Your sensory system is in alert detection mode, but your focus at this point, your figure, is buying shoes. Therefore, most of this information is receded to a homogenised background, what you are picking out most clearly are signs above shoe shops, they are standing out, and occasionally you might see shoes on people's feet and think to yourself that they are nice or not. You have looked in shoe shop windows and you're getting closer to making a choice, it's still a figure for you, when suddenly you realise you need to pee.

Your need to pee is a new figure, and it has taken precedence over the former as it is a natural need which demands your attention. Had you been close to paying for a pair of shoes you might have chosen to desensitise yourself to the urge to pee for a few minutes. This new figure is quite insistent. With your new figure, you are no longer seeing shoe shops, now you're actively looking for the nearest toilet. Your brain has stopped seeing shoe shops and signs which point to shoes, now it has switched to finding toilets. Toilet found you make full contact with your need to pee, you then feel satisfied, you withdraw from that experience and now you are free to form a new figure.

Now, at this point, you may pick up the old figure of buying shoes, or you may find something else more pressing, you may have realised you need to eat, or need to rest your feet, you may see a friend across the street you want to talk to. It matters little. All we need to realise is that your figure, your bright point of focus, the reason for making contact, changes from time to time, spontaneously arising from the field of our environment as the point of bright attention. Once a figure has formed the contact cycle will need to resolve itself, if left unresolved it will keep attempting to get resolution, even if you are unaware of it.

We will explore further how important aspects of the self if left without full contact, or if the resolution of the contact cycle is interrupted, these interruptions will form aspects within neurotic behaviours.

What Is Contact?

It could be described as spontaneous concentration. Where the figure is sharp, and we can give it our full attention without running from or losing a sense of self within it. This contact would be experienced at the contact boundary with the senses, coupled with an internal somatic response. This is a phenomenological experience of the interaction between I and otherness which stimulates a reaction within me that I am aware of and remain present to; the remaining present to is usually described as awareness.

We all have a contact boundary. For now, it is enough to know that contact happens where I end and you begin, the point at which we meet. It may be physical touch, or my ears may pick up your sound, my nose may catch your scent etc. That meeting will create excitement of some description, allowing that excitement to be without interrupting before its time to withdraw, is the essence of healthy contact.

You may have experienced being out of contact without really realising what it was. If you were ever talking with someone and not finding them or the subject interesting, but you were too polite to say anything, so you stood and nodded and said yes or hmm in appropriate places. You were perhaps wondering how to get away, to find someone else to talk to or to introduce the boring person to someone else so they could become bored instead of you. During this moment you were not in contact with the person talking, or in contact with your authentic self and its desire to change the subject or find something of interest. Instead, you were focusing on finding a polite solution, playing a role which society said you should play. Certainly not in contact with the conversation or the person in front of you.

The Contact Cycle

The contact cycle, as seen above describes the continual process of human interaction with ourselves, each other and the environment we inhabit.

It is a cycle of self-regulation, meaning that to maintain organismic balance we regulate ourselves through contact, as expressed in the contact cycle. A perceived imbalance between the organism and the environment creates a new figure. This starts a new cycle and balance returns when the cycle is complete, ready for the emergence of a new figure and the next cycle to begin. Interruptions to the cycle create unfinished situations which the organism continues to try and finish in order to achieve organism/environment balance. We might call this unfinished situation a fixed Gestalt.

In the above image, you can see the various stages of healthy contact, these are written on the outer edge of the diagram. Each phase leads smoothly on to the next unless it is interrupted. The interruptions are shown in the centre of the image and the position of the terms correspond directly to the point in the contact cycle which has been interrupted. Although as we will see as the description unfolds, some interruptions are not always limited to breaking one point of the cycle. What is important is understanding how these interruptions disrupt otherwise healthy contact.

Most of this is ordinarily out of our awareness, automatic behaviour and interactions. Much of the work I do is to help expand awareness to incorporate more experience, thus with more information, healthier, more aware choices can be made. Every one of these interruptions can be seen as avoidance, and nothing is ever gained from avoidance except in the case of real danger.

Aware/unaware

By way of an example of the aware/unaware paradigm consider vocalisation, you have access to or commonly use at least 5-6000 words, and your language is composed of many times that; day to day the average person utilises a smaller common section of the available language. You speak, the words come, you don't consciously drag the words out one by one, they are out of your awareness, at no point are you aware of them all constantly like some giant encyclopaedic dictionary, but you have access to them all the same. This means when you read a word you know but don't often use, its meaning comes back to you, and it also allows most of us to talk freely without the need for detailed, constant full awareness of your vocabulary. In the same way, throughout our waking lives we are constantly being and doing without awareness, and not all this doing is healthy.

Sensation

When we talk about sensation, we are talking about the first spark, the first physical tell that something in our environment has become a bright figure. Something has grabbed our attention. This feeling is quickly formed into an awareness. For this example, I am going to use hunger. I felt a pang in my gut, a physical manifestation of an imbalance between me, my organic self and my environment, perhaps a slight tremor in my limbs and sense of weakness.

Awareness

Next comes the awareness, I feel my pang and interpret that as hunger, now my awareness is my new figure, I am hungry, I am aware of my hunger. That seems simple enough, although all too often we misinterpret these signals. How often do you think you have taken something to eat when you really needed a drink? How often have you had something to eat when you really needed a hug? This is where interruptions come into play, and I will look at those in some detail shortly.

Awareness, as described here, is limited to how it relates to the contact cycle. Throughout this book I use the term awareness a lot. What I want to impress is that awareness is bigger than just the first step in this cycle. It is the person becoming cognisant of the entire field and the self as an interrelated, constantly changing co-created phenomenon. The contact cycle awareness is a descriptor for the first awakening and understanding of the somatic responses to a given situation. Awareness in its more general form must be present throughout the cycle, and in every aspect of being human.

Mobilisation

After awareness comes mobilisation. The body releases chemicals to garner the energy to enable action, in the case of hunger I might need that energy to hunt, more likely in modern society I just need to walk to the store, or the fridge and prepare myself some food. In this instance, the energy released is mobilising the body toward Action.

Action

To action. I have realised I am hungry; I will get up off my chair and find food. I move toward food, I find it, kill it, pick it, buy it, I prepare it, put it in my mouth, chew, etc. In short, I act toward my goal which is to satisfy my need, in this instance, hunger.

Contact

Contact, at last, this is the contact cycle after all. I make contact with my food, I touch it, I bite, I start to break it down with my teeth and I swallow it. During eating I smell it, taste it, experience its texture, it's a sensual experience on which I depend, and from which I can derive much pleasure if I allow full contact.

There is an enormous amount going on inside right now, my brain is releasing various chemicals to reinforce pleasure pathways, hormones are being released to help process the food. My gut is preparing for the influx of nutrition, insulin has been released to deal with the carbohydrates, my brain is working out if this is safe to ingest and as I taste each morsel the same occurs as a continuous process. This is the moment of contact, when I am fully aware and tasting my food, when I am fully involved in satisfying my hunger.

Satisfaction

Satisfaction, well at some point hopefully my body will say, I'm done, that's enough, I don't need more than that right now, I am satisfied. If we can self-regulate, we notice this change and our need for food is no longer a bright figure.

Withdrawal

Withdrawal from the food occurs as soon as we are satisfied, the awareness of hunger has done its job, we are back in balance, now we can withdraw from that experience and allow a new figure to emerge, a new sensation, then awareness, a new cycle begins.

The entire process has taken us on a brief journey, from our internal world to contacting the external environment in order to satisfy something innate and personal, an organic felt need to address an imbalance. Each time we develop a new figure it is created by us alone; it is our perception of our experience. Yet our experience is not created in a vacuum. We are part of, influenced by and in part created by our environment; while we, in turn, co-create our environment, and that includes the people around us, our partners, our friends and family. It is these links with our environment and their role in creating or sustaining neurosis I have attempted to detail throughout the main body of the text.

Withdrawal, as part of the contact cycle, may also include some form of mourning. you may have enjoyed something fully, then wished it could last forever, the moment of withdrawal has an element of letting go of what was, a temporary state of mourning may become apparent. I would argue it is often an essential part of the withdrawal process, particularly where an object of devotion is no longer available.

In a nutshell that's it, seems simple enough right? Except there are plenty of interruptions, and nothing is as simple as it seems.

Interruptions to contact

As you see in the diagram of the contact cycle there are interruptions at every stage of the cycle. The interruptions are listed on the inside of the cycle corresponding to one aspect of contact. This positioning is usually, but not always the case, you can start to be confluent in the awareness phase for example, but it more often happens in the withdrawal phase. It is arguable that desensitisation always happens before sensation because its goal is to prevent it. Yet I could also become desensitised to satisfaction which may result in preventing or limiting withdrawal. It's not super important for a basic overview of Gestalt theory. The important part for us is recognising how people interrupt the cycle and trying to support them to complete the cycle where possible. I personally don't like using cycle as a behavioural diagnostic tool. In doing so we restrict our own contact with the client, who may present in a thoroughly unusual way. It's good as a guide, but it's not all-encompassing.

Sensation – Desensitisation

Desensitisation is a way to prevent yourself from becoming aware of something. There are many mechanisms that can be brought to play in order to not feel, all of which result in a lack of awareness. Usually expressed as a physical manifestation. In the case of hunger above, suppression of that initial pang so that I never fully feel hunger may result in an unhealthy relationship to food or the inability to experience other needs or desires.

In many cases people will recount a lack of sensation and a total lack of awareness. Often there is no awareness of the lack of sensation too, the missing bit isn't even missed, it's just accepted that it is not there. Oftentimes it seems as though a pain killer has been administered, there is no longer any awareness of pain, emotional usually, and sometimes physical; but neither is there awareness of anything else. You may frequently find it expressed in the stoic amongst us, holding oneself still physically to prevent movement, holding one's breath etc. all promote desensitisation. One of my options as a therapist is to attempt to foster awareness of the deadness, to the mechanism of suppression and thus to the conflict it has been masking. As Fritz Perls said when discussing yogic teachings and breathing techniques, in Perls, Hefferline and Goodman's Excitement and Growth in the human personality:

"The Indian tries to overcome suffering and conflict by deadening sensation and thus insulating himself from the "environment." Let us on the other hand, not be afraid to enliven feeling and response to stimulation and stir up such conflict as may be necessary in order in the end to achieve a unitary functioning of the whole man." (1951, 76)

Having read Perls extensively I will mention that I am not sure he fully understood the yogic traditions or breathing methods. However, I do agree with him that breathing is key to feeling. We must breathe fully in order to feel fully. Much anxiety is caused by interrupting our breath, or shallow breathing. Frequently we will find by correcting this, the anxiety reorganises into another feeling, another excitement. Perls was against the deadening of sensation, which can be achieved through some breathing techniques, and I think rightly so, as this deadening limits our experience of the world and becomes a proxy for actual felt reality.

This does not mean that as a therapist I arbitrarily and unilaterally push clients into sensation where there has been a lack thereof, I do encourage attention to the gaps, it is in these gaps or the boundaries around them that we will find the key to the mysteries of our interactions, or avoidance thereof. Through greater awareness, we have greater choice about how we behave in the future and can decide if it is healthy for us now, at this moment. Desensitisation is there to guard against pain, awareness of the deadness inexorably leads to awareness of the pain, if not immediately then eventually, through dreams or other unaware means. A client has avoided such pain for good reason, but the avoidance does nothing to resolve the unfinished business or help the client move to a different understanding and acceptance of their felt reality.

Awareness - Deflection

We now come neatly to the delights of deflection of awareness. Deflection is the pushing away of awareness, it might be laughing off a hurtful comment, or changing the subject. Distraction is a common one, and currently with our social media driven world and phones which link us to the internet, distraction is expected and encouraged. Any behaviour which ignores the current interaction and pushes it out of awareness would be classed as a deflection. Often done with grace and wit it can be hard to spot, and hard to catch, easy to fall in with (confluence).

There are many awareness exercises you can find online; the internet is full of mindfulness and awareness techniques. I can't stress enough how important it is as therapists that we are pushing our own awareness, attending to our boundaries and blind spots. What is good for the goose is good for the gander. We as therapists are constantly using our own awareness, it is in many respects our only tool. Sitting with awareness at our contact boundary and witnessing the events unfolding before us; Awareness of the content and process as well as our inevitable reaction to it is principal to making timely interventions. Our excitement in those moments of contact will drive our creative selves to explore, through experimentation, other contact options. It is these experiments at the contact boundary which will heighten awareness for our clients as well as for ourselves.

Our clients lack of awareness is there for a reason, be mindful that if we push for awareness before someone is ready it may be traumatising for them. Not all awareness is useful all the time, and if the time becomes apparent, it's your choice as a therapist to attend and encourage awareness. It is also your responsibility if you promote awareness to support the client to deal with the consequences. In the same way no matter how frustrated you may be that your client just cannot see what you think you see, forcing awareness is rarely useful, often damaging, and may drive the person away or into a more serious pathological psychological position.

Awareness is a strange beast; it is so very subjective. I need to become aware of my hunger, sure, we all do, but I also need to be aware of what my hunger is for, do I need food? Or a drink? Or maybe my hunger has nothing to do with food! do I need sex? Do I really need sex, or do I need close contact and affection? I would like to relate this back to figure formation. In *Creative Process in Gestalt Therapy* (1951),

Joseph Zinker said:

"The healthy individual is able to clearly experience and differentiate something in his foreground which interests and captivates him from that which is not interesting. He experiences the sharpness and clarity of the figure with little interest in a homogenised ground." (93)

We move through life having blurred the boundaries of our awareness in order not to feel difficult emotions. Once blurred it is hard to tell what that sensation really is, and if behaviour like eating when I really want affection is reinforced by societal rules and norms, while the going out and finding for myself, affection or pleasure is frowned upon, I can quickly become embroiled in a hazy half felt half desensitised reality. This reality is likely to be neither fulfilling nor healthy; As a result, I never fully feel what I desire or fully engage with the environment to get what I truly need. The organismic imbalance is never truly addressed.

Deflection is one mechanism by which awareness is nullified. If I push away that which I do not wish to know or engage with I prevent full contact, I avoid the inevitable unpleasantness by not engaging or by actively pushing away. For example, if I smile at someone who is angry with me, I may frustrate their attempts to fight me, I can reduce the chances of conflict, and if conflict is intolerable to me then deflection has done its job. In all likelihood it's a coping mechanism which probably served me well in my youth. But now as an adult, I do it automatically, I smile as soon as there is a hint of disharmony, it looks incongruent to the observer, but it's a source of frustration to the other party, who just wants resolution and does not see the fear behind my mask.

Deflection then is to bat away that which I am afraid to engage with; Those who deflect at the point of awareness are not aware that they do so, it is so automated, instituted and ingrained that a response like "it's just what I do" " it's how I am" or "that's just part of my personality" are all comments regularly made by deflectors. These comments are in themselves deflections of the awareness offered, in order that it may be forgotten if it's pushed aside.

Mobilisation – Introjection

As mobilisation of energy in the body for action is essential to move into action, preventing mobilisation by diverting the energy into a new cycle is a complex and creative way to avoid contact.

Introjection is the underpinning mechanism by which this is most commonly accomplished. Introjection is a rule or social norm, perhaps a familiar unwritten insinuation that something is wrong or will be wrong if we follow a certain path of action. This introject sits out of our awareness for the most part, perpetuating the promise that all will be well if we only do this, or we don't do that.

Perls and Goodman describe introjection as the process of swallowing whole, without digesting or chewing up, which would ordinarily tell us if something was digestible or palatable. Naturally, in this instance, we are talking about mental food, words and behaviours, but Perls also pointed out that interjectors commonly eat actual food in the same way, without adequate chewing, tasting or contact with. In his book, Ego Hunger and Aggression (1947) Perls states "Introjection means preserving the structure of things taken in, whilst the organism requires their destruction." (p5, 129). Erving and Mirium Polster say it clearly in their book Gestalt Therapy Integrated:

"If his environment is indeed trustworthy, the material coming in will be nourishing and assimilable, be it food or personal treatment. But food is shoved hurriedly down throats, doctors say the needle won't hurt, and shitting is called dirty and disreputable. The shoulds begin early and often have little congruence with what the child senses his needs to be. Eventually, a soul is worn down. The child's confidence is depleted by external authorities whose judgements set in, eroding his own clear identity and opening him to adult conquistadors who take over the territory." (1974, 72)

An example of an introject might be "women are slags if they seek sex outside of marriage." or one of the many variations on the theme. There are many elements to how this one works. Once embedded, the shame of seeking pleasure or enjoying one's own body is not something which one can easily turn off. Just because a person has now got married, if they lived with that particular injunction, they may well experience shame or guilt at asking for sex, seeking pleasure or even recognising their own sexual impulse. The introject itself bears no relationship to authentic behaviour. It is born of an ideology which objectifies and treats women as property. The authentic behaviour, to seek satisfaction of one's sexual desires is lost in a cloud of societal ideals and judgements.

Introjects are rules, codes of conduct, swallowed whole because it was dangerous for us to not follow those rules when we were younger. A common one for men is "big boys don't cry", "don't cry, be strong." In many ways it's cliché, we have heard it so often, 'Big boys don't cry' has even been the title of songs. Yet any man who grew up being told not to cry or having that subliminally reinforced by the males and females around them will find it very hard to be sad or allow their sadness to reach full expression. Sadness is so off-limits that they are likely to jump straight into being angry instead, being seen crying is likely to evoke profound feelings of shame. Again, the authentic self, the part that needs to be sad or moved to tears, is lost under the layers of roles we need to play in order to fit into other people's ideas of what we "should" be.

Interestingly introjects do not need to be said, it is highly probable that a person would learn that nothing they do is good enough if while seeking appreciation from caregivers no appreciation is offered, no comments made; the caregiver would not necessarily need to verbalise criticism for created content, just withholding praise where praise is due is enough to invoke the sense that the thing produced was not adequate, for if it had been the requisite praise would have been offered. Beyond that is a further issue, why would my creativity need others' approval at all? If we can remove that layer there is no need for the former. In actuality my self expression and the effort of trying is far more important than the content created.

Introjects force the contact cycle to short circuit, compelling us to choose another action, fear instead of anger, anger instead of sadness or any other combination. Confusingly enough there will be another layer behind that which is the genuine feeling still trying to gain expression, which in most will provoke shame, fear and anxiety.

In couples therapy we see introjects interfering in all areas of relationships, you can see how any of the above examples might directly hinder contactful expression and communication, limiting intimacy and healthy self-regulation. But we have also introjected rules and social norms which shape how we expect others to behave, they shape our expectations of what partners will be like, and while hidden away they hinder us at every turn. If the partner does not follow the same rule, then conflict is inevitable, a strong emotional reaction is likely to be the result.

Fortunately, we will see, introjects are not immutable. They sit foreign and undigested, and as we now know by the wonders of neuroplasticity, our brains can change and develop throughout our adult life, what was once assumed to be unchangeable and set, we know we can change; we can adapt and adopt new behaviours right through our adult lives.

Raising awareness to the point of figure realisation is necessary but moving on from that we need our clients to regurgitate that which is foreign and undigested, chew it up, keep the bits they like, the bits that still work, and spit out the bits they don't like or that no longer work for them. Again, we see how awareness and choice go hand in hand with changed behaviour and the possibility of healthier contact. Bear in mind always that these behaviours were learned from a young age, as an initial adaptation to early life experience, these introjected norms were learned to keep us safe, undoing them takes courage and an understanding that we no longer live with the same threats.

Action – Projection

Projection is common enough psychologically speaking, we all do it to some extent. Projection is taking your thoughts and feelings and attributing them to someone or something else. Something? Yes something, you might wonder how a thing has a feeling, which of course it does not and cannot. Well, how often have you heard someone say that a room was full of tension, or anger? Now, we all know the room can't have any anger or tension, we know that it has no sympathetic nervous system, the room being a solid physical object made from inanimate materials.

Rather, the person experiencing tension is uncomfortable and wants to disown that discomfort, so by describing it as part of the room, a psychological trick is played, magically dispelling the tension from 'me' to 'it'. By making the tension 'other' I perceive it as less threatening, I no longer have to take responsibility for it and therefore it is experienced as distant, less immediate.

Alternatively, if I own the projection, I have to say I feel tense, I am tense or even I am making myself tense. In owning the tension as mine I make it knowable; in short, I risk becoming aware of why I am tense, perhaps I want to avoid conflict? Perhaps I feel socially awkward, and the room is full of people, onto whom I am projecting my internal judgements.

That is the other face of projection, projecting my own thoughts onto another person, rather than an object. In assuming that if I hold the belief that I am foolish or stupid, clumsy, lacking social wit or grace or some other judgement I have collected as introject, that others perceive me in the same way. Which on further investigation they invariably do not. Often if we take the time to ask, we find the others are also tied up with their own internal wrangling and projecting onto the others too. They are contending with their introjected judgements of self and in all probability, they didn't even notice me, let alone fulfil my projected judgmental fantasy. By extension, even if they are judging me, who cares? I mean why would it matter what others think anyway? I am not as others perceive me; I am me.

How does this interfere with action? Will I enter a room full of people and experience being in contact with them? Or will I enter and feel self-conscious and full of anxiety remaining in contact with my introspective anxiety and projections? Certainly, the latter, if I am giving them my judgements, I short circuit the contact cycle and experience my excitement generated by contact as anxiety instead.

In all relationships, we see projection limit intimate contact on several levels. The inability to make contact with our true need to act on awareness, urges, desires, brings severe limitations to the quality of contact we experience. If we live with someone who habitually projects onto us, we can start to feel a lack of connection and a growing sense of incongruence and frustration with the relationship.

If I have spent years projecting my lack of desire onto my spouse so that I see them as the cause for my lack of emotional connection; If I never get to the point of saying "I have not desired full contact with you" I can never get to the awareness beyond that. I never ask the questions required to create a sharp figure; what drives my lack of desire? How did I choose a partner who has no desire for me? What do I derive from this relationship and what does it help me avoid? What behaviours have I learned that stop me wanting emotional connection? What introjects sit behind my lack of desire? I would discover that I cannot tolerate full contact with you or how I deaden my need for affection or intimacy. In effect, How do I keep myself disengaged.

If I am projecting, then all the above becomes the responsibility of the other, and I never get past seeing others as the cause of my woe.

Difficulties arise in discerning which bits are me and which bits are you. There is always something which fits the projected person, which is why it's easy to project onto them in the first place. There may be some similarity between that person's behaviour and my own, enough for me to convince myself it's them not me. 20 odd years ago my mentor once said, "There is always a peg to hang the hat on," and I've never forgotten it, it's proven so true. That is not to say the screen onto which I project my judgments is making the same judgments, it just means there is something similar in their interactive styles that makes it easy for me to project onto them, and with my projection, apportion blame.

Contact – Retroflection

Retroflection is the act of doing to self what we want the environment to do to us or doing to self what we want to do to the environment, or even doing to the environment what we want the environment to do to us. That's not always a bad thing, I should say that too. As with introjects like "don't hurt people." Clearly, that's not a bad thing, so a retroflected action like holding back a punch, might lead to a lot of tension, it might lead to aches and pains temporarily and you might need to go and punch something else, but at least you will not be physically attacking another person. For safety's sake, it's important to notice that sometimes it's a good thing to retroflect.

In the collection of Essays *Gestalt Therapy Now* (1970) John B. Enright describes retroflection as follows:

"Retroflection describes the general process of negating, holding back, or balancing the impulse tension by additional opposing sensorimotor tension. The concept includes most of what is referred to as repression and inhibition..." (128)

We see then that repression of impulse and inhibition of our natural desires holds us back from ever making good clear contact with the environment, including our family, friends and lovers. In effect, the contact is negated by holding back with equal force the action that we desire. I want to stroke your hair, but I am inhibited, I retroflect my desire and stroke my own hair instead or I hold my arm back with a force equal to that that would impel it to action. Or perhaps I reach out to hold you when I want to be held. All of this is out of awareness, all I am aware of is a dull ache in my arm, shoulder or neck from the tension created by this energetic clinch. I am unlikely to remain with the awareness that I am retroflecting.

When clients describe a lack of physical intimacy, they are likely to describe either a deadening of sensation or physical aches and pains too. Physical aches and pains are frequently an indicator of retroflected action. If I really want to say something and choose not to, either with or without awareness, the action of holding back my words is another retroflection. Like its more muscular counterpart, the act of not verbalising also creates tension, often resulting in sore throats, tight necks, tension headaches or even nausea as we attempt to hold in that which is unpalatable. In some cases, it may even lead to stammering. You may have experienced a lump in your throat when you need to cry, this is caused by holding back your tears and sobs rather than letting them flow as they must. Its a retroflection, the lump sensation is the tension expressed in your neck.

Helping people become aware of times in which they retroflect action or desire, helping them explore other ways of expressing or creatively experimenting with different modes of being is often a feature of therapy. Perhaps raising awareness of the fears sustaining the behaviours will lead to a desire to explore those fears and undo some of the unhealthy behaviours that have been learned. We find that as awareness grows the behaviour must be transformed. The old behaviour now seen for what it is, becomes less and less tolerable. Exploring or experimenting with ways to do things differently, and to tolerate the difference is just one goal of therapy when dealing with retroflection.

Satisfaction – Egotism

When egotism takes over conceit and self-absorption are the order of the day, satisfaction is often prolonged, highly prized and sought after by egotistical people who may have trouble acknowledging the role of others in satisfaction or seeing another's full humanity. Other people become objectified, and an egotistical person will struggle to even acknowledge another's need for satisfaction full stop. Taking the credit for all but also an unwillingness to withdraw from the situation lest the satisfaction and their conceit be undone.

As Egotism takes over people may become stuck on satisfaction, it will be the focus of contact, and the idea of moving through and then away from satisfaction will be an anathema to most egotistical people. Egotism could be described as an excessive preoccupation with self. As though my thoughts, behaviours and feelings take a central stage, with little or no regard for my effect on others. This may lead to egotistical people becoming preoccupied with their own world view to the exclusion of others, and an inability to accept or see the difference clearly. I will expand on this in the section on single-dimensional viewpoints later in the book.

I'm hoping it's obvious from the above description why such people might prove difficult to live with. These people will be unlikely to foster growth in others unless that will in some way enhance their own standing in society or give them satisfaction or gravitas. Egotists are unlikely to see another's personal growth as important and will be happy to take the limelight. Of course, if you want to hide in another's shadow and live vicariously through another's achievements then this kind of person might make a good partner for you, so a partner to a person like this might resist active change too. "I don't want him to change, I just want him to stop having affairs." is a phrase I have heard more than once in couples therapy.

Withdrawal – Confluence

Confluence is marked by a merging of the boundaries between two individuals. I will talk about the contact boundary a lot in therapy. What we are discussing is our proprioception, our understanding and monitoring of where we end and the other begins. There is a clear demarcation between you and I; I know where I end and you begin, this is my personal space, thus far no further, I can step into your boundary by talking, I make your eardrums rattle, and if you're ok with that invasion, you will reciprocate. But if I stand to close while I talk perhaps, I am stepping over a boundary and you will experience discomfort. We monitor our boundaries constantly via our senses, it's part of our threat recognition system, but it is also where we do all our conscious interaction. We also have psychological boundaries; this is where confluence plays out.

The merging of boundaries between people is primarily a way for couples and families to avoid conflict or disharmony. If you and I are the same there will be no discomfort between us. It is commonly experienced in the withdrawal or awareness part of the cycle. In the awareness phase, it may be experienced as people step over their awareness and into a contract with another before allowing full comprehension. To avoid contactful conflict they rush in and smooth things or make all disagreements okay before they arise. In the withdrawal phase, it's the opposite, where healthy separation and withdrawal are required; these may be experienced as anxiety-producing so an urge to maintain or hold onto, without letting go takes over in the looming threat of isolation. What we want to see as therapists is a fluid movement between relationship and separation, in confluence we might see merging and fear of isolation replacing healthy separation.

Confluent people are often so unaware of themselves, of their own personal power as an agent in the environment, that they will see all external agents as threatening or overpowering. It's as though they fear they will be lost to the external power. This prevents them from applying their own power in equal measure to hold the clear boundary between and as a result they do indeed lose part of the self in the exchange.

It's a peculiar thing to see in action, have you ever wondered why a couple would both wear the same shoes, trousers, coat, hat etc. often all at the same time? It's a blurring of the boundaries, if there was healthy differentiation both would more than likely have their own style. Clothing choice is a function of the ego, it's saying to people looking on, this is me, this is my style, this is how I choose to dress and appear to the world. Identically dressed people are saying the exact opposite.

Confluence happens when the awareness of the difference between two people is lost. The ability to tolerate difference or ambiguity is diminished. I would suggest that confluent people tend toward retroflected behaviour too, in order to stay merged and similar, many parts of self-expression must, perforce, be suppressed/retroflected. In this way, we will often see an overlapping of interruptions, such as retroflection and confluence.

The contact between confluent people is often far from loving, though it may appear so on the outside, there may be very little seen of the authentic other, the merging of boundaries does not allow for difference to exist.

Relationships built in this way can be stifling and barren with spontaneous interaction and creativity often lost to homogenised safety.

I should also add that it is also necessary at times to have confluence, in the same way, it is sometimes healthy to retroflect, or deflect, I don't want to give the impression these behaviours are always bad. Good sex, for example, requires a certain degree of merging with the other, allowing ourselves to be given over to pleasure and abandon our boundaries to some extent with the person we trust to not overstep them in ways which we find harmful. It requires a degree of ruthlessness too though, which balances out the merging and allows for healthy separation when the time comes to withdraw from contact.

Theoretical Overview

Although I have included these aspects of theory above, I have not added much more detail on Gestalt theory and the therapeutic process beyond anecdotal case studies and brief comments in the rest of this book. If you are interested in Gestalt theory, I recommend reading the two books cited earlier as a place to start, though there are many more worth reading to follow up. It should be recognised that Gestalt therapy is not a series of skills you can learn, it is the enabling of contact in the here and now to facilitate the completion of unfinished business which leads hopefully to greater integration of the psyche.

About the Author

Steven Eserin is a Gestalt psychotherapist with a private practice on the south coast of England. He began working in mental health in 1993 whilst training to be a counsellor for alcohol and drug addiction. In 1996, while working at the Woodhurst Avenue Project, a therapeutic community in Watford, Hertfordshire, he began training in Gestalt Therapy with the Irish Gestalt Centre (now Irish Gestalt Institute) Graduating in 2002.

The majority of Steven's practice is 1-1 individual and couples' psychotherapy, though he also offers group work for personal development and specific conditions such as Bipolar, often co-facilitating with other therapists.

Steven also runs continued professional development training days for counsellors, therapists and trainee counsellors. He also supports other organisations as a freelance trainer. Alongside these professional development courses, Steven also runs a monthly counsellors professional development group in Eastbourne, East Sussex.

If you have any questions arising from this book and wish to create or join a discussion group or training event related to the subjects covered, or for your continued psychotherapy or training needs please contact: Steven via www.steveneserin.com

References

American Psychiatric Association. *Diagnostic and Statistical Manual of Mental Disorders (DSM-5)*. Washington: American Psychological Association, 2013.

Becker, Ernest. *The Denial of Death*. New York: Simon and Schuster, 1997.

Buber, Martin. *I and Thou*. New York: Scribner, 1937.

Carrol, Robert. *The Bible*: Authorised King James Version. Oxford: Oxford University Press: 2008.

DeYoung, Patricia A. *Understanding and Treating Chronic Shame*. Milton Park: Taylor and Francis, 2015.

Freud, Sigmund. *Moses and Monotheism*. New York: Knopf Doubleday Publishing Group, 1939

Fromm, Eric. *The Fear of Freedom*. Abingdon: Routledge, 1951.

Fromm, Eric. Man for himself: An Inquiry in to the Psychology of Ethics. Abingdon: Routledge, 1999.

Fromm, Eric. *The Anatomy of Human Destructiveness*. New York: Holt, 1976.

Fromm, Eric. Psychoanalysis and religion. Yale: Yale University Press, 1950.

Gaiman, Neil. "Why our future depends on libraries, reading and daydreaming." October, 2013.
https://www.theguardian.com/books/2013/oct/15/neil-gaiman-future-libraries-reading-daydreaming .

Kafka, Franz, *Aphorisms*. Foreward by Daniel Frank. New York: Knopf Doubleday Publishing Group, 2015.

Maslow, Abraham H. *A Theory of Human Motivation*. Washington: American Psychological Association,194. https://doi.org/10.1037/h0054346

May, Rollo. *Power and Innocence*. New York: Norton, 1972.

May, Rollo. *The Cry for Myth*. New York: Norton,1991.

May, Rollo. *The Discovery of Being*. New York: Norton, 1986.

May, Rollo. *Existential psychology*. New York: Random House, 1969.

Nietzsche, Friedrich, Michael Tanner. *Ecce Homo: How One Becomes What One Is*. London: Penguin, 1992.

Perls, Fritz S. *Ego Hunger and Aggression: A Revision of Freud's Theory and Method*. Brentwood: Knox Publishing Company, 1944. The Gestalt Journal Press, 1992.

Perls, Fritz S, Ralph F.Hefferline, Paul Goodman. *Gestalt Therapy: Excitement and Growth in the Human Personality*. London: Penguin, 1973. The Gestalt Journal Press, 1994.

Pirsig, Robert M. Zen and the Art of Motorcycle Maintenance: An Inquiry Into Values. New York: Harper Collins, 2005.

Phillipson, Peter. *British Gestalt Journal* 1998 vol. 7, no. 1, Nottingham, UK, 1998.

Polster, Erving, Miriam Polster. *Gestalt Therapy Integrated*. Abingdon: Routledge, 1973.

Polster, Erving. *Population of selves*. Hoboken: Wiley, 1995. The Gestalt Journal Press, 1995.

Schopenhauer, Arthur. *Two Fundamental Problems of Ethics*. Cambridge: Cambridge University Press, 2009.

Tzu, Lao, Stephen Mitchell. *Tao Te Ching*. Narrated by Stephen Mitchell. Frances Lincoln Adult, Audio, (The Quarto Group, Inc.), London, UK. 2009.

REFERENCES

Wallin, David J. *Attachment in Psychotherapy*. New York: Guildford Publishing, 2007.

Yalom, Irvin D. *Existential Psychotherapy*. New York: Basic Books, 1980.

Yalom, Irvin D. *Staring at the Sun*. Hoboken: Wiley, 2009.

Zinker, Joseph C. *Creative Process in Gestalt Therapy*. Abingdon: Routledge, 1977.

www.ingramcontent.com/pod-product-compliance
Lightning Source LLC
Chambersburg PA
CBHW010729270326
41930CB00018B/3416